ROUTLEDGE LIBRARY EDITIONS:
INDUSTRIAL ECONOMICS

Volume 16

THE LARGE INDUSTRIAL ENTERPRISE

THE LARGE INDUSTRIAL ENTERPRISE

Some Spatial Perspectives

H.D. WATTS

Routledge
Taylor & Francis Group
LONDON AND NEW YORK

First published in 1980 by Croom Helm Ltd

This edition first published in 2018
by Routledge
2 Park Square, Milton Park, Abingdon, Oxon OX14 4RN

and by Routledge
711 Third Avenue, New York, NY 10017

Routledge is an imprint of the Taylor & Francis Group, an informa business

British Library Cataloguing in Publication Data
A catalogue record for this book is available from the British Library

ISBN: 978-1-138-30830-5 (Set)
ISBN: 978-1-351-21102-4 (Set) (ebk)
ISBN: 978-1-138-57100-6 (Volume 16) (hbk)
ISBN: 978-0-203-70305-2 (Volume 16) (ebk)

Publisher's Note
The publisher has gone to great lengths to ensure the quality of this reprint but points out that some imperfections in the original copies may be apparent.

Disclaimer
The publisher has made every effort to trace copyright holders and would welcome correspondence from those they have been unable to trace.

The Large Industrial Enterprise

SOME SPATIAL PERSPECTIVES

H.D. WATTS

CROOM HELM LONDON

Croom Helm Ltd, 2–10 St John's Road, London SW11

British Library Cataloguing in Publication Data

Watts, H D
The large industrial enterprise.
- (Croom Helm series in geography and environment).
1. Big business
2. Geography, Economic
I. Title
338.6'44'091722 HD2731

ISBN 0-7099-0267-0

Printed in Great Britain by
Biddles Ltd, Guildford, Surrey

CONTENTS

TABLES

FIGURES

ACKNOWLEDGEMENTS

The author and publishers gratefully acknowledge permission received from the following to make use of copyright materials in the illustrations listed below. Full citations of the source material will be found in the captions to the illustrations.

The Geographical Association and *Geography*, Figure 5.1; Dr A.C.M. Jansen, Koninklijk Nederlands Aardrijkskundig Genootschnap, and *Tijdschrift voor Economische en Sociale Geografie*, Figure 4.2; Pergamon Press and *Geoforum*, Figure 5.2; Dr M.J. Taylor, the Regional Studies Association and *Regional Studies*, Figure 6.1; Koninklijk Nederlands Aardrijkskundig Genootschnap and *Tijdschrift voor Economische en Sociale Geografie*, Figure 6.2; Regional Studies Association and *Regional Studies*, Figure 6.3; John Wiley & Sons Ltd, Figure 8.1.

TO MY PARENTS

PREFACE

Large industrial enterprises play an important role in most advanced Western economies. Not only do the enterprises produce their own spatial patterns in provision of employment, in the location of production capacity and in the flows of materials and information; they also, through these, influence the spatial characteristics of the industries in which they operate and the economies of the towns and cities with which they are associated. The initial stimulus for this book arose from the contrast between the small single-plant firm, which is the actual or assumed centre piece of many industrial location studies, and the large multi-plant industrial enterprise which is depicted daily in the mass media of newspapers and radio. It seemed to me that by the mid-1970s some very interesting work had been published on the spatial behaviour of large industrial enterprises and it was an opportune time to take an overview of what was known about them and their effects on industrial location patterns, regions and city systems.

The enterprises often dominate the industrial sector or sectors in which they operate and, just as economists have found it necessary to develop special approaches to deal with firms operating in oligopolistic environments, so the geographer must develop a framework for understanding industrial locations where a small number of firms dominates an industrial sector. Such a framework will complement earlier approaches to industrial location, which are still very relevant for industries characterised by small firms.

This discussion of the spatial behaviour of large industrial enterprises may interest students of economics and business who, as yet, have given little consideration to the topic, but the book is aimed primarily at University, Polytechnic and College students who have completed introductory courses in either economic geography or industrial location. They will find here a review and analysis of the behaviour of large enterprises in space, based mainly on geographical enquiries in North America and the United Kingdom, but also drawing out the spatial implications of some ideas taken from business studies and industrial economics. Readers interested primarily in general concepts may omit Part Three which introduces some new case analyses of large enterprise behaviour in the UK brewing industry.

The scope of the book is confined deliberately to the developed world, and within that area the discussion is restricted primarily, but not exclusively, to the behaviour of private-sector enterprises. These enterprises are examined only within national boundaries; the multi-national spread of the large industrial enterprise would justify a study in its own right. Moreover, this is not a book about decision making in large enterprises; it is, as indicated above, about their observed behaviour patterns. The research available to date just does not allow a close examination of decision-making procedures in these very large organisations.

Inevitably, the book owes much to those who have taught me. W. Barnard, at Fakenham Grammar School in Norfolk, aroused my interest in industrial geography, and this was stimulated later by the teaching of Kenneth Warren, then at the University of Leicester. In my post-graduate work at Hull, Jay Appleton supervised my first attempts at research, and Peter Mounfield, when he and I were colleagues at the University College of Wales, Aberystwyth, encouraged me to develop my ideas in this area. My students too, especially those in the final-year industrial geography groups at the University of Sheffield, have criticised and contributed to the arguments presented in the pages that follow.

Particular thanks are also due to those who assisted in the compilation and interpretation of the data relating to the large industrial enterprises in the UK brewing industry. Margaret Wilkes and Verity Brack assembled lists of firms and plants and I was most fortunate in being able to talk to a number of senior members of the brewing industry. They included the following former or present members of the large industrial enterprises: Mr F.A.O.G. Bennett (Whitbread), Lt-Col P.L. Bradfer-Lawrence (Bass-Charrington), Mr T. Bunting (Courage), Mr A. Elliott (Bass-Charington), Mr J.L. Mills (Allied Breweries), Sir Gerald Thorley (Allied Breweries), Mr C. Tidbury (Whitbread), and Mr M.G.T. Webster (Watney-Mann). The Campaign for Real Ale kindly allowed me to consult the past numbers of

What's Brewing at their St Albans headquarters. The points of view expressed in the discussion are entirely my own and are very much those of an observer looking at the enterprises from the outside. They should not be attributed to any one of the individuals acknowledged here.

The final form of the book has benefited considerably from the help of Peter Dicken, Michael Healey and David North who struggled through early drafts of the manuscript and saved me from a number of injudicious statements and confused arguments. To them, a special thanks. Diana and David Connolly applied their combined business expertise to a later draft and enlightened some points of business behaviour that had been ignored. My wife, Suzanne, has read the chapters in draft and suggested a number of improvements. I also owe a very special debt to Professor R.O. Buchanan who throughout the preparation of the manuscript acted as a helpful and wise counsellor and who in the final stages turned many an awkward phrase into a more felicitous expression. In the Department of Geography my colleagues' trenchant criticism during research seminars and their good humoured interest has in no small way contributed towards the completion of the manuscript. What is more, they agreed to undertake my teaching and administrative duties during a term's study leave granted to me by the University of Sheffield in Autumn 1977. The University also provided a grant to cover some of the expenses incurred in collecting the empirical data.

The cartographers in the Department of Geography, Steve Frampton and Sheila Ottewell, drew the illustrations for publication, and Wendy Mann converted a very messy manuscript into the final typescript.

To one and all, many thanks. Of course, the usual caveat applies.

H.D. Watts
Sheffield

1 INTRODUCTION

> The most important of . . . [the] fundamental changes in the world industrial environment during the past half century . . . is the rise of large scale organisations . . . to dominate the management of urban, regional, national and international industrial systems.
>
> F.E.I. Hamilton, 1976[1]

In the United Kingdom 2.5 million workers are employed by only 100 large industrial enterprises. The same enterprises control more than 3,000 different industrial establishments.[2] The five largest enterprises in an average industry account for over two-thirds of the industry's output.[3] These figures indicate quite clearly that large industrial enterprises, whether large in an absolute or in a relative sense, are established features of the UK economy. This situation is not unusual. The 100 largest industrial corporations in the United States employ 9.4 million workers, and the 100 largest manufacturing firms control nearly half the assets of all manufacturing firms.[4]

These large industrial enterprises are not new phenomena but they have been growing steadily in importance over the last few decades. The 52 enterprises in the United Kingdom with over 10,000 employees in 1935 had risen to 74 by 1958, and to 85 by 1972.[5] Moreover, increases have been recorded in the share of net output attributable to the 100 largest concerns. In 1948 they accounted for around 21 per cent of net output and by 1970 for 45 per cent.[6] Similarly, between 1965 and 1973, the number of workers employed by the 100 largest industrial enterprises in the United States rose by almost 2.5 million, and the 100 largest manufacturing firms' share of the assets of all such firms rose by 7.4 percentage points between 1948 and 1972.[7] If these trends continue, Jay has suggested that 'the small private corporate kingdom controlled by its proprietor will be as rare an anachronism in the future as the landed aristocrat is to-day'.[8]

Not surprisingly, the importance and increasing dominance of large industrial enterprises has attracted considerable attention. One of the first popular works to describe them was Galbraith's *The New Industrial State*,[9] and more recently substantive research such as Prais's *The Evolution of Giant Firms in Britain*,[10] Hannah's *The Rise of the Corporate Economy*[11] and Sobel's *The Age of Giant Corporations*[12] has appeared. The enterprises have figured also in more general works such as Bannock's *The Juggernauts*.[13] The majority of the accounts concentrate upon the absolutely large enterprise but Hannah & Kay's *Concentration in Modern Industry*,[14] and Aaronovitch & Sawyer's *Big Business*[15] redress the balance by focusing on industries where a few firms control a high proportion of the output. A similar task was undertaken in the United States in Blair's study of *Economic Concentration.*[16] The work of industrial economists has been paralleled by students of business behaviour. Examples are Chamberlain's *Enterprise and Environment*[17] and Channon's *The Strategy and Structure of British Enterprise*[18], which developed from Chandler's seminal study of *Strategy and Structure.*[19] This listing of a selection of works on the large industrial enterprise is indicative of the interest it has aroused in the academic community.

Politicians have expressed an interest too, fearing particularly the sheer power of these large organisations. As Prais observes,

> if the greater part of the investment policy of the country is in relatively few hands, and if the greater part of the country's employment is controlled by relatively few employers, then the market mechanism is increasingly by-passed and replaced – ultimately by the administrative decisions of a few powerful men, whose aims and responsibilities are often not clear.[20]

Early concern is seen in the anti-trust legislation in the United States, and very much later in the setting up of the Monopolies Commission in Britain. The very largest enterprises in several Western countries have been taken over by the state. In addition to the power of these organisations, much of the political interest comes from the role they play in a national economy in investment, wage and price policies and in export activities. Within Britain in the 1970s both major political parties recognised the need for special treatment of these very large concerns. This is reflected in the Labour Party's proposals to take an increased financial stake in private industry through the National Enterprise Board and to make Planning Agreements with the largest firms.[21] Similarly, in their White Paper on Prices Policy the Conservative Party selected for special treatment Category One firms with turnover in excess of £50 million at 1973 prices.[22] There appears to be agreement that these enterprises need to be monitored carefully by the state, a point of view expressed forcefully by Holland.[23]

The geographical study of large industrial enterprises grew out of the geographer's traditional concern with explaining and predicting spatial patterns. In geographical enquiries an attempt is made to understand the spatial patterns created by the enterprises, both in aggregate and individually, and to examine their influence on the location of different industries and on city-systems and regions. The effective starting point was McNee's pioneering attempt to put the geography of large industrial enterprises into perspective.[24] In subsequent papers, Krumme[25] and McNee[26] have touched upon some of the essential spatial characteristics of large enterprises, but there has been no major review of the field. Since 1960 progress in this area has been slow, so that while McNee regarded 'the enterprise approach [as] relatively new',[27] so also Krumme argued nine years later that 'in economic geography – particularly manufacturing geography – relatively few attempts have been made to take the phenomenon "enterprise" into account'.[28] Since 1969 an increasing number of studies of individual firms such as the British Steel Corporation,[29] the Royal Hoesch Union,[30] Siemens,[31] Watties Industries,[32] Creusot-Loire,[33] Harland & Wolff,[34] Triumph[35] and Boeing[36] have appeared. These works have been paralleled by the examination of small groups of large enterprises operating in specific industries such as fertilisers,[37] beet-sugar processing,[38] petrochemicals,[39] forest products,[40] together with the whole series of enterprises examined by Rake.[41] Despite this 'rapidly increasing interest in the spatial implications of large enterprise behaviour',[42] Dicken was right to argue that the 'study of the spatial behaviour of business organisations is as yet in its infancy'.[43]

The lack of detailed geographical studies of large enterprises until the 1970s probably mirrors two factors. The first is related to the quantitative paradigm which has dominated geography. It has been fashionable to approach geographical problems by computer-based assaults on large data sets. Yet the large enterprise is often not amenable to this kind of approach. The population of enterprises in any one industry is too small for the appropriate use of many quantitative techniques, and statistical inference is an almost impossible task. Cross-industry studies, while permitting an increase in the number of firms examined, raise a number of difficult problems, the most important being that the results can be influenced markedly by technological contrasts between different industrial sectors. The second factor is the lack of any well-developed theory from which to begin. Admittedly a lack of theoretical developments has not stopped some geographers in the past, but industrial geography has had the classic locational literature on which to draw. Regrettably, but not surprisingly, the majority of this literature is concerned with small, single-plant firms.

Theories about large enterprise behaviour in space are still undeveloped, but with increasing interest in behavioural approaches to geography (for example, Pred[44]) and in location decision making (Stafford,[45] Townroe[46] are examples) interest turned away from industries and plants to decision-making units. One such decision-making unit is the large industrial enterprise.

Large Industrial Enterprises

The isolation of a type of organisation for discussion is relatively unusual in economic geography, and until quite recently industrial geographers were constrained within the frameworks of standard industrial classifications of economic activities. In these classifications manufacturing is divided into classes based on the physical characteristics of either inputs or outputs. While this approach has considerable merit, Krumme has suggested that the 'classification of firms other than to industrial categories . . . [is] . . . increasingly important'.[47] The basic argument of this book is that a large industrial enterprise, whatever the industry or industries in which it operates, has more in common with other large enterprises, in the same or different industries, than with small firms operating in the same industry (or industries) as itself. Whether a motor vehicle assembly enterprise can be compared with a brewing enterprise of the same size is a moot point, but the spirit of research in studies of the enterprise is that such comparisons are valid and are likely to lead to significant generalisations.[48]

Once large industrial enterprises are recognised as distinct phenomena, there is one very important reason why economic geographers should consider their spatial behaviour. In one way or another, they impinge on the lives of most members of advanced Western economies.

Large industrial enterprises influence a wide range of social and economic activities because of their size and the geographical distribution of their plants. Not only are these enterprises important employers in their own right, they may also, by input and output links, affect the location of smaller firms. Their decisions to abandon or expand certain plants can modify the economic base of specific towns, and their long-term investment strategies can influence the degree of regional differentiation in a national space economy. Individuals may feel that they have little power over these enterprises, whether this is because they are redundant as a result of a rationalisation policy or because their home environment is changed suddenly by the arrival of a new plant or the expansion of an existing one. An understanding of the spatial behaviour of large industrial enterprises may permit effective attempts to modify their behaviour where it clashes with community or regional needs. Similarly, if management can be made aware of some of the spatial repercussions of their decisions, a path can be laid for a spatially as well as a socially responsible enterprise.

In the ensuing discussion, the central focus is large industrial enterprises and their subsidiary firms. An enterprise is made up of one or more sites under common ownership or control. In the words of Penrose it is 'an autonomous administrative planning unit, the activities of which are inter-related and co-ordinated by policies which are framed in the light of their effect on the enterprise as a whole'.[49] It is usual to distinguish between an *enterprise*, which is a unit of ownership, and a *firm*, which is the legally constituted entity under which a particular site, or group of sites, operates. An enterprise is treated conventionally as controlling a firm if it owns 50 per cent or more of its shares. These definitions are not without their problems. Some subsidiary firms may have a high degree of autonomy and receive little direction from the enterprise, while other enterprises may influence the behaviour of firms in which they have only a small shareholding. A further difficulty is that the word 'firm' tends to be used in different ways by various writers. To clarify the discussion it is used here to refer to all industrial companies or, more usually, to small companies outside the large industrial enterprise category.

As an essential simplification, attention is focused on those enterprises which are concerned predominantly with industrial activity, with particular reference to the location of their production, research and head-office sites. Warehousing, retail outlets and sales offices owned by such enterprises receive only limited attention. Since most enterprises have a mix of functions, which may include, for example, mineral extraction or retail sales, it is difficult to identify enterprises which are purely industrial enterprises. Indeed, it may be unwise to attempt such an identification, but there are three reasons for treating industrial enterprises as a separate category. First, a considerable number of the enterprises originated, and still see themselves, as primarily manufacturing organisations. Second, the literature on the spatial behaviour of enterprises in the primary, tertiary and quaternary sectors is not, as yet, extensive. Third, to try to explain the behaviour of all enterprises, at one step, would result in unwarranted complexity in a comparatively unexplored area. Of course, in the long run, explanation of the behaviour of all types of large organisation should be the aim. Some confusion may be created by the use of the term industrial; it is used to describe only those activities which are ascribed to Order III to Order XIX of the 1968 Standard Industrial Classification, that is the two-digit categories from 20 to 39 of the United States classification.

Defining a *large* industrial enterprise is beset with problems. Size, for example, can be measured in several ways – number employed, net assets (capital employed), value added (net output), turnover, issued capital and market capitalisation. An enterprise scoring high on one parameter will not necessarily score as highly on another. For example, the tenth ranking UK enterprise by turnover in 1976 was ranked fortieth in terms of capital employed. Further, large is not only an absolute but also a relative concept: an enterprise may be small when compared with all enterprises, but large when compared with other enterprises in the industrial sector in which it operates. Whatever measure is used, and whether it is relative or absolute, the dividing line between large and small is necessarily arbitrary.

Large is used in this account in both the absolute and the

relative sense. Not only is it concerned with the absolutely large enterprises – defined here whenever possible by the number employed – but also with those enterprises which though small when set against all industrial enterprises are large in relation to the industrial sectors in which they operate. Of course, many firms are large in both the absolute and relative sense.

These large industrial enterprises have six characteristics which, apart from size, differ from those of small single-plant firms and which may have an influence on their behaviour in space. These characteristics are the separation of ownership from control, formal organisational structures, special relationships with government, multi-regional operations, diversified outputs, and some are controlled by enterprises based overseas.

An increase in size tends to lead away from the personal control of the enterprise by the owner-entrepreneur and his family. Although it is a view which has been challenged by Manne,[50] the managerialist approach to the study of enterprises, seen in the work of Berle & Means[51] and Marris[52], stresses the dominant role of the managers in guiding enterprise behaviour. The rise of the managers reflects the fact that they have the necessary expertise to control the enterprise, and that the absentee shareholder can have only a limited influence on the way an enterprise is run. This process is aided by the fact that an enterprise tends to become self-financing through retained earnings. The limited importance of family control is seen in the absolutely large enterprises. Only 30 out of the 100 largest industrial enterprises in the United Kingdom contained 'significant elements' of family control in 1970,[53] and in Belgium only 8 out of 41 large enterprises had families as their main owners.[54] Admittedly some of the enterprises which are large only in the relative sense may still be under the control of their owners and, while not owning their enterprises, some individual industrialists heading specific enterprises may have a major influence on their policy. Nevertheless, evidence from Scott suggests that the personal role of any one individual is played down in the large enterprise.[55] The point was developed by Krumme, who drew attention to the fact that it was possible for 'organisations and their individual members to terminate their relationship with each other'.[56] This allows an enterprise to increase adaptability by exchanging decision makers and permits the individual executive to make 'personal' location decisions without affecting the location of the organisation.

To control operations within the large enterprise a system is developed to monitor its activities. Such a system is based upon an enterprise's organisational structure. These structures are discussed in more detail later (pp. 57–60) but it is important to note that 'corporate bureaucratic organisations differ significantly from company to company . . . in their officially recognised structure'[57] and that such differences may have an important influence on their behaviour.

A further consequence of size is that a large enterprise's behaviour is constrained by government policy rather more than that of smaller enterprises. This topic is explored in the final chapter, and it is sufficient at this stage to note that a government may attempt to influence the location and timing of plant expansions, contractions, branches, and closures and will also monitor carefully proposed merger activity.

Such government interest may be heightened where an enterprise displays the fourth characteristic – foreign ownership. The proportion of enterprises under foreign control need not be high, but there is always the underlying suspicion that, with their international flexibility and their lack of strong ties with the host nation, they may work primarily for their own interests. Since they probably form a not insignificant sub-set of large industrial enterprises, they are examined in Chapter 3.

The fifth characteristic is that large industrial enterprises are, inevitably, multi-plant enterprises, and are usually multi-regional ones. This is well illustrated by UK data. The 195 enterprises employing over 5,000 workers controlled on average 38 plants each, a total of 7,506 establishments. Particular industrial groups reflect this overall pattern. The five largest enterprises manufacturing bolts, nuts and screws operate five plants each, while the three largest wire manufacturing enterprises operate 11 plants each.[58] Similarly, among the largest employers, one operates in 29 different towns in the United Kingdom, and another operates in 42 principal manufacturing centres.[59]

The sixth and final characteristic is the diversified nature of a large industrial enterprise's outputs. The general trend is for such enterprises to become increasingly diversified. Inevitably, the notion of diversification is dependent upon the definition of product. While accepting this as a difficulty, the development of an enterprise has been envisaged as a move from single product, through dominant product to unrelated product activities. This pattern is to some extent confirmed by Channon, who shows that, whereas in 1950 24 per cent of the top 100 manufacturing enterprises in the United Kingdom were diversified, by 1970 the percentage had reached 60.[60] Similarly, Hassid showed that between 1963 and 1968 the average index of diversification for enterprises in UK manufacturing industry rose by about 20 per cent.[61] While this pattern may be true in general, enterprises in some sectors (for example, in the automobile industry) have shown little tendency to diversify and have remained essentially single-product concerns.

This listing of the six special characteristics of large industrial enterprises is not claimed to be exhaustive, but it is sufficient to indicate their special nature.

In examining the spatial outcomes of the behaviour of these large industrial enterprises, classical location theory suggests that the size and location of their plants and the linkages generated by material and information flows from and to those plants should be the principal objects of interest. These two spatial aspects of an enterprise's activities – plants and linkages – are explored in the following chapters, with the emphasis placed on the former rather than the latter. This is not indicative of the relative importance of the two aspects but mirrors data availability and the nature of the published research work on linkage, which although extensive, does not necessarily distinguish the plants operated by large industrial enterprises.

It is recognised that space can be related to the behaviour of these enterprises in two distinct ways. Sometimes spatial considerations have an important influence on behaviour. A plant is closed because it is some distance from an enterprise's other activities or a linkage is strengthened because the supplier is in close proximity to an existing plant. Admittedly, this kind of behaviour may occur infrequently, but it is still important to understand it. In contrast, the behaviour of an enterprise may often be implicitly rather than explicitly spatial. An example here might be a decision to drop a certain product line, resulting in the closure of two plants manufacturing the product. Although the plant closures represent a distinct spatial outcome, spatial considerations did not influence the decision. It seems particularly important to draw attention to the spatial consequences of these aspatial decisions.

In sum, a spatial perspective on large industrial enterprises involves looking at those aspects of their behaviour which express themselves in a spatial form. It is much wider than a study of new locations. It is a study of the spatial outcomes of what Dicken termed spatial decisions,[62] and includes analysis of plant closures, *in situ* expansions (and contractions), acquisition of plants through mergers and changes in the products manufactured by specific plants as well as the better-known location decisions linked with the establishment of branch plants. Associated with these characteristics are the important inter- and intra-enterprise linkage systems of both materials and information.

Method of Approach

Both Averitt[63] and Galbraith[64] have proposed the recognition of two broad classes of firm within advanced Western-type economies. The former suggests a distinction between 'centre' and 'periphery' firms, while the latter distinguishes between firms operating within the 'industrial system' and those operating within the 'market system'. Similarly, in the more specific UK context, Holland[65] has argued that there is a group of firms making up the 'meso-economic' element of the economy. The view that this group of meso-economic or centre firms operating in the industrial system are different in kind from the remainder of the economy has not gone unchallenged either by economists,[66] management scientists[67] or businessmen.[68] Nevertheless, it is clear that the large enterprise, which usually operates in a multi-regional and multi-national context, is an established feature of many economies. Traditional industrial location theory, with its emphasis on the single-plant firm, remains the most appropriate starting point for handling some of the problems posed by periphery firms operating in the market system, but it does not seem sufficiently well developed to handle the problems posed by large industrial enterprises operating in the industrial system, except to assist in the selection of branch plant locations.

Once a move is made towards the study of these enterprises, it is important to recognise that they differ from the smaller firm and are a different species.[69] Not only do they differ in the six characteristics described earlier, but they operate in a contrasting environment. As Chamberlain has argued, large industrial enterprises are 'obviously not pushed and pulled . . . by market forces which overwhelm them; rather they demonstrably choose to follow certain courses of action'.[70] Often they operate in oligopolistic (few firm) environments where they influence and are influenced by one another's behaviour. The image of a firm at the mercy of its environment has to be replaced by that of the enterprise with its purposive actions to modify the environment. Because of these differences Pred argues that 'it would not seem potentially fruitful to continue primarily to employ forms of locational analysis which focus on single location, single function firms, where multi-locational, multi-functional firms rule the economic roost'.[71]

Steed believes that 'the complex geographic behaviour of [these] multi-plant corporations requires a different line of approach',[72] different, that is, from the approach to the single-plant firm. In the absence of a well-developed theory, such an approach tends to put empirical work first and model building and theory second. This places 'a premium on individual and specific corporate case studies',[73] and once such studies are complete 'it should prove possible to move beyond individual cases to a more general interpretation'. Similarly, Evan sees the case study as invaluable 'for generating insights and propositions'[74] but it is difficult to generalise from them to large populations. It seems false, however, to assume that generalisation is a later stage and that it would be premature until numerous case studies have been completed. The process of generalisation begins with the ordering of material within the case study. Support for this approach comes also from Lipsey, who has argued that 'what is required is much more empirical knowledge of how firms actually do react in small group situations'.[75] Such knowledge will permit the identification of characteristic types of behaviour by large industrial enterprises. This does not mean that a search for a theory of small group behaviour should be abandoned, but that a piecemeal approach to the problem may produce elements that could be incorporated into a theory of the spatial behaviour of large industrial enterprises.

The closest parallel to the approach suggested here comes from studies of business policy. In the 1950s and 1960s students of business policy depended upon the case study. It was argued, in the then relatively new area, that only by studying examples of particular policies in the context of particular firms could all the relevant considerations emerge. By the late 1960s as evidence of business policies accumulated and questions to be asked were identified, so greater emphasis was placed on the study of populations, but the old case study approach has not been abandoned. In business policy an enterprise is viewed as something worth studying in its own right, and not only as a member of a class of enterprises with certain features in common. In the mid-1970s business schools like Harvard had a 'two pronged' approach to business policy – the case study and the population.[76]

In the following discussion evidence is drawn from two kinds of source material and it is important to distinguish between them. First, there are the case studies of specific large enterprises or small groups of large enterprises. Second, there are investigations of specific types of behaviour which perhaps occur more frequently among large enterprises than among small firms, for example the acquisition of another firm or the establishment of a branch plant. Incorporation of the results of the first kind of evidence into a study of large industrial enterprises presents few problems, but the second type of evidence is drawn from a much wider population of firms and of necessity includes some firms which would not fall within the definition of the large industrial enterprise given earlier. Although Hamilton has asked whether 'more case studies are really justified'[77] it is the case study which provides much of the evidence used in this volume because the geography of the large industrial enterprise is still in a relatively early stage of development.

The nature of the enterprises examined means that most of the material discussed relates to the observed behaviour of the enterprises rather than to the decision-making process. It moves away from traditional questionnaire-based studies because in larger enterprises information from one or two individuals is unlikely to reveal the motives of other members of the group or groups involved in that decision. Analysis of a decision process within a large enterprise based on the views of one or at the most two contributors to that process seems to be unwise. Inevitably, the enterprise is treated as a black-box and the behaviour inside the enterprise does not fall within the scope of this study. Studies of decisions within large enterprises will necessitate detailed study of all the individuals involved in the decision process. In essence, the emphasis here is on analysis of the spatial patterns produced by large industrial enterprises rather than on processes internal to the enterprise.

A further difficulty is presented by the sheer complexity and multi-product nature of an enterprise. In an exploratory study such as this the problem has been overcome by examining predominantly either single-product enterprises or one product group of a larger enterprise. This is not unrealistic, for as Dicken observes, in the large diversified enterprise there may be 'little or no direct connection between units operating within different product markets, though each unit makes a discrete contribution to the overall enterprise and each is sustained by the whole enterprise'.[78]

Perhaps the major problem facing the study has been the very limited availability of data, and, to no small extent, data have determined which enterprises are studied, how they are approached and the methods of analysis used. This is not the ideal way to approach the problem, but it is the only one that was open. Some might argue that one ought to wait until better data are available, but this seems a negative attitude which, if applied widely, would ignore many important social and economic problems. Hopefully, a study using limited data may pin-point areas where more data are wanted, and the exact form those data should take. A plea for more data is by itself not enough; some initial studies plus some careful thinking about theory are needed to indicate the data required.

Access to data has governed also the location of the principal case studies, which are drawn from the United Kingdom, although the literature review covers primarily the English speaking developed world. These cases complement the work already completed in the North American context, and develop many of the ideas in a rather different cultural and institutional framework. Too often both North American and British students accept the North American situation as being typical of the developed world, but Granick's study of managerial behaviour showed important contrasts between enterprises in the United Kingdom, United States, and France.[79]

Earlier in this chapter a distinction was drawn between behaviour influenced by space, and behaviour which had a spatial outcome even though spatial considerations had not influenced the form it took. Much of the emphasis in this book, especially in the detailed empirical studies, is on those enterprises where spatial considerations influence behaviour. Examples tend to be drawn from agricultural and forest-product-processing industries, or industries serving consumer markets. These are the industries in which distribution costs or material assembly costs tend to form a high proportion of net output, where there tend to be marked economies of scale and the resulting barriers to entry are high. Of course, enterprises operating in these industries make up only a small proportion of total industrial employment, but they are a group of enterprises where one would expect the influence of space to be most marked. Other enterprises may not display the features discussed in such a distinct form, but some elements may still be present. Clearly, enterprises manufacturing electronic components will react to space in a less marked way than a forest-product-processing enterprise. All enterprises, however, whatever their industry or industries, and regardless of their reaction to space, will eventually express themselves in space.

Hamilton has argued that the most fundamental need in studies of large enterprise behaviour is to concentrate research upon three elements: first, the character and explanation of the spatial structure of, and the inter-relationships among, the units that make up the industrial organisation; second, the processes and reasons for change in the spatial structure of organisations; third, the relationship between the organisations and their environment.[80] These three elements are reflected in the overall structure of the ensuing discussion.

A study of large industrial enterprises from a spatial perspective raises many intriguing questions. What is the spatial distribution of the plants of these large enterprises? How are these plants linked by material and information flows? Is it possible to produce a typology of site activities? Can the spatial separation of functions within an enterprise be explained? Do foreign-owned enterprises have distributions and linkages which differ from those of indigenous concerns? These are essentially questions about static spatial features and attempts are made to answer them in Part One.

The more these questions are investigated, the more the answers and explanations can be seen to be intermingled with the way an enterprise has grown. Explanations have to be sought, in part, in an historical context, as the spatial structure of an enterprise at one point in time is the end product of a continuous process of change and at the same time a spring board for change yet to come. In Part Two attention is turned to questions concerning the process of change. Do different methods of growth by an enterprise result in different spatial patterns? How do enterprises adjust their spatial structures as they grow? To what extent do organisational structures influence spatial change? In what ways do enterprises interact with one another in space as they grow? Part Two concludes with a discussion of attempts to model the evolution of an enterprise, with particular reference to a development sequence which depicts spatial growth and locational adjustment in enterprises with high distribution costs and marked economies of scale.

Part Three presents detailed analyses of some large enterprises in the UK brewing industry. It attempts to explore many of the points raised in Part One and Part Two as well as illustrating some of the difficulties of studying large enterprise behaviour. Inclusion of this material in a book-length discussion allows it to be presented in rather more detail than would be possible elsewhere and, more importantly, there is room both to relate the enterprises to one another and to their total industrial context.

The discussion is concluded by Part Four, which asks questions concerning the social and regional consequences of large industrial enterprises. Do intra-regional linkage patterns of large industrial enterprises differ from those of other firms? What are the effects on the system of the increasing number of white-collar jobs in these enterprises? How has the state influenced their spatial behaviour by legislation? Have the large industrial enterprises been more or less responsive to regional policies than their smaller counterparts?

Tentative answers to these questions and others derived from them are put forward in the subsequent chapters; in some cases it is possible to indicate only where such answers might be found. They are not the only questions that can be asked. For example, there is a need to know much more about the relationships between large and small firms; nor is the approach used the only one that could be adopted. In the future, aggregate data may be available to allow a more quantitative examination of large enterprises as a group, instead of analysis of a few enterprises within a narrow range of industries as is done here. What is presented in the chapters that follow is a review of the spatial aspects of the behaviour of large industrial enterprises that had emerged from research published before the end of 1976.

Notes

1. F.E.I. Hamilton, 'Modern Problems of Industrial Location Analysis' in F.E.I. Hamilton (ed.), *The Organisation of Spatial Industrial Systems*, IGU Working Group (Novosibirsk) on Industrial Geography, 1976, London, p.1.
2. Business Statistics Office, *Census of Production, 1972*.
3. K.D. George, 'A Note on Changes in Industrial Concentration in the United Kingdom', *Economic Journal*, 85, 1975, pp.124–8. For the purposes of this introductory statement only, sales are treated as output.
4. *Statistical Abstract of the United States, 1974*, pp.486–7.
5. These figures are taken from the UK Census of Production data.
6. L. Hannah, *The Rise of the Corporate Economy*, 1976, London, p.216.
7. *Statistical Abstract of the United States, 1974*, pp.486–7.
8. A. Jay, *Corporation Man*, 1972, London, p.275.
9. J.K. Galbraith, *The New Industrial State*, 1967, London.
10. S.J. Prais, *The Evolution of Giant Firms in Britain*, 1976, Cambridge.
11. Hannah, *Corporate Economy*.
12. R. Sobel, *The Age of Giant Corporations: a Micro-economic History of American Business*, 1972, Westport, Conn.
13. G. Bannock, *The Juggernauts*, 1971, London.
14. L. Hannah and J.A. Kay, *Concentration in Modern Industry*, 1977, London.
15. S. Aaronovitch and M.C. Sawyer, *Big Business: Theoretical and Empirical Aspects of Concentration and Mergers in the United Kingdom*, 1975, London.
16. J.M. Blair, *Economic Concentration: Structure, Behaviour, and Public Policy*, 1972, New York.
17. N. Chamberlain, *Enterprise and Environment: the Firm in Time and Place*, 1968, New York.
18. D.F. Channon, *The Strategy and Structure of British Enterprise*, 1973, London.
19. A.D. Chandler, *Strategy and Structure*, 1962, Cambridge, Mass.
20. Prais, *Giant Firms in Britain*, p.22.
21. Department of Industry, *The Regeneration of British Industry*, Cmnd.5710, 1974, London.
22. *Counter Inflation Programme. Operation of Stage Two*, Cmnd.5267, 1973, London.
23. S. Holland, *Capital Versus the Regions*, 1976, London; S. Holland, *The Regional Problem*, 1976, London.
24. R.B. McNee, 'Towards a More Humanistic Economic Geography: the Geography of Enterprise', *Tijdschrift voor Economische en Sociale Geografie*, 51, 1960, pp.201–5.
25. G. Krumme, 'Toward a Geography of Enterprise', *Economic Geography*, 45, 1969, pp.30–40.
26. R.B. McNee, 'A Systems Approach to Understanding the Geographic Behaviour of Organisations, Especially Large Corporations', in F.E.I. Hamilton (ed.), *Spatial Perspectives on Industrial Organisation and Decision-Making*, 1974, London, pp.47–75.
27. McNee, 1960, 'Towards a More Humanistic Geography', p.201.
28. Krumme, 'Toward a Geography of Enterprise', p.30.
29. D.W. Heal, 'Ownership, Control, and Location Decisions: the Case of the British Steel Industry Since 1945', in Hamilton (ed.), *Industrial Organisation and Decision-Making*, pp.265–86; D.W. Heal, *The Steel Industry in Post-War Britain*, 1974, Newton Abbott; K. Warren, 'Recent Changes in the Geographical Location of the British Steel Industry', *Geographical Journal*, 135, 1969, pp.343–64.

30. D. Fleming and G. Krumme, 'The Royal Höesch Union: Case Analysis of Adjustment Patterns in the European Steel Industry', *Tijdschrift voor Economische en Sociale Geografie*, 59, 1968, pp.177–99.
31. G. Krumme, 'The Inter-regional Corporation and the Region', *Tijdschrift voor Economische en Sociale Geografie*, 61, 1970, pp.318–33.
32. R.B. Le Heron and E.C.R. Warr, 'Corporate Organisation, Corporate Strategy and Agribusiness Development in New Zealand', *New Zealand Geographer*, 32, 1976, pp.1–16.
33. F. Derrieux-Cecconi, 'Les espaces de la firme: le cas de Creusot Loire', *L'Espace Géographique*, 2, 1973, pp.21–36.
34. G.P.F. Steed, 'The Changing Milieu of a Firm', *Annals of the Association of American Geographers*, 58, 1968, pp.506–25.
35. G. Krumme, 'Corporate Growth Through Spatial Decentralisation: Triumph's Expansion Path', *International Geography, Volume 1*, 1972, Montreal, pp.554–6.
36. For example R.A. Erickson, 'The Regional Impact of Growth Firms: the Case of Boeing, 1963–68', *Land Economics*, 50, 1974, pp.127–36; G. Krumme and R. Hayter, 'Implications of Corporate Strategies and Product Cycle Adjustments for Regional Employment Changes', in L. Collins and D.F. Walker, *Locational Dynamics of Manufacturing Activity*, 1975, London, pp.325–56.
37. K. Warren, 'Heavy Industry With Special Reference to the Chemical Industry', in M. Chisholm and G. Manners (ed.), *Spatial Policy Problems of the British Economy*, 1971, Cambridge, especially pp.194–211.
38. H.D. Watts, 'The Location of the Beet-Sugar Industry in England and Wales, 1912–36', *Transactions of the Institute of British Geographers*, 53, 1971. pp.95–116.
39. K. Chapman, 'Corporate Systems in the United Kingdom Petro-Chemical Industry', *Annals of the Association of American Geographers*, 64, 1974, pp.126–37; and K. Chapman, 'Agglomeration and Linkage in the United Kingdom Petro-Chemical Industry', *Transactions of the Institute of British Geographers*, 60, 1973, pp.33–68.
40. R. Hayter, 'Corporate Strategies and Industrial Change in the Canadian Forest-Products Industries', *Geographical Review*, 66, 1976, pp.209–28.
41. D.J. Rake, 'The Economic Geography of the Multi-Locational Industrial Firm With Special Reference to the East Midlands', unpublished PhD thesis, University of Nottingham, 1972, summarised in *East Midland Geographer*, 6, 1974–76, pp.1–16, 51–65, 173–84 and 265–74.
42. Hayter, 'Corporate Strategies and Industrial Change', p.209.
43. P. Dicken, 'Some Aspects of Decision Making Behaviour in Organisations', *Economic Geography*, 46, 1970, p.434.
44. A. Pred, *Behaviour and Location, Part I*, 1967, Lund; A. Pred, *Behaviour and Location, Part II*, 1969, Lund.
45. H.A. Stafford, 'The Geography of Manufacturers', in C. Board *et al.*, *Progress in Geography*, 4, especially pp.207–13; H.A. Stafford, 'The Anatomy of the Location Decision: Content Analysis of Case Studies', in Hamilton (ed.), *Industrial Organisation and Decision-Making*, pp.169–87.
46. P.M. Townroe, *Industrial Location Decisions: a Study in Management Behaviour*, 1971, Birmingham.
47. Krumme, 'Toward a Geography of Enterprise', p.32.
48. The final sentence is adapted from W.H. Starbuck, 'Organisational Growth and Development', in W.H. Starbuck (ed.), *Organisational Growth and Development*, 1971, Harmondsworth, p.11.
49. E. Penrose, *The Growth of the Firm*, 1959, Oxford, p.15.
50. H.G. Manne, 'Mergers and the Market for Corporate Control', *Journal of Political Economy*, 83, 1965, pp.110–20.

51. A.A. Berle and G.C. Means, *The Modern Corporation and Private Property*, 1968, New York (first published in 1932).
52. R.L. Marris, *The Economic Theory of Managerial Capitalism*, 1964, London.
53. Channon, *Strategy and Structure*, p.75.
54. M. de Vroey, 'The Owners' Intervention in Decision-Making in Large Corporations: a New Approach', *European Economic Review*, 6, 1975, pp.1–15.
55. B.R. Scott, *Stages of Corporate Development, Part I*, Harvard Business School, mimeographed, 4–371–294, BP 998, 1971.
56. Krumme, 'Toward a Geography of Enterprise', p.36.
57. McNee, 'Towards a More Humanistic Geography', p.203.
58. Department of Industry, *Report of the Census of Production, 1968*, *Part 158, Summary Tables: Enterprise Analysis*.
59. The enterprises are Philips (42 centres) and Plessey (29 centres). Data from Expenditure Committee, *Regional Development Incentives, HC327*, 1973, London, pp.480 and 500.
60. Channon, *Strategy and Structure*, pp.237–8.
61. J. Hassid, 'Recent Evidence of Conglomerate Diversification in U.K. Manufacturing Industry', *Manchester School*, 4, 1975, pp.372–95.
62. Dicken, 'Some Aspects of Decision Making Behaviour', p.427.
63. R.T. Averitt, *The Dual Economy*, 1968, New York.
64. Galbraith, *New Industrial State*.
65. Holland, *Capital Versus the Regions*.
66. H. Demsetz, 'Where is the New Industrial State?', *Economic Inquiry*, 12, pp.1–12.
67. Scott, Part II.
68. F. McFadzean, *The Economics of John Kenneth Galbraith*, 1977, Centre for Policy Studies, London.
69. Bannock, *The Juggernauts*, p.5.
70. Chamberlain, *Enterprise and Environment*, p.47.
71. A. Pred, *Major Job-Providing Organisations and Systems of Cities*, Commission on College Geography, Resource Paper No. 27, Association of American Geographers, 1974, p.3.
72. G.P.F. Steed, 'Internal Organisation, Firm Integration and Locational Change: The Northern Ireland Linen Complex, 1954–1964', *Economic Geography*, 47, 1971, p.372.
73. McNee, 'Towards a More Humanistic Geography', p.205.
74. W.M. Evan, *Organisational Experiments*, 1971, p.1.
75. R.G. Lipsey, *An Introduction to Positive Economics*, 1975, London, p.284.
76. B.R. Scott in 'Foreword' to D.F. Channon.
77. F.E.I. Hamilton, 'A View of Spatial Behaviour, Industrial Organisation and Decision-Making', in Hamilton (ed.), *Industrial Organisation and Decision Making*, p.14.
78. P. Dicken, 'The Multi-Plant Business Enterprise and Geographical Space: Some Issues in the Study of External Control and Regional Development', *Regional Studies*, 10, 1976, p.408.
79. D. Granick, *Managerial Comparisons of Four Developed Countries: France, Britain, United States, Russia*, 1972, Harvard.
80. F.E.I. Hamilton, 1976 *Spatial Industrial Systems*, pp.4–5.

Part One

THE LARGE INDUSTRIAL ENTERPRISE IN SPACE

2 SPATIAL STRUCTURES

The large industrial enterprise is a difficult organisation to identify, especially where there is no attempt to foster an enterprise identity. Some British readers will probably need reminding that many of their soups come from Unilever, that much of their bread is manufactured by Associated British Foods and that a large quantity of their beer is produced by Grand Metropolitan Hotels. Not surprisingly, Turner called these enterprises 'invisible Empires'.[1] In this chapter, the first part is devoted to discussing examples of large industrial enterprises. The second illustrates the distribution of employment provided by large industrial enterprises both in aggregate and individually. The third examines the plant and linkage structures of an enterprise. The fourth and final part reviews the attempts to explain the location of an enterprise's head-office and research activities.

Large Industrial Enterprises in the UK

Table 2.1 lists the industrial enterprises employing over 65,000 workers in the United Kingdom in 1975–6.[2] Of the three largest enterprises, only GEC is still privately owned, as both British Steel and British Leyland belong to the public sector. The large enterprises operate in a variety of industries which the industrial groups in the table tend to hide. Unilever, for example, produces frozen foods, ice-cream and animal foods; GEC owns Elliott Automation, Marconi, Hotpoint and Osram, while Playgirl Nylons, Susan Small dresses and Aristoc Hosiery are just some of the many products from Courtaulds.[3] Similarly, the Imperial Group divides its activities into four main sections – Tobacco, Food, Brewing and Paper,[4] while GKN's activities in Britain are grouped into Automotive and General Products sectors.[5] There is no complete listing of the 100 largest employers of labour, but *The Times 1000* provides a list of the largest enterprises ranked by turnover.[6] In the top 100 are the major brewing enterprises (Allied Breweries, Bass-Charrington and

Table 2.1: Industrial Enterprises Employing Over 65,000 Workers Within the United Kingdom, 1975–6

Enterprise		000's
British Steel Corporation	Metals	210
General Electric (GEC)	Electrical Engineering	166
British Leyland	Vehicles	154
Imperial Chemical Industries (ICI)	Chemicals	125
Courtaulds	Textiles	114
Unilever	Chemicals	91
Imperial Group	Food & Tobacco	87
Thorn	Electrical Engineering	82
Guest, Keen and Nettlefolds (GKN)	Engineering	73
Hawker-Siddeley	Aerospace	71
Ford	Vehicles	69
Lucas Industries	Engineering	69

Source: *The Times 1000, 1976–7* and *Annual Reports*.

Whitbread), food manufacturing enterprises (Cadbury Schweppes, Rowntree Mackintosh, Brooke Bond Liebig, Ranks-Hovis-McDougall), aerospace concerns (British Aircraft Corporation) and representatives of the electronics industry (Plessey, IBM), as well as the older electrical engineering companies (Philips). All these are in addition to the enterprises listed in Table 2.1. The large number of sectors in which these enterprises operate means that there are few industries in which they do not have some influence. Indeed, the distribution of the top 100 (quoted companies) among industries is 'more even than might . . . [be] . . . expected'.[7]

These absolute size measures give no indication of the relative size of an enterprise to the industry or industries in which it operates. Relative size is assessed usually by the extent to which an industry shows signs of concentration. Concentration is used here *not* in the spatial sense, but as an indication of the extent to which ownership is concentrated in the hands of a few enterprises. A number of sophisticated measures have been developed to measure concentration, but in many empirical studies reliance is placed on the relatively straightforward *concentration ratio*.[8] This describes either the percentage of the market for a particular product that is supplied by 'n' enterprises, or the percentage of an industry's output produced by 'n' enterprises. The size of 'n' depends on data availability. The most commonly used values of 'n' are 3, 4 and 5.[9]

A detailed insight into industrial concentration is provided by analyses of the 1968 *Census of Production*, which became available only in 1974. Concentration data were published for 324 industries, and no fewer than 73 per cent had a five-firm concentration ratio in excess of 50, and over a third had ratios in excess of 80 per cent. Despite the fact that industries accounting for 25 per cent of sales were excluded because of lack of data, Aaronovitch and Sawyer concluded that the figures

Table 2.2: Weighted Five-Firm Sales Concentration Ratios, United Kingdom, 1968

Industry Group	Weighted Concentration Ratio
Vehicles	93.4
Food, drink and tobacco	81.5
Chemical and allied industries	78.9
Electrical engineering	75.9
Metal manufacture	75.3
All Manufacturing	69.4
Bricks, pottery, glass, cement	65.4
Other	60.7
Metals n.e.s.	58.3
Plant, machinery and instrument engineering	53.9
Textiles	52.8
Paper, printing and publishing	52.4
Leather, clothing and footwear	32.2
Timber, furniture	23.4

Source: Based on the calculations in K.D. George, 'A Note on Changes in Industrial Concentration in the United Kingdom', *Economic Journal*, 85, 1975, p. 126. Since concentration data relate to products rather than industry groups, the figures for each group are derived from the concentration ratios of the products in the group, the contribution of each product to the overall industry figure being adjusted (weighted) to take into account its contribution to the total sales of the industry group.

provide 'a reasonably accurate picture of all manufacturing industries'.[10]

The variation in concentration levels among thirteen different industry groups has been calculated by George (Table 2.2).[11] To some extent, the industries with above average concentration ratios are those in which the absolutely large enterprises are operating. The enterprises that contribute to these high levels of concentration have been described in detail by Hart, Utton & Walshe[12] and Walshe[13] for the United Kingdom. One typical example will suffice. The British Sugar Corporation, although employing only 5,500 workers and coming 239th in *The Times 1000*, accounts for over one-third of the UK sugar output. While small in the absolute sense it is clearly large in the relative sense in that it is an important enterprise in the sugar industry.

This identification of large industrial enterprises in the UK has indicated the kind of enterprise with which this account is concerned. Similar lists can be assembled readily for other economies. It is now possible to turn to the spatial structures created by large industrial enterprises.

Spatial Structures

Several studies have been made of spatial changes within large industrial enterprises as will be illustrated in Chapters 4 to 6, but few have asked questions relating to an enterprise's spatial structure at one point in time. Consequently, while it is possible to trace patterns of change in some selected parts of an enterprise's system, an overall view of the essential characteristics of the spatial structure of an enterprise is difficult to obtain. By concentrating on the dynamic before the static, studies of large industrial enterprises are to be contrasted with other areas of industrial geography where analyses of static patterns are well developed. The collection of essays edited by Collins and Walker shows some of the cautious first steps that are being made into the field of dynamics.[14] The emphasis on change in enterprise studies reflects possibly an awareness of the economic, social and political consequences of these changes. These consequences appear to be of more immediate relevance than the description of an existing system, but there are dangers in examining change before a thorough understanding of the spatial structure of an enterprise has been achieved, as that structure may well guide any change that takes place.

The examination of the spatial structure of large industrial enterprises is concerned with the location of their operating sites and the interactions taking place between those sites. As the preliminary stage in an investigation of these spatial features, it is important to specify some of the questions that ought to be asked about an enterprise's spatial structure. Some questions might be as follows. Where is the employment provided by these large organisations? What is the characteristic spatial pattern of a single enterprise? Can an attempt be made to classify the spatial framework within which an enterprise operates? Do the functions at different sites lend themselves to any classificatory system? How are the sites related by intra-organisational material flows? What are the alternative ways by which information flows hold the enterprise together? Once descriptive questions such as these have been answered it should be feasible to move towards an explanation of at least some of the features that they have established.

Aggregate Data

Most previous studies of the distribution of employment in large industrial enterprises have been able to draw only on data relating to a few concerns. It is, of course, difficult to make generalisations from such data and analysis of the employment patterns of all large enterprises in a particular economy is more useful. Special tabulations were prepared for this study by the Business Statistics Office (BSO) of the United Kingdom showing the regional distribution of employment in the thirteen largest private-sector enterprises in 1972. Like most BSO data merchanting, transport and warehouse activities are excluded wherever possible but head-offices which were engaged mainly in the administration of production units are included.

The regional distribution of employment in these enterprises is shown in Figure 2.1. It includes all the enterprises listed earlier in Table 2.1 with the exception of British Steel, but it is not possible to identify the two remaining enterprises with any degree of accuracy. This new data set presents an intriguing picture. These enterprises alone provide almost 15 per cent of UK manufacturing employment. Half their employment is in the West Midlands and the South East (49.9 per cent), while these two regions plus East Anglia, the South West and the East Midlands account for 62.5 per cent. Only 14.1 per cent is in the

Figure 2.1: Employment in Private-Sector Enterprises With Over 50,000 Employees, 1972

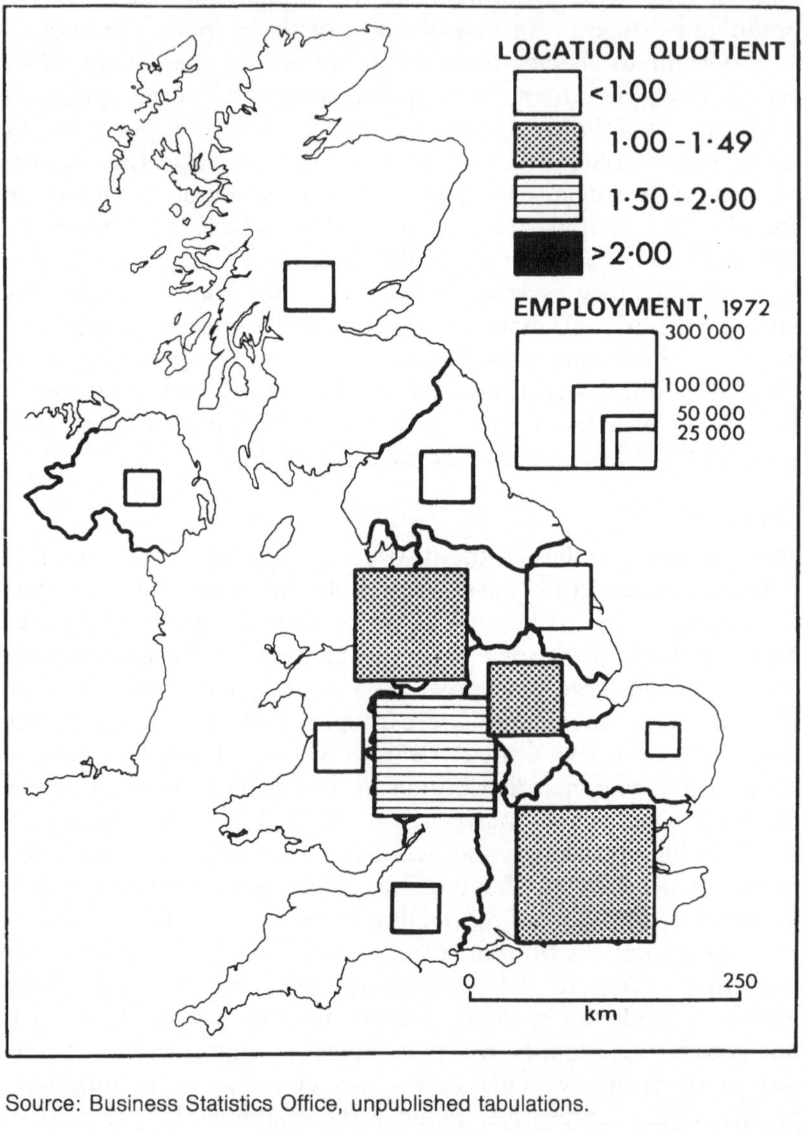

Source: Business Statistics Office, unpublished tabulations.

peripheral areas of Northern England, Wales, Scotland and Northern Ireland. In the West Midlands no less than 24 per cent of the manufacturing jobs are controlled by these thirteen enterprises.

The overall pattern of over- and under-representation of large enterprises in relation to smaller firms is indicated by a location quotient. The South East has just about its expected share, as has the East Midlands, while East Anglia and the South West are under-represented. The only marked over-representation occurs in the West Midlands and the North West. This pattern of location quotients, and consideration of the firms involved, suggests that much of the difference between large and small firms reflects the distribution of the motor vehicle industry and the inclusion of Ford and British Leyland in the top thirteen employers. Presumably if adjustments for industrial structure could have been made, the differences between large and small firms would have been reduced and indeed have become negligible.

It might be objected that these results are extremely sensitive to the positioning of the enterprise's plants in relation to regional boundaries, and that closure or expansion of only a few plants would radically alter the pattern that has emerged. To overcome this difficulty it can be assumed that the existing eleven regions are only one of n possible ways of dividing the country into eleven subdivisions and thus permit treatment of the eleven regions as a sample of all possible regions. On this basis it is possible to see whether there is a significant association between the employment distribution of large and small firms. In view of the positively skewed distribution, a non-parametric test of association (Spearmans R) was used. Overall the distribution of large and small firms is highly correlated ($R_s = +0.911$) and the association is significant ($p < 0.01$). Certainly these large enterprises show no more marked tendency than the remainder of manufacturing to concentrate in the more developed parts of the regional system. Admittedly, if the line between large and small were drawn at another point, a contrasting result might emerge.

On this evidence, the overall distribution of employment in large enterprises is markedly concentrated in the leading regions of the UK economy, but this is true of smaller firms too.

A similar pattern is shown in Figure 2.2, which depicts the distribution of industries in which the weighted five-firm sales concentration ratio was above the national average. Over a quarter of the employment is in the South East, with the North West and West Midlands accounting for another 30 per cent,

Figure 2.2: Employment in Industries With Above Average Concentration Ratios, 1972

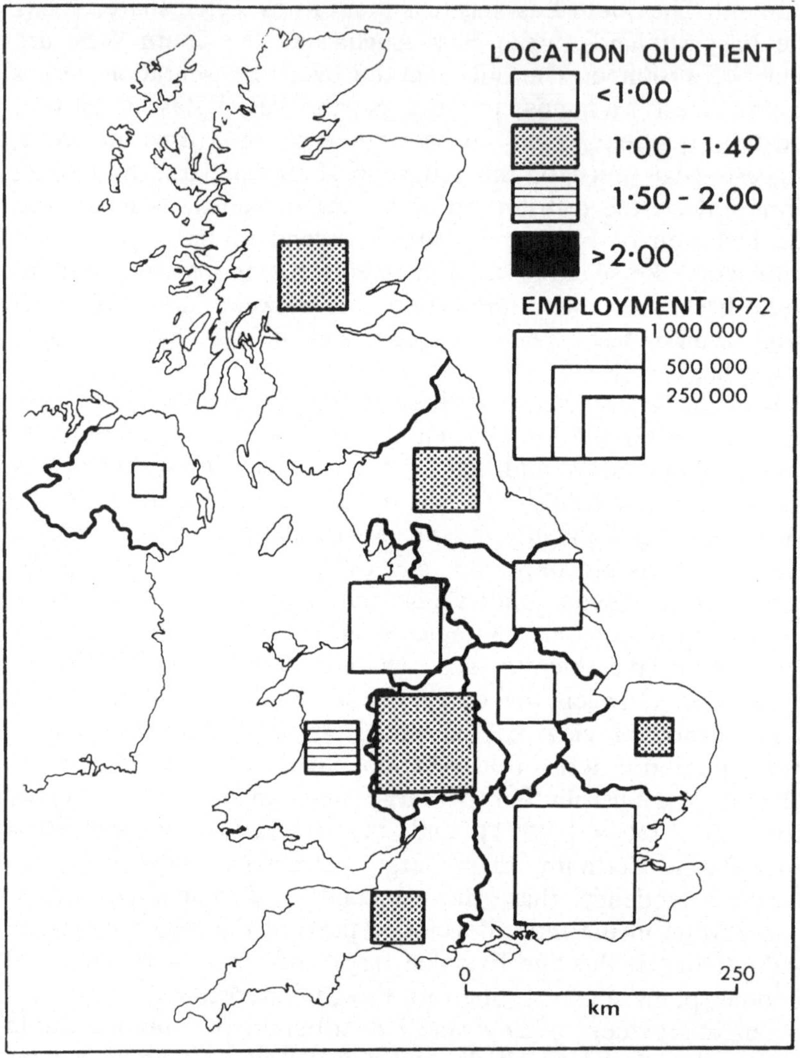

Source: Business Statistics Office, *Report on the Census of Production, 1972*, PA 1002.

but this pattern, like that of the very large enterprises, differs little from that of the remaining industries. No location quotient[15] exceeds 2, and only Wales and the Northern region have quotients in excess of 1.18. The higher values here presumably reflect the shares of metal manufacture in Wales, and metals and chemicals in the Northern Region.

These two data sets produce an important conclusion that, in aggregate and at this spatial scale, large industrial enterprises, whether measured in an absolute or in a relative sense, do not produce spatial patterns which differ markedly from their smaller or less concentrated contemporaries. This suggests that in the long run both large and small enterprises produce similar patterns. It does not follow that the patterns are produced by similar processes.

Enterprise Data

Maps of the employment provided by individual enterprises are not very common but, as Pred has argued, 'studies of the recently and presently existing spatial structures of organisations should be given a high priority'.[16] Enterprise sites, but not employment, are depicted by a number of writers. Rees has shown the UK sites of ICI and the North American sites of Procter & Gamble;[17] other examples are provided by Moore's description of Paccar[18] and Warren's illustration of the sites of Shell and Fisons.[19] Further examples are provided in Chapter 9. Some published maps of employment provision do exist. Keeble was able to produce corporate maps of both Chrysler and British Leyland,[20] while Osborne produced a map of Rolls-Royce based on data collected by Rake.[21] The sheer size of the organisations and the nature of the information held at head-office levels militates against the ready availability of spatially coded employment data.[22] The two corporate maps reproduced here (Figures 2.3 and 2.4) are drawn from special tabulations prepared for a government enquiry. For that report only two other enterprises (Ford and Vauxhall) produced detailed breakdowns of employment data.[23] Although the spatial structures of the individual enterprises have changed since 1972, their patterns illustrate some of the important spatial characteristics of large industrial enterprises.

Figure 2.3 shows the distribution of the plants of Cadbury Schweppes. Cadbury Schweppes is about thirty-sixth in size by turnover among enterprises operating primarily in manufacturing industry and employs around 26,000 workers. It is one of five enterprises which account for 83 per cent of the sales of cocoa products. Figure 2.3 depicts clearly the

Figure 2.3: Employment at the Main United Kingdom Sites of Cadbury Schweppes, 1972

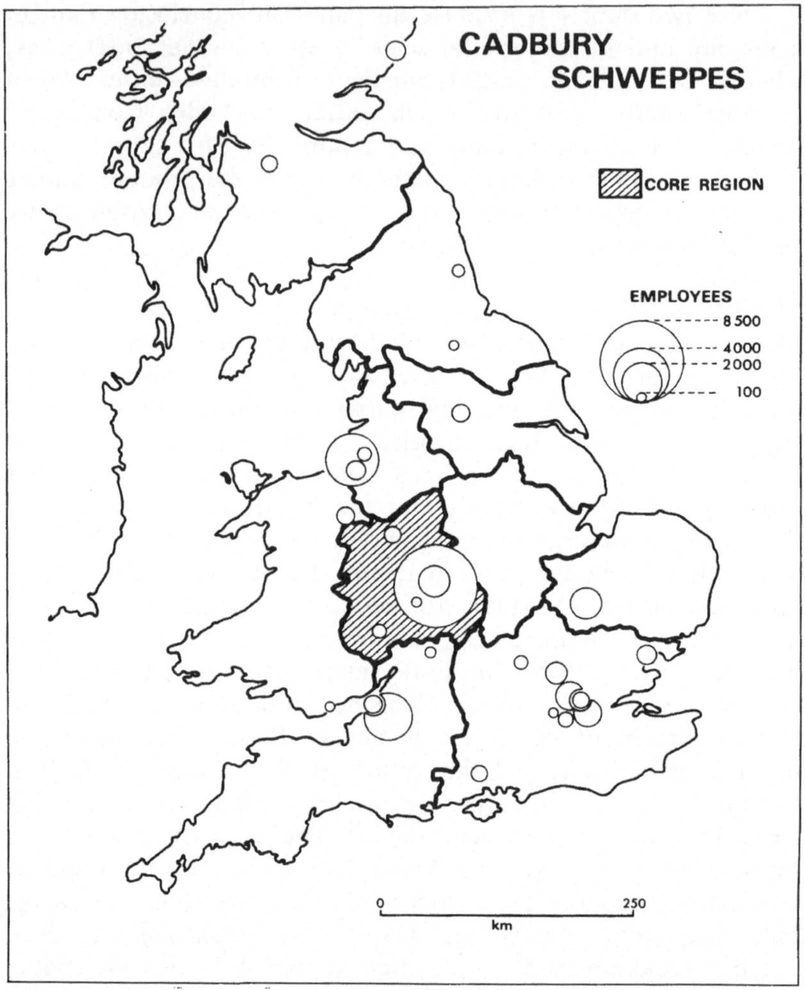

Source: Expenditure Committee, *Regional Development Incentives HC 327*, p. 486.

enterprise's multi-plant and multi-regional character, as it lacks plants only in Northern Ireland and the East Midlands. The enterprise is essentially West Midlands based, with three other regions (South East, South West and North West) of subsidiary importance. The West Midlands includes the massive Bournville complex employing 8,500 in the manufacture of chocolate confectionery, while a further 1,000 employees work at the Typhoo plant in Birmingham. The North West and South West are each dominated by one major plant; in the North West, the Moreton (Liverpool) works employs around 3,000 workers in food products and chocolate biscuits, while in the South West the major plant is Fry's confectionery works between Bristol and Bath. Although the enterprise has over 3,000 workers in the South East they are employed in a number of small units, an example of which is the manufacture of lime juice at St Albans. In plant size, Cadbury Schweppes is characterised by a number of small scale operations, and almost two-thirds of its 28 plants employ fewer than 500 workers. Nevertheless, three plants employ over 2,000 workers each.

The distribution of Dunlop's activities shown in Figure 2.4 is described less easily in verbal terms. Overall it has 36,000 employees engaged in manufacturing and is one of the five enterprises supplying 93 per cent of the sales of rubber products. Again, it is multi-regional in its scope, with plant absent only from Northern Ireland and the South West. Its two major production areas are in the North West and the West Midlands, with the Northern region also of considerable importance. In this case it is possible to allocate activities to one of four product divisions within the enterprise: a tyre group, consumer group, industrial group and engineering group. Each group shows a rather different pattern. At one extreme the engineering group has plants in only two regions; the consumer group has plants in some seven regions. Further, while the activities in the core region and North West are diversified, Wales and Yorkshire & Humberside depend heavily on the fortunes of the consumer group, just as the Northern Region depends on the industrial group. Overall, the 35 plants within the Dunlop organisation are large, three have over 2,000 employees and another seven have over 1,000.

From this brief description of the spatial patterns of the plants of the enterprises two distinctive features emerge. First, they are multi-plant, multi-regional concerns, and second, although there is a wide dispersal, the employment figures alone identify a clear core region and for both this is the West Midlands. Dunlop's West Midland activities employ around one-third of their total employees and a similar proportion of Cadbury Schweppes' employees are in the same area. Similarly, there are one or two

Figure 2.4: Employment and Product Divisions of the Major Dunlop Factories in the United Kingdom, 1972

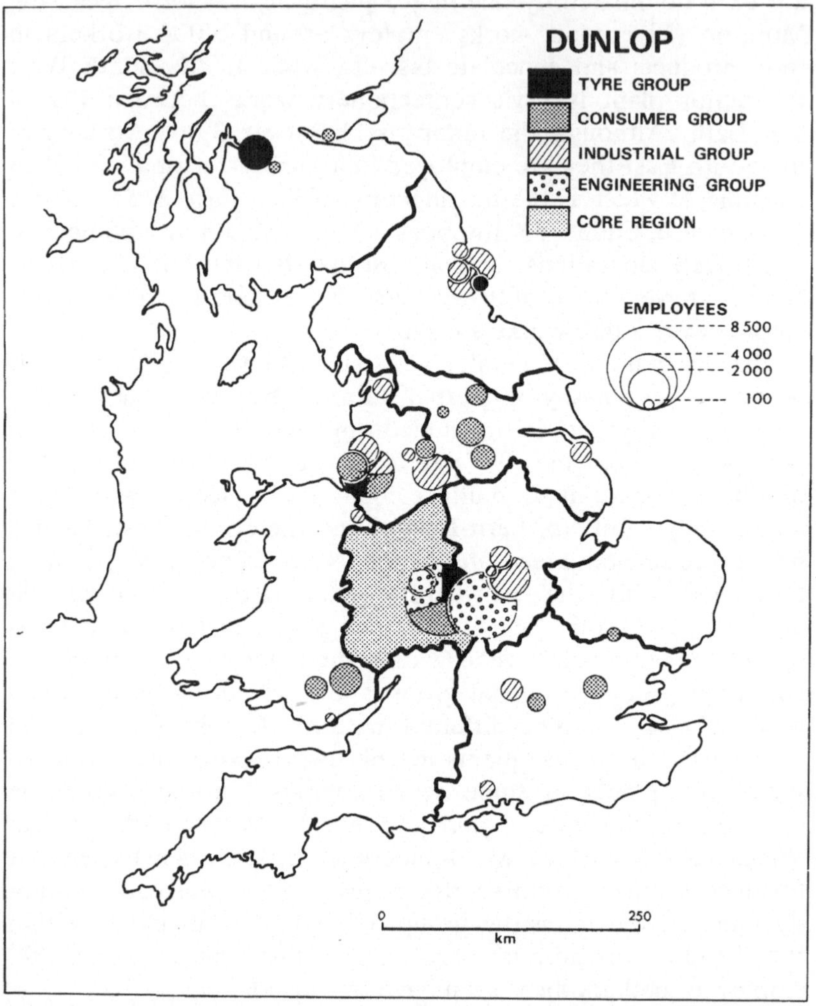

Source: Expenditure Committee, *Regional Development Incentives*, Session 1972–3, HC 327, p. 494.

plants which are much bigger than the remainder of those in the enterprise. Cadbury Schweppes' Bournville operations are three times the size of the next biggest plant, while Dunlop's Coventry activities are just less than twice the size of the next largest set of activities. It is within the core region that the interaction between the different activities of the enterprise is expected to be most intense.[24] While this may be true for the explicitly manufacturing operations, in both these enterprises at least some of the head-office functions are undertaken in London and not in the core region. It is impossible to explore the varying degrees of interaction within these two enterprises as the data are simply not available. Instead, attention is turned away from the individual enterprise towards generalisations about some of the more important features of corporate spatial structures.

Plant Characteristics

Labasse has argued that within any geographical area an enterprise 'imparts a structure by the siting of its plants . . . [and] the distribution of its markets'.[25] Preliminary ideas about this structure were developed by Dicken[26] and McNee,[27] but the most elaborate discussion is by Taylor.[28] He describes operational space, action space, information space and decision space, but these terms present difficulties, and it seems more useful to talk of three readily identifiable zones.

(1) The market area: simply, the area or areas within which an enterprise's products are sold.

(2) The supply area: the area or areas from which an enterprise receives its material inputs.

(3) The plant space: the area or areas within which an enterprise has located its plants.

Perhaps an apology is needed for introducing yet another classification of the space within which an enterprise operates, but it does provide a workable classification for phenomena for which data are not over abundant. Clearly, these areas will overlap and within each area there will be varying degrees of interaction, for, as studies of linkage of both inputs and outputs have shown, interaction tends to be very marked immediately around the plants of an enterprise.[29] Further, within the plant space of an enterprise the two examples have shown it is possible to see a core region which may contain a considerable proportion of an enterprise's plants and employees. In enterprises with high distribution costs there may be little difference between market areas and plant space – this is seen in Chapter 8 – but in those enterprises where the friction of distance is less important there can be marked contrasts in the spatial extent of the three categories.

The spatial arrangement and inter-relationships of plants within an enterprise's plant space is an almost unexplored topic in the geographical literature, yet Krumme has argued that the 'spatial structure of a corporation, as well as its size . . . [is a] . . . factor of great significance with respect to a firm's ability to adjust to and generate change'.[30] What is more, Steed believes there is a great need for locational analysis 'to place a given plant within its own corporate environment'.[31]

It is likely that the behaviour of these multi-plant enterprises differs from that of a single-plant firm in at least two important ways. First, a plant within a multi-plant enterprise must be considered not as an independent unit, but as part of an enterprise's total operations; its relationship with other plants within the enterprise may be more important than its links with plants in the same industrial group or within the same region. In McNee's words, the value of a location to an enterprise 'depends not only on the inherent advantage of its site and position, but also on its corporate position'.[32] Second, the survival of any plant does not depend on profit or loss criteria alone. An enterprise 'may recognise external benefits stemming from the existence of an establishment and may decide to "adopt" and subsidize it'.[33] As long as the enterprise makes some profit or works steadily towards some other goal, loss-making plants can survive through the use of cross-subsidisation. Further, an enterprise will not make decisions about investment at a particular site in terms of whether a profit can be made there, but in terms of whether it will offer a bigger contribution to profits than investment at other sites belonging to the enterprise.

In attempting to generalise about the spatial pattern of an enterprise's plants what is needed is a classification of the sites belonging to an enterprise. Such a classification may help to identify important patterns in the location of an enterprise's activities, for it does not seem unreasonable to propose that plants in different categories may have different types of location. It may also be the first step towards establishing the long-term employment prospects of different types of site. The classifications discussed below are based on a single parameter. In the long run research will perhaps move towards the ideal proposed by Wood, where sites can be categorised in 'a multivariate classification . . . according to their position within a chain of production, their organisational status, or their ownership background'.[34] Three possible taxonomies are proposed, based on the product cycle, best-practice techniques and functional mix. They are discussed in that order.

The product-cycle approach to plant classification was developed in relation to international trade,[35] but both Krumme & Hayter[36] and Dicken[37] have argued that it might be used in relation to large industrial enterprises. The concept in an *intra*-national context is undeveloped, but the idea behind it is a simple one. Most products pass through a series of recognisable stages in the course of their life, but it seems most useful in this case to distinguish between the growth and mature stages. In the growth stage the product has been successfully developed but it still depends upon an important number of technological inputs and a skilled labour-force. In the mature stage the product is manufactured by mass production techniques utilising primarily an unskilled or semi-skilled labour-force. The different requirements of the two stages appear to have important implications for the location of the stages of a product cycle within an enterprise's plant space.

First, it might be expected that in the early and growth stages of a product's life it will be manufactured in that part of an enterprise's system that can be monitored carefully by management or perhaps by the research and development department. In contrast, products that have reached the mature stage may well be located in the more peripheral parts of the system. Second, contrasts between enterprises may arise as a result of their differing attitudes to new products. An innovating enterprise could have a series of plants associated with products in their growth stage in its core region, together with a more widely dispersed set of plants handling the mature stage of the product cycle. On the other hand, enterprises concerned mainly with the mature stage of the product cycle may have less incentive to concentrate plants near the centre of the corporate system and will show overall a very dispersed set of production plants. Such suggestions remain to be tested.

An alternative approach to plant classification is to use the best-practice concept. The term 'best-practice' appears to have been introduced by Grosse[38] and best-practice techniques, as defined by Salter, are techniques 'which employ the most recent technical advances and . . . [which are] . . . economically appropriate at current factor prices'.[39] The best-practice concept has been extended beyond technological phenomena to include the organisational aspects of innovation. For example, best-practice techniques may include an improved accounting system. The process and managerial innovations can be inter-related. The introduction of best-practice technology may depend on co-operation from the labour-force, which in turn may be obtained only where a best-practice labour relations policy is being followed.

Identification of best-practice plants in a corporate system is by no means straightforward, but Le Heron argues that this can be done by both a technological criterion and an efficiency criterion.[40] In his work the problem was simplified by looking at single-product plants. The same criteria could probably be applied to multi-product plants, although the practical difficulties might well be greater. The technological criteria were based on the type of equipment used by a plant and the efficiency criteria on the output per man. Using these criteria, Le Heron was able to classify plants in the veneer and plywood industries into 'best-practice' and 'other' categories.

Such a classification scheme would not be independent of a product-cycle classification. It seems easier to operationalise than the latter, but there are no clear indications as to the kind of pattern the best-practice plants would take up within a corporate system, although one might expect best-practice plants to be located in the core region, thus reinforcing the effects of the product cycle.

These two classifications have been concerned primarily with the manufacturing sites of an enterprise. Tornqvist[41] classified *all* an enterprise's activities into two groups: the administrative or control functions and the operating functions. The administrative or control functions relate to head-office and research departments, while operating functions cover the primarily manufacturing plants. A development from this is Norcliffe's recognition of five principal functions that are undertaken by manufacturing organisations.[42] These five functions can be envisaged also as the broad categories of activities that might be undertaken by large industrial enterprises. The functions listed by Norcliffe are administration and research (control functions), processing, fabrication and integration (operating functions). The distinguishing of some of the operating functions may need clarification. Integration is essentially the assembly of components made at the fabrication stage; fabrication is the treatment of processed raw materials from the processing stage. The listing of the functions in this order indicates their hierarchical nature; atop the hierarchy sit the control functions, which monitor the movement of materials from the processing to the integrative stage.

The recognition of these functional types appears to have important repercussions for understanding the spatial structure of an enterprise. The reasons for this are two. First, the economies-of-scale in each function may differ, and thus the minimum efficient scale of operation can differ as well.[43] The spatial implications of the difference are that for any given level of enterprise output the ideal number of sites to fulfil each function might vary from function to function. Inevitably, for each function there will be a different number of plants to allocate to specific sites. Thus, to some extent some kind of functional separation will be inevitable. Second, although all functions could be on the same site, each function might have different locational requirements. Some processing plants, for example, tend to be attracted to material sources, while an assembly (or integrative) plant, with a need for large quantities of labour, will be attracted to or develop in a large conurbation. Similarly, high personal contact needs of control units may necessitate a major urban location.

A consideration of the functional characteristics of sites goes some way to understanding the reasons behind their spatial arrangement, but allocating a site's activities to one of these five functions is not always easy, with the exception of the research and administrative categories. Nevertheless, this final classification is the only one which so far permits a move towards a more general understanding of the spatial structure of large enterprises. It is considered again in the final part of this chapter.

Linkages

Classification of plants and sites gives very little idea of their inter-relationships within an enterprise's system, nor does the spatial distribution of an enterprise's plants give any indication of the extent to which such plants are linked into regional and city systems. These two aspects are encompassed by a study of linkages. An enterprise's external links are discussed in detail in Chapter 10, and this chapter examines only the material and information linkages among an enterprise's own sites.

Study of material linkage within an enterprise system depends on provision of fairly full data by the enterprise or enterprises under study. Ideally an inter-plant flow matrix for the enterprise would give an indication of the extent to which any one plant was linked into an enterprise's system. It might even be possible to measure the extent to which the plant is an integral or peripheral part of that system or, viewed the other way, the extent to which an enterprise is linked into a cohesive unit by a series of interlocking material flows. Where detailed information is lacking, the linkage question may be attacked in a more general way. For each plant data could be obtained to illustrate the proportion of outputs sent to other parts of the enterprise, and the proportion of inputs received from the enterprise. This has the advantage over the inter-plant flow matrix in that it allows intra-enterprise material links to be related to material links with other enterprises.

Very little information is available about inter-plant linkages within large industrial enterprises. Moore, for example, depicts corporate flows within an individual enterprise, but does not break it down to flows between specific plants.[44] Cartographic depiction of inter-plant links normally shows presence or absence of links and their nature, but gives no indication of quantities. Both Goodwin[45] and Keeble[46] depict flows between motor vehicle plants, and Chapman[47] provides similar information for some petro-chemical plants. Aggregate data on new plants established from 1964 to 1967, however, show that those plants established by enterprises in *The Times 500* depended more on intra-enterprise inputs and on intra-enterprise sales than did most other plants in the sample.[48] This suggests, albeit in a tentative manner, that plants within large enterprises are more closely integrated with each other than those of smaller concerns. Some further supporting evidence is found in Taylor & Wood's study of the West Midlands metal industries, where 'head-quarters and branch plants of multi-plant firms . . . are concerned mainly with national patterns of contact' instead of with local linkages.[49]

Some early results from Healey's research into the behaviour of multi-plant enterprises within the clothing and textile

Table 2.3: Internal Linkages of Plants in Multi-plant Enterprises

Material Inputs from Within Enterprise (per cent)	Per Cent of Plants
Nil	41.0
1–10	9.7
11–50	12.9
>50	36.4
Material Outputs to Enterprise (per cent)	
Nil	49.7
1–10	9.4
11–50	16.1
>50	24.8

Source: M.J. Healey, 'Changes in the Location of Production in Multi-Plant Enterprises', work in progress for doctoral thesis, University of Sheffield.

industries illustrates dramatically the striking contrasts in intra-enterprise dependency.[50] Table 2.3, based on his work, shows that over one-third of the plants in his sample received more than 50 per cent of their inputs from within the enterprise, and almost a quarter sent over half their output to other parts of the enterprise. In contrast, many of the plants have few intra-enterprise links in either inputs or outputs. These differences are indicative of the marked variations in the extent to which individual plants are linked into an enterprise's production system.

This very limited evidence on intra-enterprise material linkages indicates how very little is known about the topic, but in turning to information flows some ideas can be derived from the work of those concerned with organisational behaviour. The flows of information within an enterprise are channelled formally through communication systems described by organisation charts of the kind shown in Figure 2.5. Only the formal information flows are discussed here, but the importance of other primarily informal links should not be forgotten.[51]

These organisation charts cover normally the whole communication system within an organisation, but in this context only the upper levels of the hierarchy are important, usually the principal control unit and one level below it. This is

Figure 2.5: Three Basic Organisational Structures in Large Industrial Enterprises

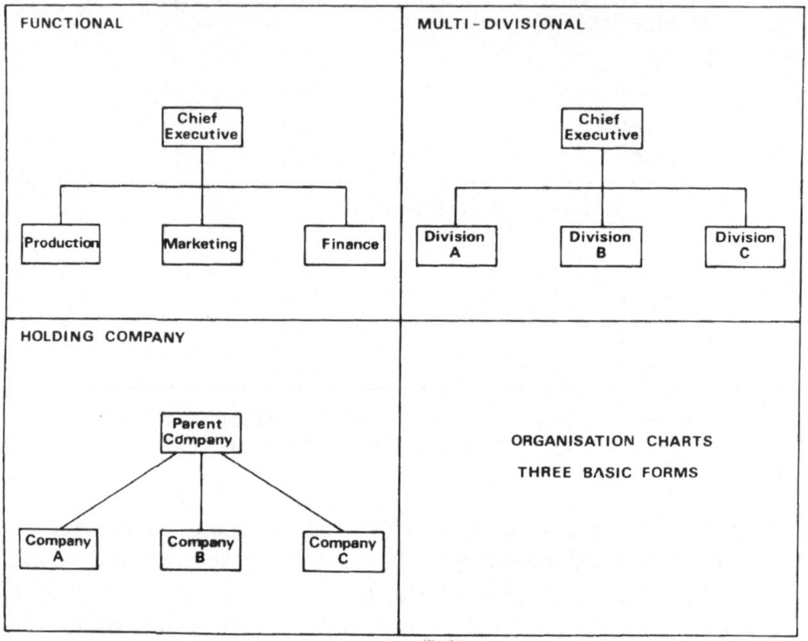

Source: derived from D.F. Channon, *The Strategy and Structure of British Enterprise*, 1973, London, pp. 50-2.

because much spatial behaviour arises from what Simon terms strategic or non-programmed decisions.[52] The routine or programmed decisions (for example, to repair a machine) are handled at lower levels of the organisation, but decisions to invest in major new capacity or to alter radically linkage patterns fall within the higher level, non-programmed category; at least, they ought to fall within this category even if they do not always do so. The actual dividing line between the categories can be defined by maximum spending limits imposed upon the lower levels of the organisational hierarchy.

The organisational structure influences the information received by an organisation and different structures filter that information in different ways as it proceeds to the top of the administrative hierarchy where the non-programmed decisions are usually made. Chandler was able to show how the strategies and structures of an enterprise were inter-related,[53] and following from this it is argued that the organisational structure not only influences the way in which a locational problem is perceived, but may also guide the nature of the spatial policies that are implemented.

The functional structure is headed by a chief executive whose principal role is to co-ordinate the work of specialist functions, which might, for example, include production, marketing and finance. The production activities are controlled by one department and presumably spatial decisions will be concentrated in this department. If production extends beyond a single or a few related products, it becomes extremely difficult for the single department to co-ordinate the differing needs and requirements of each product, and an organisation's ability to cope with changes in a product environment will be limited. As a consequence of this, spatial change by an enterprise may be slow.

The second structure, the holding company structure, is still fairly common. Although the nature of these structures can vary, one form is shown in Figure 2.5. The members of the executive board of the holding company sit on the boards of the subsidiaries and provide the only co-ordinating link between them. There is little attempt to devise an overall enterprise strategy and, where different subsidiaries operate within the same industry, it could be almost impossible for an overall enterprise view of its activities in that industry to emerge. Spatial decisions may well be taken with little reference to the total enterprise.

In the multi-divisional structure an executive board services and monitors each of the operating divisions. Each of these divisions operates within overall constraints of a budget set by the enterprise as a whole, but they have a considerable degree of autonomy.

Of the three basic organisational structures depicted in Figure 2.5 the multi-divisional structure is most frequently associated with large industrial enterprises. Data from 94 of the 100 largest industrial enterprises in the United Kingdom in 1969–70 showed that no less than 71.3 per cent had a multi-divisional structure, 21.3 per cent had a holding company structure and only 7.4 per cent had the functional structure which is more characteristic of small firms.[54] The distinction between the holding company and multi-divisional structures is not always clear cut, and Granick argues that many European enterprises with a multi-divisional structure act as though they were only holding companies for 'there was a lack of detailed planning control [of the divisions] by the headquarters organisation'.[55]

The principles upon which divisionalisation is based are a critical influence on the pattern of information flows within large enterprises. A territorial divisionalisation, where each plant reports to a regional office, may result in very different spatial outcomes from a product divisionalisation, where each plant reports to an office controlling the manufacture of a particular product. The former system may result in solutions to spatial problems being sought within the region for which the division is responsible, whereas the latter may seek solutions on an inter-regional basis.[56]

Information through these organisational structures represents the formal information links that hold an enterprise together and supplement the more readily measured material links. It will be shown in Chapters 5 and 9 how variations in these organisational structures can have an important influence on the spatial behaviour of large industrial enterprises.

This part of the second chapter has taken up some questions introduced initially in Chapter 1 and has illustrated them with reference to large enterprises both in aggregate and individually. Classificatory schemes of an enterprise's space, its plants and its linkage system have been presented. In this last part of the chapter, attention is turned to the functional classification of sites, as in this area some important empirical work has been completed.

Functional Separation

Once the spatial separation of functions is recognised as a characteristic of the spatial structure of an enterprise, the concept of spatial separation has to be clarified. Essentially, the problem is separation at what scale? Are two functions spatially separate if they are undertaken in plants on either side of a road? If not, how far apart do they need to be before they are regarded as separate? Definitive answers to these questions cannot be given, but to avoid problems arising from confusion introduced by imprecise use of the term 'separation', separation is discussed here only at UK planning region scale (Function A is in a different region from Function B) or at urban scale

(Function A is in a different town from Function B). Separation at planning region scale implies inevitably separation at urban scale, but obviously separation at urban level does not necessarily imply separation at regional scale.

Interest in the separation of administrative from other functions dates back to the mid-1960s, while interest in research functions dates from the early 1970s. The concern with the separation of administration (control) from manufacturing activities arises out of the work on regional development[57] and from attempts to distinguish between different types of city.[58] The theme was then developed in investigating the role of multi-locational organisations in guiding the development of a city-system[59] and in influencing regional disparities between one part of a nation and another.[60] In the present context, the principal questions to which answers are being sought are first, what is the empirical evidence for the separation of head-office and research activities from manufacturing activities in large industrial enterprises, and second, how have these disparities been explained? The implications of this separation for city and regional systems are examined in more detail in Chapter 10.

Detailed work on the distribution of head-offices of large enterprises is provided by Parsons.[61] Using data from 69 enterprises, it can be shown that the distribution of the head-offices differs significantly ($p < 0.001$) from the distribution expected from the number of plants controlled by the offices in each region (Table 2.4). Evidence of similar concentration is found also in Johnston's work on Australia,[62]

Table 2.4: Head-Offices and Plants of a Sample of Large Industrial Enterprises in the United Kingdom, 1970

	South East	Other Centre[a]	Periphery[b]
Group Head-Office	51	10	8
Expected Offices[c]	19	22	28

Notes: $\chi^2 = 74.7$***

a. South West, West Midlands, East Midlands, East Anglia.
b. Wales, North West, Yorkshire and Humberside, Northern, Scotland, Northern Ireland.
c. Expected related to the proportion of an enterprise's plants in each region.

Source: Based on data in G. Parsons, 'The Giant Manufacturing Corporations and Balanced Regional Growth in Britain', *Area*, 4, 1972, pp. 99–103.

Johnston and Rimmer's on New Zealand[63] and Pred's survey of the United States and summary of research on West European countries.[64] Most of these works are based upon directory evidence and thus may over-emphasise the dominance of large centres. Several large companies have a small head-office in the major metropolitan centre with most control work carried out elsewhere, but Westaway believes this will be offset because some enterprises with head-offices elsewhere may undertake some of their typical head-office activities in the capital city.[65]

There are some inter-industry variations in degree of separation of administration from other functions. Regionally oriented enterprises may retain their head-offices in the region with which they are associated. Therefore, it might be expected that industries which are highly localised (e.g. hosiery, footwear, in the United Kingdom) will be less likely to be controlled by distant head-offices. It may be inferred that regional specialisations in New Zealand may have influenced head-office location in clothing, food, cement and fuel to be over-represented in the South Island cities;[66] similarly in Australia control of the food industry was over-represented in Hobart and the manufacture of vehicles in Adelaide.[67] It is not perhaps surprising that several of the industries, where administration remains in regional centres, are those dependent on resources with a restricted geographical distribution.

On research functions, analysis by Buswell & Lewis of UK data indicates that the South East and West Midlands taken together had 56.6 per cent of research establishments and 44 per cent of all manufacturing employment.[68] There is some over-representation present, but if allowance is made for the fact that research establishments tend to be associated with new industries which are concentrated in these regions anyway, the share of research establishments in these regions is not unduly high. Crum & Gudgin, in contrast, discovered 61 corporate R & D laboratories separate from production sites, with a total employment of about 27,500 jobs. Of these, some 75 per cent are in the South East.[69] Parsons's data show that the West Midlands and South East had 69.8 per cent of the research units of respondent enterprises, but had only 43.3 per cent of the plants controlled by these enterprises.[70]

The general evidence seems to suggest that there is a tendency for control units concerned with research and

Figure 2.6: Employment of Administrative, Technical and Clerical Employees in Private-Sector Enterprises With Over 50,000 Employees, 1972

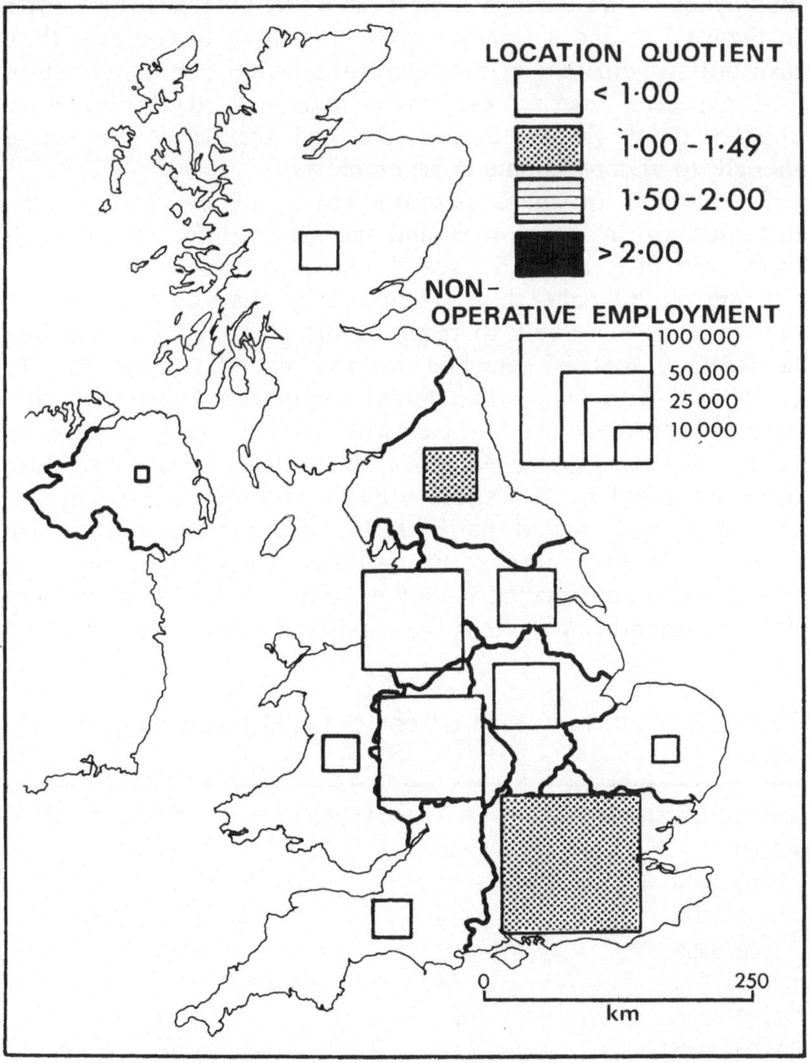

Source: Business Statistics Office, unpublished tabulations.

administration to be more spatially concentrated than operating units. A more subtle shift in enterprise activities may accentuate this effect in that the occupational mix of employees on different sites will vary from one area to another. The distribution of the administrative, technical and clerical employees of the thirteen largest industrial enterprises is shown in Figure 2.6, and a location quotient is used to compare their distribution with that of the operatives in the same enterprises. The expected over-representation mainly in the South East appears quite clearly, despite the fact that this data set is thought to under-estimate these employees.

Explanation of these patterns seems to lie in both the increased size of enterprises and the special information needs of the administrative and research functions.

Crum & Gudgin show (Table 2.5) that an increase in enterprise size is likely to result in the creation of a detached head-office, that is detached from a manufacturing site. In enterprises with fewer than 5,000 employees, fewer than half have a detached head-office; with over 50,000 employees, nearly all have a detached office. The effects of size have also been illustrated by Watts. He utilised data on all non-financial enterprises and showed that both the large and the medium-size firms have a distribution of head-offices which differs from that which would be expected if they were distributed in accordance with all employment, but the smallest enterprises show no

Table 2.5: Detached Head-Offices of UK Manufacturing 'Firms', 1975

Total UK Employment	Number of Firms	Per Cent Detached
<2000	146	44
2000–2999	107	43
3000–4999	119	42
5000–9999	95	65
10,000–19,999	54	63
20,000–49,999	39	79
50,000–99,999	17	88
⩾100,000	4	100

Source: Based on R.E. Crum and G. Gudgin, *Non-Manufacturing Activities in UK Manufacturing Industry*, 1976, p. 45.

significant difference between the observed and expected frequencies. The control of smaller firms is distributed in accordance with distribution of the working population. While there is no magic size at which administrative and manufacturing activities are separated at regional scale, it seems likely that where a UK enterprise's turnover exceeds £10 million (at 1971 prices) control is separated from the production sites.[71]

In the majority of cases the detached head-office or control unit tends to be located in the principal metropolitan area. For example, in the United Kingdom 93 per cent of the detached head-offices of firms employing over 30,000 people were in central London.[72] The logic of a control unit located in a major metropolitan centre has two aspects.

First, the centre itself provides the optimum area for access to other parts of the country, and indeed overseas. For example, the existing communication network in the United Kingdom makes London the most convenient location for a head-office for a multi-regional concern. Evans illustrates this from the pre- and post-nationalisation pattern in the UK steel industry. The seven major steel companies prior to nationalisation had head-offices in Glasgow, Teesside, Sheffield, Port Talbot and Chester; following nationalisation British Steel's head-office became London. Before nationalisation most of the steel companies' plants were confined to a particular region and the head-office was in the same region. Only when the enterprises became part of a multi-regional concern was the head-office of the major enterprise moved to another site. Further, for organisations with overseas sales, London provides the best site for overseas contacts by air.[73]

The second factor favouring concentration in one area is that 'contact intensive' functions require reasonably close spatial proximity to operate well. The control units in which these functions are located depend upon flows of information, particularly flows of a non-routine nature. Direct personal contacts (i.e. face-to-face) between the members of different control units provide the rationale both for the separation of control from production and the clustering of control units in specific locations. These direct personal contacts usually have the advantage of good, two-way transmission of messages, leave less room for misunderstandings and permit the use of a variety of senses and techniques such as the interpretation of facial expressions or the use of diagrams and other bulky records.[74] Goddard's analysis of office linkages in central London provides an example of the importance of this interaction.[75]

There seem to be good reasons too for locating separate research establishments in a major urban area, but out of 165,000 jobs in 1975 in research departments in UK enterprises, only about 20 per cent are on non-production sites. Whether it is best to keep research away from production sites is open to debate. If they are combined, research may become overwhelmed with minor production problems; if they are separate, an ivory tower mentality may develop among research scientists. Crum & Gudgin argue the bigger the department or firm, the more likely is a separate R & D facility and they attribute the concentration in the South East to the fact that head-offices are already there, that in the immediate post-war years country houses were available to become research centres, that the South East is the most accessible area of the United Kingdom in both the national and the international sense, and that there is an increasing number of research establishments in the region.[76] The region is in that part of the United Kingdom where contact potential is at a maximum.

One factor which escapes their attention is that there is some evidence (albeit subjective) that the South East appears to offer a more attractive environment than other parts of Britain. Buswell & Lewis see this as a particularly critical factor.[77] To maintain a successful research establishment it is important to be able to develop and keep a team of research scientists and technicians, and some managers think that a location in the South East, or a town within it, may help an enterprise meet this aim. Honeywell, for example, when selecting a location for a high technology plant (admittedly not a research establishment but with similar labour demands) selected the South East because 'of the need to attract an unusually large number of graduate engineers'.[78]

Conclusion

This chapter has identified some of the absolutely and relatively large enterprises operating within the United Kingdom economy. It has described, at Planning Region scale, the distribution of the employment of the very largest enterprises and the most concentrated industries. The pattern did not differ from that of the smaller firms or less concentrated sectors. The examples of Cadbury Schweppes and Dunlop show clearly that while most enterprises are multi-locational and multi-regional they have a clearly distinguished core region. The core region stands at the heart of what is termed the plant space, which is itself set within the market and supply areas of an enterprise. A number of typologies for plant classification are suggested, these being based on the product cycle, the best-practice concept and site functions. Little is known of the intra-enterprise material links, but the literature of organisational behaviour suggests that information flows may be focused through one of three types of organisational structure: the functional, the holding company and the multi-divisional. The use of different principles in divisionalisation is thought to influence an enterprise's reactions to spatial problems.

Only the distribution of functions is examined in detail. Both administration and research (control functions) are shown to separate from production sites and to concentrate in major metropolitan areas. This is particularly characteristic of multi-regional and very large enterprises. Clustering of head-offices in the metropolitan core of an economy is shown to reflect both the high accessibility of that core from all parts of an economy, the concentration itself mirroring the necessity for inter-enterprise face-to-face contact by the very top executives. The clustering of research activities is less readily explicable.

One aspect of the large industrial enterprise is probably conspicuous by its absence from this discussion, and it is to the spatial pattern of the foreign-controlled large enterprise that attention is turned in the next chapter.

Notes

1. L. Turner, *Invisible Empires*, 1970, London.
2. Below 65,000 employees are a substantial group of enterprises with over 50,000 employees recorded in their *Annual Reports*.
3. *Who Owns Whom*, 1975.
4. Imperial Group Ltd., *Imperial Group Products, 1976*. The full title of the group is Paper, Board, Packaging and Plastics.
5. Guest, Keen and Nettlefolds Ltd., *GKN Facts and Figures*, 1976.

6. Times Newspapers Ltd., *The Times 1000, 1976–1977*, 1976, London.

7. G. Whittington, 'Changes in the top 100 Quoted Manufacturing Companies in the United Kingdom, 1948–68', *Journal of Industrial Economics*, 21, 1972–3, p. 25.

8. Commission of the European Communities, *A Study of the Evolution of Concentration in the United Kingdom Paper Industry*, 1975, Brussels.

9. Concentration ratios relate usually to the sales or output of firms manufacturing in the area for which the ratio has been calculated; they exclude the role of imports. Further a three-firm ratio with the remainder of the market supplied by two firms, depicts a very different situation from that where thirty firms supply the rest of the market.

10. S. Aaronovitch and M. Sawyer, 'The Concentration of British Manufacturing', *Lloyds Bank Review*, 114, 1974, p. 21.

11. K.D. George, 'A Note on Changes in Industrial Concentration in the United Kingdom', *Economic Journal*, 85, 1975, p. 126.

12. P.E. Hart, M.A. Utton and G. Walshe, *Mergers and Concentration in British Industry*, 1973, Cambridge.

13. G. Walshe, *Recent Trends in Monopoly in Great Britain*, 1974, Cambridge.

14. L. Collins and D.F. Walker, *Locational Dynamics of Manufacturing Activity*, 1975, London.

15. Location quotient calculated by comparing the region's percentage of concentrated industries with region's share of other industries.

16. A. Pred, 'The Growth and Development of Systems of Cities in Advanced Economies', in A. Pred and G. Tornqvist, *Systems of Cities and Information Flows*, 1973, Lund, p. 63.

17. J. Rees, 'The Industrial Corporation and Location Decision Analysis', *Area*, 4, 1972, p. 201; J. Rees, 'Decision-Making, the Growth of the Firm and the Business Environment', in F.E.I. Hamilton (ed.), *Spatial Perspectives on Industrial Organisation and Decision Making*, 1974, London, p. 201.

18. C.W. Moore, 'Industrial Development Linkage Paths', *Tijdschrift voor Economische en Sociale Geografie*, 64, 1973, p. 97.

19. K. Warren, 'Growth, Technical Change and Planning Problems in Heavy Industry With Special Reference to the Chemical Industry', in M. Chisholm and G. Manners (eds.), *Spatial Policy Problems of the British Economy*, 1971, Cambridge, p. 196.

20. D. Keeble, *Industrial Location and Planning in the United Kingdom*, 1976, London, pp. 188-90.

21. R.H. Osborne, 'Place and Man', *East Midland Geographer*, 5, 1970–3, pp. 182-3.

22. Attempts were made to collect plant employment data for the largest employers of labour, but while lists of operating sites could be obtained readily, the enterprises often did not hold detailed employment data for each site.

23. Expenditure Committee, *Regional Development Incentives*, HC327, Session 1972–3, 1973, London, p. 85 and p. 464.

24. R.B. McNee, 'A Systems Approach to Understanding the Geographic Behaviour of Organisations, Especially Large Corporations', in Hamilton (ed.), *Spatial Perspectives*, p. 55.

25. J. Labasse, 'The Geographic Space of Big Companies', *Geoforum*, 6, 1975, p. 114.

26. P. Dicken, 'Some Aspects of Decision Making Behaviour in Business Organisations', *Economic Geography*, 47, 1971, pp. 426-37.

27. McNee, 'A Systems Approach'.

28. M.J. Taylor, 'Organisational Growth, Spatial Inter-Action and Locational Decision Making', *Regional Studies*, 9, 1975, pp. 313-23.

29. M.J. Taylor, 'Local Linkage, External Economies and the Iron-Foundry Industry of the West Midlands and East Lancashire Conurbations', *Regional Studies*, 7, 1973, pp. 387-400.

30. G. Krumme, 'Toward a Geography of Enterprise', *Economic Geography*, 45, 1969, p. 40.

31. G.P.F. Steed, 'Plant Adaptation, Firm Environments and Location Analysis', *Professional Geographer*, 23, 1971, p. 327.

32. R.B. McNee, 'Towards a More Humanistic Economic Geography: the Geography of Enterprise', *Tijdschrift voor Economische en Sociale Geografie*, 51, 1960, p. 204.

33. Krumme, 'Toward a Geography of Enterprise', p. 36.

34. P.A. Wood, 'Industrial Location and Linkage', *Area*, 1969, No. 2, p. 38.

35. L.T. Wells, *The Product Cycle and International Trade*, 1972, Harvard.

36. G. Krumme and R. Hayter, 'Implications of Corporate Strategies and Product Cycle Adjustments for Regional Employment Changes', in Collins and Walker, *Locational Dynamics*, pp. 325-46.

37. P. Dicken, 'The Multi-Plant Business Enterprise and Geographical Space: Some Issues in the Study of External Control and Regional Development', *Regional Studies*, 10, 1976, pp. 409-10.

38. A.P. Grosse, 'The Technological Structure of the Cotton Textile Industry', in W. Leontief *et al*., *Studies in the Structure of the American Economy*, 1953, New York, p. 264.

39. W.E.G. Salter, *Productivity and Technical Change*, 1966, Cambridge, p. 26.

40. R.B. Le Heron, 'Best Practice Firms and Productivity Changes in the Pacific North-West Plywood and Veneer Industry, 1960-72: Some Regional Growth Implications', *Environment and Planning* A, 8, 1976, pp. 163-72.

41. G. Tornqvist, *Flows of Information and the Location of Economic Activities*, 1968, Lund; and *Contact Systems and Regional Development*, 1970, Lund.

42. G.B. Norcliffe, 'A Theory of Manufacturing Places', in Collins and Walker, *Locational Dynamics*, pp. 43-4.

43. Since in many industries there is no distinct size of output at which costs cease to fall with increased size, it is usual to define minimum efficient scale by an arbitrary point after which decline in costs with increased size is relatively insignificant. For example, this could be defined as the point at which a doubling of plant would reduce total average unit costs by less than 5 per cent. Thus the minimum efficient scale for a plant would be the smallest plant which, in doubling its size, reduced the costs by less than 5 per cent. For a full discussion see C.F. Pratten, *Economies of Scale in Manufacturing Industry*, 1971, Cambridge, p. 26.

44. Moore, 'Linkage Paths', p. 103.

45. W. Goodwin, 'The Structure and Position of the British Motor Vehicle Industry', *Tijdschrift voor Economische en Sociale Geografie*, 56, 1965, pp. 145-56.

46. D. Keeble, ibid.

47. K. Chapman, 'Oil Based Industrial Complexes in the United Kingdom', *Tijdschrift voor Economische en Sociale Geografie*, 61, 1970, pp. 157-72.

48. Expenditure Committee, *Regional Development Incentives*, Session 1973-4, HC 85-I, 1973, London, p. 659.

49. M.J. Taylor and P.A. Wood, 'Industrial Linkage and Local Agglomeration in the West Midlands Metal Industries', *Transactions of the Institute of British Geographers*, 59, 1973, pp. 147-8.

50. M.J. Healey, 'Changes in the Location of Production in Multi-Plant Enterprises', work in progress for doctoral thesis, University of Sheffield.

51. W. Brown, *Exploration in Management*, 1965, Harmondsworth, pp. 47-8. I am indebted to Suzanne Richbell for drawing my attention to this reference.
52. H.A. Simon, *The New Science of Management Decision*, 1960, New York, pp. 5-6.
53. A.D. Chandler, *Strategy and Structure: Chapters in the History of the Industrial Enterprise*, 1962, Cambridge, Mass.
54. D.F. Channon, *The Strategy and Structure of British Enterprise*, 1973, London, pp. 51–2.
55. D. Granick, *Managerial Comparison of Four Developed Countries: France, Britain, United States, Russia*, 1972, Boston, p. 40.
56. J.L. Gibson, J.M. Ivancevich and J.H. Donnelly, *Organizations, Structure, Process, Behaviour*, 1973, Dallas, pp. 145-52.
57. P. le Fillâtre, 'La puissance economique des grandes agglomerations françaises', *Études et Conjoncture*, 19, 1964, pp. 3-40.
58. W. Goodwin, 'The Management Centre in the United States', *Geographical Review*, 55, 1965, pp. 1-16.
59. A. Pred, *Major Job Providing Organisations and Systems of Cities*, Commission on College Geography, Resource Paper No. 27, 1974, Washington, D.C.
60. J. Westaway, 'Contact Potential and the Occupation Structure of the British Urban System', *Regional Studies*, 8, 1974, pp. 57-73; J. Westaway, 'The Spatial Hierarchy of Business Organisations and its Implications for the British Urban System', *Regional Studies*, 8, 1974, pp. 145-55.
61. G. Parsons, 'The Giant Manufacturing Corporations and Balanced Regional Growth in Britain', *Area*, 4, 1972, pp. 99-103.
62. R.J. Johnston, 'Commercial Leadership in Australia', *Australian Geographer*, 10, 1966, pp. 49-52.
63. R.J. Johnston and P.J. Rimmer, 'Commercial Leadership in New Zealand', *New Zealand Geographer*, 23, 1967, pp. 165-8.
64. Pred, *Major Job Providing Organisations*.
65. Westaway, 'Contact Potential', p. 71.
66. Johnston and Rimmer, 'Commercial Leadership in New Zealand'.
67. Johnston, 'Commercial Leadership in Australia'.
68. R.J. Buswell and E.W. Lewis, 'The Geographical Distribution of Industrial Research Activity in the United Kingdom', *Regional Studies*, 4, 1970, pp. 297-306.
69. R.E. Crum and G. Gudgin, *Non-Manufacturing Activities in UK Manufacturing Industry*, Report by the School of Social Studies of the University of East Anglia, 1976, Norwich, p. 179.
70. Parsons, 'Giant Manufacturing Corporations'.
71. H.D. Watts, 'Further Observations on Regional Growth and Large Corporations', *Area*, 4, 1972, pp. 269-73.
72. Crum and Gudgin, *Non-Manufacturing Activities*, p. 166.
73. A.W. Evans, 'The Location of the Headquarters of Industrial Companies', *Urban Studies*, 10, 1973, pp. 390-1.
74. Tornqvist, *Contact Systems*.
75. J.B. Goddard, 'Office Linkages and Location: a Study of Communications and Spatial Patterns in Central London', *Progress in Planning*, 1, 1973, Part 2.
76. Crum and Gudgin, *Non-Manufacturing Activities*, pp. 179-81.
77. Buswell and Lewis, 'Geographical Distribution', p. 177.
78. Expenditure Committee, *Regional Development Incentives*, p. 177.

3 INDIGENOUS AND FOREIGN ENTERPRISES

In many economies an important sub-group of large industrial enterprises are under foreign control. Among the leading employers in the United Kingdom, Ford has its headquarters in the USA and Philips in the Netherlands. Similarly, in some highly concentrated industries, foreign enterprises account for a high proportion of home-produced sales – examples from the United Kingdom are provided both by breakfast cereals (73 per cent foreign controlled) and vacuum cleaners (79 per cent).[1] These features are characteristic of other developed countries with the exception of the United States. Concern with the spatial characteristics of foreign-controlled enterprises within the United States has been minimal, but it is US-based enterprises which play an important role in economies outside their home country. The description and explanation of the distribution of foreign-controlled large enterprises within an economy have raised considerable interest and some of the limited evidence relating to their spatial characteristics is brought together in this chapter.

The interest of geographers in multi-nationals has been stimulated by the work of Vernon[2] in the United States and Dunning[3] in the United Kingdom. Much of this work has focused upon the selection of locations at an international scale; for example, this is the primary concern of both Blackbourn[4] and Hamilton.[5] This problem is not explored here; instead, attention is focused upon the spatial structures of foreign-controlled large enterprises *within* a particular economy.

There are two very important limitations to the evidence presented in this chapter. First, while most countries record the employment in plants owned by foreign firms, they rarely distinguish between the sizes of either the owned or owning firm. The important repercussion of this is that the evidence relates to all foreign firms (regardless of size) and it follows that, while the general discussion is in terms of *enterprises*, the evidence relates to *firms*. Until more appropriate data are available this is all that is feasible, but since it seems that employment in plants owned by foreign firms is dominated by large multi-national enterprises they must play a major role in shaping the spatial patterns created by foreign-owned firms. Second, in comparing foreign and indigenous firms the data are not available in a sufficiently disaggregated form to allow for structural differences between the two groups to be taken into account. These two difficulties are stressed as they clearly impose important limitations on the extent to which it is possible to generalise about the spatial behaviour of foreign-owned large industrial enterprises from the evidence presented here.

The chapter first sets out the extent and characteristics of foreign-owned manufacturing activities in various countries and puts forward a number of reasons for expecting the spatial behaviour of foreign-owned large industrial enterprises to differ from that of similar indigenous concerns. The evidence is then examined to see whether the expected differences do occur and the chapter concludes with a brief review of the efforts made to explain the observed differences.

Foreign Enterprises

Extent of Foreign Control

There is little doubt that foreign enterprises are an important sub-set of large industrial enterprises. In 1971 foreign firms provided employment for over three-quarters of a million employees (804,100) in the United Kingdom, that is 11.4 per cent of employment in private-sector firms.[6] Similarly in the Netherlands, de Smidt suggests that from 1950 to 1964 new foreign manufacturing establishments accounted for 16 per cent of the total increase in employment.[7] Likewise between 1945 and 1965, of the 575,000 jobs in the United Kingdom involved in inter-regional moves, some 18.9 per cent originated abroad, and this *excludes* inter-regional moves by foreign firms already established in the country.[8] These figures relate to all manufacturing, and were data available for large industrial enterprises; no doubt a much higher proportion of total employment would be accounted for by foreign concerns.

Foreign participation is not necessarily spread evenly over all industries; indeed, it tends to be concentrated in only a few. For example, engineering, electrical goods and vehicles alone accounted for 60.4 per cent of the employment in foreign firms in the United Kingdom in 1963.[9]

So too, the importance of the enterprises of different foreign countries will vary between one economy and another. In the Republic of Ireland from 1955 to 1969 foreign firms established 261 plants, of these 38 per cent were British, 22 per cent American and 18 per cent West German.[10] The Netherlands received 50 per cent of its plants from the United States from 1945 to 1964, and 17 and 12 per cent respectively from the United Kingdom and Northern Europe.[11] Figures for Britain relating to all employment (not just new establishments) show that of foreign-controlled employment by far the largest share is held by the United States (75.8 per cent) but significant contributions are made also by the Netherlands (7.3 per cent), Canada and Switzerland (5.2 per cent each) and France (3.3 per cent).[12]

The enterprises of particular foreign countries tend to specialise in characteristic industries, and partly as a result of this they often have distinctive plant size distributions. In the Netherlands the majority of new US plants were in the machinery industry (not electrical), the new plants from the United Kingdom were predominantly in chemicals and the North European plants predominantly in textiles and clothing.[13] In Ireland, the most important British sector was textiles, and the most important sectors for American firms were metals and miscellaneous industries.[14] Plant size variations in the Netherlands suggested the US firms built large plants. This was true of Ireland, too, where O'Farrell compared grant-aided plants in Ireland over the period 1960-73 and found that in mean floor space per establishment US plants were largest, followed by the West German and British plants.[15]

Contrasts in the degree of foreign control in different industries, variations in country of origin and in plant sizes are indicative of some of the problems of comparing the spatial structures of foreign and indigenous enterprises. Ideally, data sets would be adjusted to remove any differences resulting from the structural characteristics of the two sub-sets, but as was pointed out earlier this cannot be done with the existing sources of data and the discussion below must be read with this very important limitation in mind.

Expected Spatial Patterns

Yannopolous & Dunning, following the ideas of Vernon, argue that 'the choice of sites of foreign-based enterprises will be dominated by locational considerations that are different from those affecting similar choices of national enterprises',[16] and as a result foreign-controlled large industrial enterprises are expected to display a spatial pattern which differs from that of indigenous large enterprises.

An important reason for expecting a contrast is that the foreign enterprise does not, initially at least, have a core region within its host country. Hamilton notes that the distribution of the national enterprises is explained partly by 'successful growth where they were established by their "founding fathers"'.[17] The two enterprises discussed in the last chapter depicted this feature.

The extent of the difference will be influenced by the growth path selected by the foreign-based enterprise. Normally, a marketing unit precedes the setting up of a manufacturing operation, the latter being undertaken by acquisition of established firms or the setting up of new plants. A compromise between the two principal methods is to set up a joint company with an indigenous enterprise.

Entry by new plants appears, from evidence in Scotland, to be most common. There, Forsyth shows that only 20 per cent of the foreign firms were established by acquisition.[18] Since entry by new plants does not inherit any features from pre-existing patterns, entry by this route is more likely to result in differences between foreign and indigenous enterprises than entry by acquisition.

Decisions about growth methods and location may well be taken by 'absentee' decision makers, who are subject to constraints which differ from those operating on indigenous enterprises. The potential effects of those constraints on spatial patterns are not at all clear. While a foreign concern might select an established and prosperous region for its initial operations within a country in order to reduce the risk and uncertainty inherent in a new project, it may also be forced to depend upon government-financed information sources with their tendency to direct new investment to peripheral areas. These contrasting expectations are seen also if the foreign-based enterprise has an awareness of national space which differs from that of an indigenous enterprise. For example, the distance between Dundee and London will seem much less to a New York head-office than to one based in south-east England. This may result in a greater propensity to favour what are seen in the national context as peripheral areas, but conversely, a foreign-based management might place a premium on access to an international airport for control purposes.[19] This would tend to act in the opposite direction.

Much of the argument of the previous paragraph depends upon the assumption that non-programmed decisions are taken by overseas management. While this is usually true for initial operations within a country, the sites for subsequent expansions could be selected by national managements, perhaps subject only to ratification of the decision by head-office. Clearly, the pattern of subsequent expansion may be influenced to no small extent by the degree of autonomy that has been granted to local management.

Other contrasts may emerge as a result of differences in language, culture and social and economic institutions between foreign and host nation. Further, the foreign enterprise faces the particular difficulty that its presence in an area may not be seen as wholly good by the nation concerned. The pros and cons of foreign investment for a particular country are summarised by Hamilton and an example will suffice.[20] Foreign investment will be welcomed for the employment it provides, but on the other hand there is the fear that those jobs are under the influence of managements based abroad. The threat this presents is emphasised by Vernon, who observes that 'the enterprise whose operations are dispersed among many geographic areas may be able to reduce its commitment in the less promising areas and expand in those areas which seem more profitable'.[21] In view of the politically sensitive nature of foreign enterprises, their spatial policies may be constrained by the need to maintain good relations with the state. The influences of foreign enterprises when they present a direct challenge to the interests of indigenous concerns is illustrated by the example of Canadian Breweries in Chapter 8.

Variations in linkage patterns between foreign and indigenous enterprises may emerge for similar reasons to those outlined above. In addition, since the foreign enterprise has, by definition, plants elsewhere it might be expected to be less well integrated into a national economy than an indigenous concern, particularly if it attempts to procure materials from, and supply products to, its own plants.

This discussion indicates that it does not seem unreasonable to expect the spatial patterns of foreign and indigenous enterprises to differ, but the direction and extent of those differences remains uncertain, and can be clarified only by reference to the empirical evidence. As has been observed elsewhere, 'the elements of enterprise structure and strategy interact in so many different ways, that it is not possible to take any dogmatic position regarding the influence of the locational strategies of foreign-based enterprises'.[22]

Spatial Patterns

Inter-Regional Scale

The spatial distribution of foreign-controlled employment within an economy can be difficult to establish. For example within the United Kingdom both academic studies[23] and government-sponsored enquiries[24] have been forced to work with very unsatisfactory data sets. Nevertheless by piecing together the fragmentary evidence it is possible to explore the distribution of foreign-controlled employment in the United Kingdom, the location of new foreign-controlled plants and the pattern of overall employment change in foreign-controlled plants over the last decade.

Until this study, writers concerned with the spatial pattern of employment in foreign-owned plants were restricted to data on foreign firms as a whole. However, data specially prepared for this investigation now permit the identification of three groups of firms with direct investment in the United Kingdom. These groups are US-controlled firms, the firms controlled by the original six members of the EEC and a remainder category. Only the first two groups are discussed here and it should be noted that joint operations such as Unilever and Shell are treated as being UK-owned. The data were provided by the Business Statistics Office and are subject to the same limitations as the BSO data discussed in the last chapter. Further, the small numbers of EEC-owned plants in some regions may have caused one or two large plants to have had an undue influence on the aggregate patterns. The data also differ from those published by the Census of Production as they include estimates for non-respondents, unsatisfactory returns and small establishments of under twenty-five employees, all of which are excluded from the published figures.

The overall distribution of the foreign-controlled jobs is shown in Figure 3.1. Two-fifths of the employment is in the South East, with a further fifth in the North West and Scotland taken together. Over-representation, measured by a location quotient comparing employment in foreign-owned plants with employment in UK-owned plants, is apparent in two types of area: the periphery (Wales, Scotland and Northern Ireland) and the core, the South East, plus East Anglia. While some concentration of foreign direct investment can be found in the more developed regions of the UK economy, at the same time these firms place more than their share of employment in the peripheral areas. They are over-represented in the periphery by no fewer than 60,000 jobs. Significantly, it is the intermediate zones between the periphery and the core that fail to obtain their share of employment created by foreign firms in the United Kingdom. The United Kingdom thus fails to depict clearly the concentration in the more developed regions of a country, as has been noted by Hamilton for several other EEC members.[25]

A clearer concentration on a core region by foreign firms is seen in Ray's study of US plant in Canada. Admittedly, the spatial scale is rather different, but he was able to show that US firms were more highly concentrated in the Toronto area than Canadian ones and 'that differences in the location of Canadian and American-controlled manufacturing employment are not simply a consequence of the differences in industry type in which foreign capital is invested'.[26]

This clear concentration of US-owned firms in a core region is less well marked in the United Kingdom. The pattern is very similar to that shown in Figure 3.1 since, as was shown earlier, US firms account for three-quarters of the foreign-owned employment. Admittedly, two-fifths of the employment in US-owned plants is in the South East, but a further quarter is found in the North West and Scotland taken together.

In contrast, employment in plants controlled by firms based in the EEC shows a concentration in the South East as Figure 3.2 makes clear. East Anglia and the South East account for 47.3

Figure 3.1: Employment in Foreign-Owned Enterprises in the United Kingdom, 1971

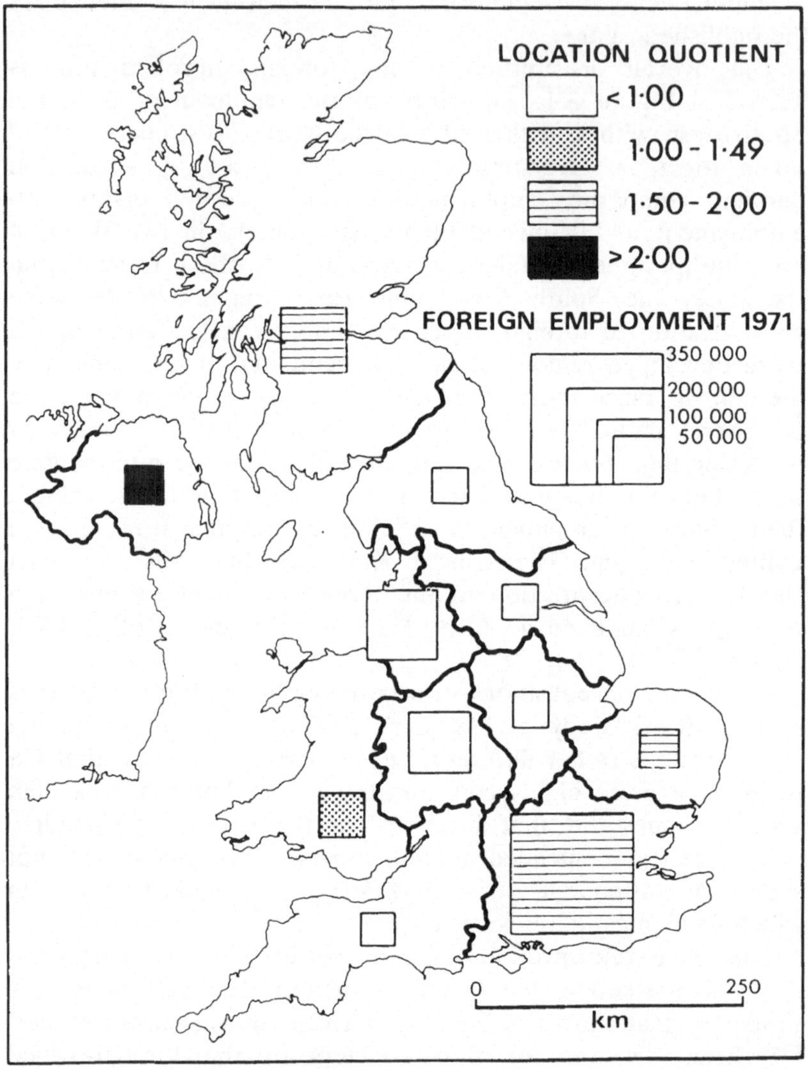

Source: Business Statistics Office.

per cent of the total and these are the only two regions, with the exception of Northern Ireland, where over-representation occurs. The location quotient for the North West is 1.00. Scotland and Wales get only 10 per cent of EEC-controlled

Figure 3.2: Employment in EEC-Owned Enterprises in the United Kingdom, 1971

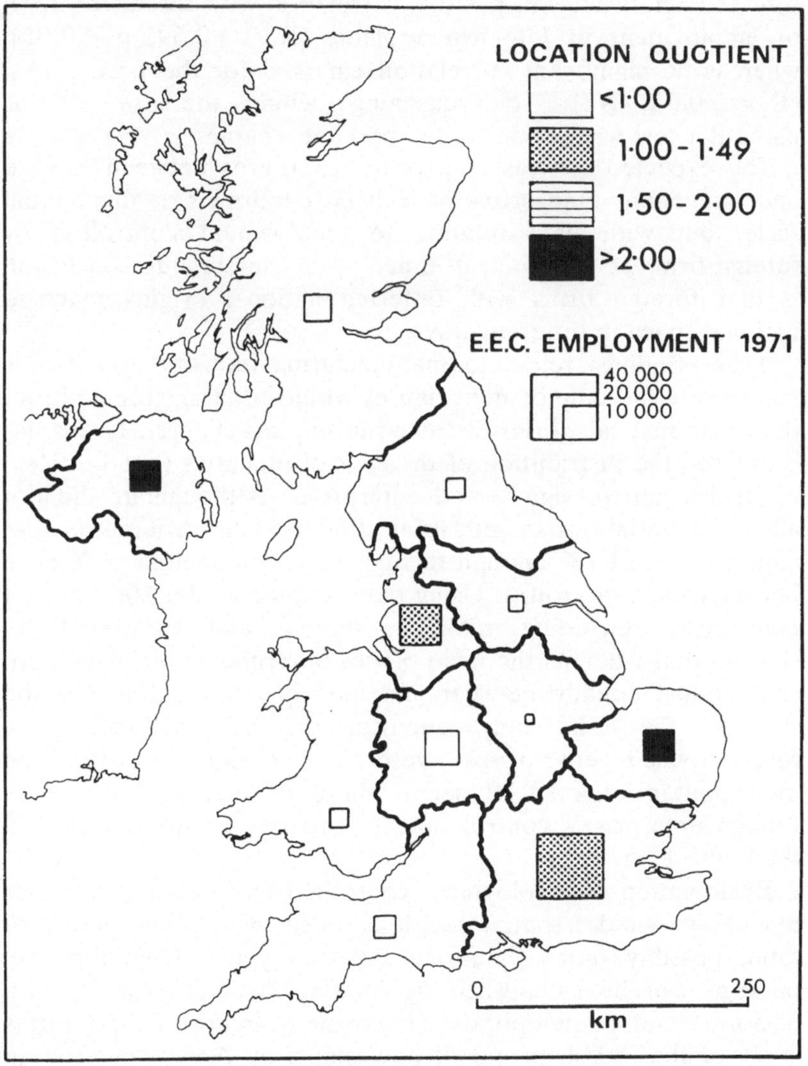

Source: Business Statistics Office.

employment compared with 18.7 per cent of US-controlled employment.

The differences in the distribution of EEC- and US-controlled employment emerge distinctly if their relationship with employment in UK-owned firms is considered. Overall, employment in plants owned by firms based in the United States shows a significant and positive correlation with the distribution of employment in UK-owned plants ($R_s = +0.69$, $p < 0.05$), whereas no significant correlation emerged for the EEC group ($R_s = +0.38$, NS). The reasoning behind the use of this particular test was set out in the previous chapter.

The expected contrasts in location patterns between foreign and indigenous enterprises have been confirmed at this spatial scale, but with data relating to employment controlled by foreign firms at one point in time. A very interesting conclusion is that foreign firms with differing national origins react to national space in different ways.

These findings relate to manufacturing industry as a whole and ideally the employment figures would be disaggregated into the functional categories discussed in the last chapter. Evans has compared the distribution of the control functions (head-offices) of British and foreign-owned enterprises. Although he did not allow for variations in industrial structure, the differences that emerged were large enough to suggest a fundamental difference between the two groups. Using data relating to the 1000 largest enterprises (including retailing, mining and transport) he showed that whereas the head-offices of British enterprises were split almost equally between the metropolitan region and the rest of the UK, only one-fifth of the head-offices of foreign-owned enterprises were in locations outside the metropolitan region.[27] It seems there is a tendency for the foreign enterprise's control functions to be over-represented in the South East.

Examination of employment controlled by foreign enterprises inevitably includes spatial decisions taken over a long period of time, possibly more than one hundred years. Contemporary patterns can be established by looking both at new location decisions and contemporary employment trends. Blackbourn's study of the establishment of new plants by American firms in Britain, France, Germany and Sweden provides some striking evidence which suggests that the location of foreign-controlled plants outside the national capital and other metropolitan areas is unusual, and that concentration is still a feature of the contemporary scene. Only in the United Kingdom is there a marked propensity to locate elsewhere.[28]

This is reflected (albeit at a rather different scale) in the UK inter-regional movement data for 1945 to 1965. Almost half the employment in firms new to the country went to Scotland (42.6 per cent) and only 15.6 per cent to the South East (Table 3.1), Northern Ireland, Wales and the North West receiving about 8 per cent of the total each. These figures are even more interesting if their regional distribution is compared with the destination of employment created by inter-regional movement, which was dominated in all probability by the branch plants of the larger enterprise. Whereas over half the internal UK movement went to Wales, the Northern region and North West, only one-fifth of the moves originating abroad went to those regions. The contrasts are yet more marked when the over-representation of moves from abroad to Scotland is examined. Scotland's share of moves from abroad was almost *four* times its share of employment received from inter-regional moves. The general pattern is confirmed by Keeble's discussion of the period from 1966 to 1971.[29] Nevertheless, while few indigenous firms set up branches

Table 3.1: Destination of Moves from Abroad and Inter-Regional Movement, United Kingdom, 1945–65

Region	Abroad	Inter-Regional	Location Quotient
	Percentage share of sub-group employment		
Northern	4.8	18.0	0.27
Yorkshire and Humberside	2.7	6.0	0.45
East Midlands	4.3	4.7	0.91
East Anglia	1.2	3.3	0.36
South East	15.6	3.1	5.03
South West	3.0	7.2	0.42
West Midlands	0.4	1.8	0.22
North West	8.8	20.1	0.44
Wales	8.3	18.1	0.46
Scotland	42.6	11.1	3.84
Northern Ireland	8.3	6.6	1.26

Source: Board of Trade, *The Movement of Manufacturing Industry in the United Kingdom, 1945–65*, London, 1968, p. 40.

in the South East, it did receive a high proportion of moves from abroad and so the contrast between indigenous and foreign firms is very marked in this region.

Data for overall employment trends exist for the United Kingdom between 1963 and 1971, but in view of the UK's atypical patterns in the location of new plants it would perhaps be dangerous to generalise from them. One of the most striking features of this data set is that while indigenous firms declined in employment by 5 per cent, or approximately one-third of a million jobs, the foreign firms recorded an increase of 37 per cent or just over 200,000 jobs. This difference must reflect in part the transfer of firms from the indigenous to foreign category by acquisition during the period examined and also the differing industrial structures of the two groups to which reference has already been made. The largest amount of foreign growth went to Scotland while the South East and the North West had approximately equal absolute gains (Table 3.2). As can be seen from the table all regions gained in foreign firm employment. In contrast, only the Northern region, the East

Table 3.2: Employment Change in United Kingdom and Foreign Firms 1963–71

	Foreign Firms[a]	UK Firms[b]
	000's	000's
Northern	+15.9	+ 29.8
Yorkshire and Humberside	+ 4.0	− 63.4
East Midlands	+ 8.1	+ 19.9
East Anglia	+13.1	+ 30.3
South East	+27.3	−158.9
South West	+15.3	+ 24.2
West Midlands	+20.9	− 50.2
North West	+27.4	−147.8
Wales	+11.5	+ 27.6
Scotland	+36.7	− 28.1
Northern Ireland	+22.1	− 14.2

Notes:
a. Firms employing 25 or more persons.
b. All firms, and includes any foreign firms employing less than 25 persons.

Source: M.D. Steuer et al., *The Impact of Direct Foreign Investment on the United Kingdom*, London, 1973, p. 197 and unpublished tabulations from the Business Statistics Office.

Midlands, East Anglia, Wales and the South West showed employment gains by UK firms.

The re-distribution of employment resulting from these changes is illustrated in Figure 3.3. In both categories the South East shows a decline in relative importance; that is its employment grew more slowly than the average for foreign firms and declined faster than the average for UK firms. Significantly the relative decline in the South East was much greater for foreign firms than for UK ones. In other central regions the differences between employment in foreign and UK-owned plants was not particularly marked, although there was a general tendency for the share of national employment in these regions in UK-owned plants to increase rather more than the share of national employment in foreign-owned plants. In other words, employment in UK-owned plants showed a more distinct shift to these regions than did employment in foreign-owned plants.

The pattern in the other regions is less clear but there were important differences in Scotland and Northern Ireland. These two regions alone accounted for 50 per cent of the gains by foreign firms, while they only just maintained their share of employment in UK-owned firms. The evidence appears to suggest that current trends in employment expansion by foreign firms are favouring the most peripheral areas of the United Kingdom.

It must be stressed again that it has not been possible to adjust for differences in industrial structure between the indigenous and foreign firms, with the exception of the study by Ray, and this could be of considerable importance in explaining the contrasts that exist at inter-regional scale. Despite this difficulty, the inter-regional contrasts seem sufficiently well marked to allow some important conclusions to be drawn.

First, foreign enterprises tend to be found most frequently in major metropolitan regions, particularly the dominant one in a country. Second, this pattern is not as marked in the United Kingdom, where foreign enterprises tend to be over-represented in the core and periphery but are under-represented in an intermediate zone. Third, the enterprises of different nations may show contrasting patterns within a specific economy. Fourth, control functions appear to be more concentrated in the major metropolitan region than operating functions. Finally,

Figure 3.3: Net Shift in UK and Foreign-Controlled Employment in the United Kingdom, 1963–71

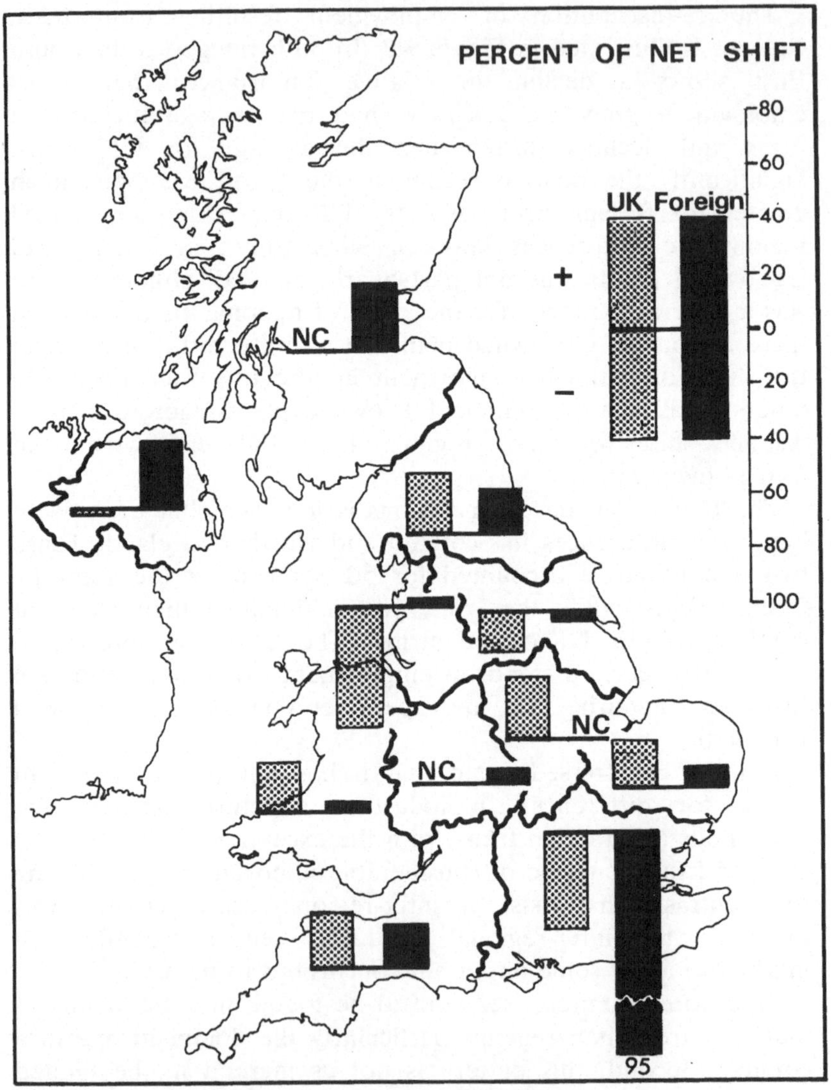

Source: Business Statistics Office and M.D. Steuer et al., *The Impact of Direct Foreign Investment on the United Kingdom*, London, 1973, p. 197.

examination of current trends through data on new plants, and employment data of all plants, indicates a continued concentration in existing metropolitan areas in Europe, while in Britain the periphery is very strongly represented. The apparently contrasting experience of the United Kingdom does illustrate some of the difficulties of drawing general conclusions about the foreign-controlled sub-set of large industrial enterprises. Some of the special circumstances must reflect in part the spatial policies followed by UK governments and these will be considered in the final chapter.

Intra-Regional Scale

To some extent, the contrasts seen at inter-regional scale are apparent also at intra-regional scale. This discussion of intra-regional patterns is based not only on foreign enterprises within specific regions of Britain, but also on countries such as Ireland, the Netherlands and Belgium whose spatial extent is comparable with a large British region. Within each region, as within a nation as a whole, the centre of interest is the spatial distribution of foreign-controlled employment compared with that of indigenous enterprises.

The most rigorous attempt to compare foreign and indigenous patterns is that by Hoare, who also adjusts for industrial structure. Unfortunately, for the present discussion, firms in the primary and tertiary sectors are included as well as manufacturing. In his study a foreign firm is defined as one with one or more foreign representatives on the Board of Directors. A clear difference emerges with a marked tendency for foreign firms to be over-represented in the western part of the South East region of Britain.[30]

A less sophisticated comparison was carried out for north-west England by Dicken & Lloyd, who confined their discussion to US firms.[31] Although high concentrations of these enterprises are apparent, with 54 per cent of US-controlled jobs found on Merseyside, this to some extent mirrors the distribution of a few large plants in the vehicles and food industries, in which, nationally, foreign enterprises have a major interest. Likewise, if the Netherlands is divided into four subdivisions, then the northern and western provinces show an over-representation of foreign firms.[32] Despite the limited nature of the data there is some evidence that, at intra-regional scale too, foreign enterprises do develop spatial patterns which differ from indigenous ones.

Differences within the 'foreign' group are again quite clear cut. In Ireland, American and West German firms, despite having similar industrial structures, chose very different locations, the American firms preferring development areas, industrial estates and peripheral areas, while West German firms preferred locations in the small remote towns of south-western Ireland.[33] In the Netherlands 'a striking feature is the concentration in the northern provinces of the . . . units of Northern European origin'[34] while West German plants were concentrated along the eastern frontier. Similar contrasts exist in south-east England where 'Northern American firms . . . show a greater concentration [than European firms] in the western part of the region'.[35]

This evidence confirms that, at this scale too, there are important contrasts between foreign and indigenous enterprises in their spatial patterns, and that enterprises based in different foreign countries may perceive regional space in different ways. It remains to be seen whether these contrasts emerge also in the other major element in spatial structures, linkage patterns.

Linkage Patterns

The evidence relating to both material and information links is rather limited, primarily because the majority of linkage studies have failed to distinguish between foreign and indigenous enterprises. Even where such a distinction has been made it is preferable, for the present study, to compare the linkages of branch plants of indigenous large enterprises with the linkages of plants of foreign enterprises. Failure to do this would mean that differences between the plants of foreign and indigenous enterprises might reflect simply the variations between large and small firms.

Some data which meet these requirements are provided by McDermott's study of the Scottish electronics industry. He compares purchases and sales of the plants of UK enterprises based outside Scotland, with plants of foreign firms. Data difficulties mean that from this point the discussion treats a plant's intra-enterprise and other linkages as one group. Whereas the UK-controlled plants sold almost half their output within the region, only 15 per cent of the US output went to the region. McDermott concludes that US enterprises were, of all enterprises, 'least integrated into the Scottish economy and the least dependent on the market provided by local manufacturers'.[36] Forsyth's study of a wider range of American firms showed a low proportion of domestic inputs and, in particular, that the longer-established American firms were not linked strongly into the regional economy.[37]

Two other studies produced similar results, but are less useful in the present context as they compare foreign plants with all indigenous plants, which may exaggerate the extent of foreign/indigenous differences within a set of large industrial enterprises. Stewart analysed a sample of 43 plants in the Limerick mid-west region of Ireland. Grouped into foreign and Irish categories, they had significantly different ($p < 0.01$) backward and forward linkage patterns, with the indigenous firms being more fully linked into the Irish economy.[38] Similarly Britton's more exhaustive study of *four* industries in southern Ontario indicated that domestic plants took advantage of a wide range of local suppliers as did some foreign-controlled firms, but 'a substantial proportion of United States-owned branches . . . [were] . . . heavily dependent on long distance, intra-company inputs' and were poorly integrated into the local economy.[39] While the Irish study did not adjust for industry type, Britton argues that variations in linkages between foreign and indigenous enterprises were in part a function of industrial differences but were also influenced strongly by foreign ownership. Further support for this point of view comes from Bater & Walker who noted that 'even on the basis of a simple distinction between foreign and Canadian-owned operations, there were observable differences in plant linkage'.[40]

This contrast is reflected also in information links as measured by Walker & Bater's 'non-goods linkages'. In their data, the percentage of non-goods linkages obtained by the metals and machinery industry of southern Ontario from the local community was higher for Canadian firms than for foreign firms.[41] Here, too, comparison is with all Canadian firms, not just the larger ones.

An additional criticism of most of these studies is that only crude measures of linkage distance are used, the categories being determined by administrative units. Different units might produce different results. Admittedly this reflects some of the practical problems of data collection. A more fundamental difficulty is that comparing long-established enterprises (predominantly indigenous) with newer ones (predominantly foreign) raises questions as to whether similar phenomena are being compared. The newer enterprise has had less time to integrate itself into the regional economy: it may of course never do so (cf. Forsyth above), but it does need time to see whether such integration will be achieved.

While some tentative evidence of differences in linkage patterns between foreign and indigenous enterprises has emerged, no final conclusion can be reached until comparisons are made between the branch plants of foreign and indigenous enterprises, standardised for both industry type and date of establishment. Clearly, this is an area where further careful investigation is required.

Towards Explanation

So far the reasons why foreign and indigenous enterprises might be expected to have different spatial structures have been considered, and some of the expected differences have been illustrated with empirical data. A full explanation of the patterns discussed is still some way ahead, and would certainly need much better data sets than those discussed here.

Explanations so far provided are generally subjective, difficult to test and contradictory. The emphasis on Scottish sites in the UK economy has been seen by Sant as being 'to a considerable degree . . . attributed to the working of regional policy',[42] while Dunning suggests it reflects the pre-existing engineering base in Scotland, effective Scottish publicity and traditional links with North America.[43] Admittedly, he was talking of a period when regional policy was less intense. Forsyth's study, like Sant's, puts government incentives as a primary attractive feature, but adds to it labour availability.[44] Since these two features were also characteristic of other peripheral areas, Dunning's is perhaps the most convincing explanation.

Traditional links between foreign countries and specific areas within an economy were seen by de Smidt as being an important reason for North European concerns in the Groningen area of the Netherlands. As in Scotland, traditional links were strengthened here by the municipal and provincial authorities aiming their propaganda mainly at Scandinavia. M. de Smidt argues that one Scandinavian firm led to another in a form of 'psychological agglomeration'.[45] This follow-the-leader effect may also have been important in Scotland when favourable reports of operations in that country reached the United

States.[46]

Despite the arguments for 'psychological agglomeration' it could be argued that the North European concentration in the north of the Netherlands reflects a distance decay effect, as do the West German enterprises in the east. Both North European and West German enterprises have tended to locate in those parts of the Netherlands closest to the home country of the foreign enterprise. It is tempting to explain the existence of EEC firms in east and south England in this way too. Traditional links between areas, which presumably influence the spatial awareness of decision takers, appear to be important explanatory variables. The quantification of such variables will pose numerous difficulties.

The distance decay effect is taken up in Ray's move towards an explanation of the location of direct foreign investment in a nation, specifically a study of US subsidiaries in Ontario. He shows that there is clear evidence that the number of subsidiaries established in Ontario by parent companies in US cities is inversely proportional to the distances of those cities from Ontario. Within Ontario plants tend to lie between Toronto and the parent city (sectoral affinity), and the further a US city is from Ontario the more likely its plant will be located in Toronto (sectoral penetration). The logic behind this behaviour is developed from basic interaction models. The concept of sectoral affinity argues that a plant is unlikely to be located beyond Toronto when Toronto is viewed from the corporate headquarters, as Toronto provides an important intervening opportunity. Sectoral penetration mirrors the fact that a US firm located near the Canadian border will move only a short distance into Ontario in order to minimise the costs of links between headquarters and the foreign plant, while distant firms will locate within the major local market centre (Toronto) because being near to the international border will be of little relevance to them. While Ray's work indicates the relationship between the location of foreign subsidiaries and the spatial pattern of urban centres in the foreign country, it does not really get at the actual processes underlying the pattern; nevertheless it marks an important step away from speculative suggestions. He subsequently extended his work to cover US subsidiaries in the whole of Canada.[47]

Hoare adopts a rather different approach and examines the

importance of one location factor (Heathrow airport) in explaining the location of foreign firms (not only manufacturing concerns) in south-east England. Over-representation of foreign firms was most marked to the west of the region but the variation in the expected/actual ratio of foreign firms explained by distance from Heathrow was low – only 7.3 per cent. This was interpreted to reflect the fact that there may not be a continuous response to distance from airport, but a marked break point with foreign firms desiring to be within a certain threshold distance. Analysis of the data by a series of χ^2 tests puts the break point at 48 kilometres, foreign firms showing a propensity to locate within 48 kilometres of the airport. This was particularly true for North American rather than European firms. There seems little doubt that within a region with a major international airport proximity to that airport will influence the location of foreign firms. It is by no means the *only* explanatory variable but, unlike so many others, it has been measured.

One difficulty with this approach is that some foreign firms may pre-date the existence of the airport and any proximity is purely coincidental, therefore analysis of current behaviour is needed to strengthen the findings. Movement of firms from Slough over the period 1963 to 1969, although small in number (23 moves) confirms the general pattern. Seventy-five per cent of the foreign firms settled within 32 kilometres of Heathrow, compared with only 40 per cent of the British firms.[48]

While some progress has been made in the search for explanation of the differences in the spatial pattern of employment of foreign and indigenous enterprises, explanations of contrasts in linkage patterns are still relatively undeveloped. This is a reflection of the fact that only in the 1970s have the linkages of foreign and indigenous enterprises been compared. Nevertheless, Britton's study of southern Ontario[49] is able to identify foreign ownership as an important explanatory variable in a study of linkage patterns, though he admits this may have been exaggerated by the small number of domestic branch plants in his sample. As described above, the general pattern was for corporate flows to replace local ones.

Conclusion

In conclusion, the two limitations to this discussion outlined at the beginning of the chapter need emphasising. First, in most cases, comparisons are between *all* firms subdivided into foreign and indigenous categories and not large industrial enterprises so divided. Since it seems reasonable to assume that foreign firms within a particular country will tend to be part of large industrial enterprises based elsewhere comparative material is relating the operations of foreign large industrial enterprises to all indigenous firms from the very smallest concerns operating within the market system to the dominant enterprises of the industrial system.

Second, both the industry and the plant size distribution of the foreign and indigenous enterprises may differ and so comparisons between them ought to be made only after allowing for these differences. Since such adjustments were not made, except for US enterprises in Canada and foreign firms in south-east England, variations between indigenous and foreign firms could be a reflection of their distinctive industrial mix and plant size distribution.

Despite these caveats some very interesting conclusions can be drawn from the discussion. Foreign multi-nationals form an important group of large industrial enterprises, but their significance varies from one sector to another. In any one economy multi-nationals based in different foreign countries will have distinct affiliations with particular industrial sectors and, partly as a consequence of this, with different sizes of plant. Intuitive reasoning suggests that there are several factors which will cause foreign enterprises to have different location patterns and linkages from those of indigenous concerns. This reasoning is not strong enough to suggest clearly the nature and direction of those differences.

Inter-regionally, empirical evidence shows that foreign enterprises place a greater emphasis on established metropolitan areas and core regions than do indigenous enterprises, and that this is especially true of their control functions. Only in the United Kingdom does there seem any marked bias towards peripheral areas. Intra-regionally (including the Netherlands and Ireland), some distinct spatial preferences by foreign enterprises may be discerned. Some very limited data on the linkage patterns of these enterprises suggest that they are less dependent on local inputs of materials and services than their indigenous counterparts.

Explanation of these contrasts has proved difficult. In most cases, differences are explained by a listing of some possible explanatory variables, but the mathematical treatment of US subsidiaries in Canada, the investigation of the influence of Heathrow airport in south-east England, and the study of linkages in southern Ontario have considerably improved our understanding of at least three possible causes of the contrasts between the foreign and the indigenous sub-sets of the group of large industrial enterprises. These cross-sectional approaches, however, do not allow full account to be taken of the evolution of the pattern of plant locations and their associated linkages. It is these processes of change to which attention is now turned.

Notes

1. Business Statistics Office, *Report on the Census of Production, 1968, Part 158, Summary Tables*, 1974, London, Table 44.
2. R. Vernon, *Sovereignty at Bay: the Multi-National Spread of US Enterprise*, 1971, London.
3. J.H. Dunning, *American Investment in British Manufacturing Industry*, 1958, London, and J.H. Dunning (ed.), *The Multi-National Enterprise*, 1971, London.
4. A. Blackbourn, 'The Spatial Behaviour of American Firms in Western Europe' in F.E.I. Hamilton (ed.), *Spatial Perspectives on Industrial Organisation and Decision Making*, 1974, London, pp. 245-64.
5. F.E.I. Hamilton, 'Multi-National Enterprise and the European Economic Community', *Tijdschrift voor Economische en Sociale Geografie*, 67, 1976, pp. 258-78.
6. Unpublished tabulation by Business Statistics Office.
7. M. de Smidt, 'Foreign Industrial Establishments Located in the Netherlands', *Tijdschrift voor Economische en Sociale Geografie*, 57, 1966, p. 15.
8. Board of Trade, *The Movement of Manufacturing Industry in the United Kingdom*, 1945-65, 1968, London, p. 40.
9. M.D. Steuer et. al., *The Impact of Direct Foreign Investment on the United Kingdom*, 1973, London, p. 196.
10. A. Blackbourn, 'The Location of Foreign-Owned Manufacturing Plants in the Republic of Ireland', *Tijdschrift voor Economische en Sociale Geografie*, 63, 1972, p. 439.
11. de Smidt, 'Foreign Industrial Establishments', p. 6.
12. Business Statistics Office, *Report on the Census of Production 1971*, Table 43.
13. de Smidt, 'Foreign Industrial Establishments', p. 5.
14. Blackbourn, 'Location of Foreign-Owned Manufacturing Plants', p. 441.
15. P.N. O'Farrell, *Regional Development Trends in Ireland, 1960-73*, 1975, Dublin, p. 42.
16. G.N. Yannopolous and J.H. Dunning, 'Multi-National Enterprises and Regional Development: an Exploratory Paper', *Regional Studies*, 10, 1976, p. 389.
17. Hamilton, 'Multi-National Enterprise', p. 266.
18. D.J. Forsyth, *US Investment in Scotland*, 1972, London, p. 39.

19. A.G. Hoare, 'Foreign Firms and Air Transport: the Geographical Effect of Heathrow Airport', *Regional Studies*, 9, 1975, p. 365.
20. Hamilton, 'Multi-National Enterprise', pp. 270-2.
21. Vernon, *Sovereignty at Bay*, p. 117.
22. Yannopolous and Dunning, 'Multi-National Enterprises', p. 398.
23. Dunning, 1958, p. 85; and Economists Advisory Group, *United States Industry in Britain*, 1972, London, p. 13.
24. Steuer et al., *Impact of Direct Foreign Investment.*
25. Hamilton, 'Multi-National Enterprise', p. 24.
26. D.M. Ray, 'The Location of United States Manufacturing Subsidiaries in Canada', *Economic Geography*, 47, 1971, pp. 389-90.
27. A.W. Evans, 'The Location of the Headquarters of Industrial Companies', *Urban Studies*, 10, 1973, pp. 391-2.
28. Blackbourn, 'The Spatial Behaviour of American Firms', p. 255.
29. D. Keeble, *Industrial Location and Planning in the United Kingdom*, 1976, London, p. 140.
30. Hoare, 'Foreign Firms and Air Transport', p. 355.
31. P. Dicken and P.E. Lloyd, 'Geographical Perspectives on United States Investment in the United Kingdom', *Environment and Planning A*, 8, 1976, p. 702.
32. de Smidt, 'Foreign Industrial Establishments', pp. 5-6.
33. Blackbourn, 1972, 'The Spatial Behaviour of American Firms', pp. 439-42.
34. de Smidt, 'Foreign Industrial Establishments'.
35. Hoare, 'Foreign Firms and Air Transport', p. 358.
36. P.J. McDermott, 'Ownership, Organisation and Regional Dependence in the Scottish Electronics Industry', *Regional Studies*, 10, 1976, p. 326.
37. Forsyth, *US Investment in Scotland*, p. 114.
38. J.C. Stewart, 'Linkages and Foreign Direct Investment', *Regional Studies*, 10, 1976, pp. 251-6.
39. J.N.H. Britton, 'The Influence of Corporate Organisation and Ownership on the Linkages of Industrial Plants: a Canadian Enquiry', *Economic Geography*, 52, 1976, p. 323.
40. J.H. Bater and D.F Walker, 'Aspects of Industrial Linkage: the Example of the Hamilton Metalworking Complex, Ontario', *Revue de Géographie de Montréal*, 28, 1974, p. 243.
41. D.F. Walker and J.H. Bater, 'Foreign Ownership and Industrial Linkage' in D.F. Walker and J.H. Bater (eds.), *Industrial Development in Southern Ontario*, University of Waterloo, Department of Geography Publication Series, No. 3, 1974, Waterloo, pp. 119-21.
42. M. Sant, *Industrial Movement and Regional Development*, 1975, London, p. 121.
43. Dunning, *American Investment*, p. 88.
44. Forsyth, *US Investment*, p. 41.
45. de Smidt, 'Foreign Industrial Establishments', p. 15.
46. Forsyth, *US Investment*, p. 231.
47. D.M. Ray, *Market Potential and Economic Shadow*, University of Chicago Research Paper, No. 101, 1965, Chicago.
48. Hoare, 'Foreign Firms and Air Transport', pp. 349-67.
49. Britton, 'Influence of Corporate Organisation', p. 323.

Part Two

THE LARGE INDUSTRIAL ENTERPRISE IN SPACE AND TIME

4 THE SPATIAL EVOLUTION OF AN ENTERPRISE: GROWTH

The previous two chapters have adopted an essentially static approach. The function of the next three is to look at the growth and development of large industrial enterprises to put the cross-sectional studies into a temporal perspective. Such a perspective may contribute towards a fuller understanding of their spatial structure. As Steed has argued, there is a need to 'give greater consideration to the factors encouraging the geographic diversification of the increasingly dominant major corporations, and to the nature of the survival capacity of their individual plants'.[1]

Spatial evolution is used here to describe the changes in the spatial pattern of an enterprise's plants and linkages that occur during some given period of time. It is made up of two elements: *spatial growth* which increases the number of plants an enterprise operates and extends its plant space and *locational adjustment* which is concerned with changes in spatial patterns with static or decreasing plant numbers. This is a rather narrower definition of locational adjustment than that proposed by Krumme.[2] To clarify the process of spatial evolution the two elements are treated separately in this and the next chapter. There are disadvantages in splitting the process into these two elements, the most important being the tendency to treat what is one process as two, but at this exploratory stage the division offers a workable framework for discussing the spatial evolution of large industrial enterprises.

The chapter is in two parts. The first reviews the motives, the strategies and the methods of growth, while the second considers the way in which these three elements affect the spatial growth of large industrial enterprises. Attention is then turned to locational adjustment in the first part of Chapter 5.

Growth of an Enterprise

Growth in absolute size and/or in market share is not a spontaneous or a random event over which an enterprise has no control; nor is it necessarily part of a corporate growth strategy or investment plan. While corporate planning is well established in the United States, as late as 1968 Argenti reported that 'in Britain only a few dozen companies are as yet using . . . [corporate planning] . . . and only a very few have been doing so for more than three or four years'.[3] No doubt the very largest enterprises are among Argenti's few dozen, and they have had and continue to have three-, five- or seven-year investment plans,[4] but for the majority of enterprises the characteristics of increased size reflect the accumulated effects of numerous non-programmed decisions taken for a variety of reasons and in response to many different kinds of conditions.

Rees has argued that 'no comprehensive framework exists to explain the growth of the firm over space',[5] and as Hayter points out 'there are few empirical studies . . . of individual corporate expansion paths over long periods of time'.[6] Therefore before proceeding to examine the spatial growth of an enterprise it is useful to look at some general aspects of growth: the motives that cause an enterprise to grow, growth strategies, and the methods of growth. Of course, different motives, different strategies, and different methods of growth may be employed at different times in an enterprise's life.

Growth Motives

In public statements, the executives of a large industrial enterprise will usually claim their goal is to maximise the shareholders' return. Investigations of enterprise behaviour indicate that this is rarely the only goal, most enterprises having multi-dimensional goals, and it is often subsidiary to a number of other objectives. An important and measurable objective is growth, but growth is usually seen as a means of reaching some other goal. The motives for growth have been summarised by Starbuck, and they can be divided into three categories.[7]

The first set of motives is concerned with the personal interests of those working in an enterprise. The motives for growth that emerge here are a desire for adventure and risk, a desire for the prestige and power that come from supervising large numbers of people, and a desire for higher salaries. Further, it could be argued that growth has become simply an accepted and fashionable goal for an enterprise's managers.

The second group of growth motives arises out of the

organisational characteristics of large industrial enterprises. Some growth may come inevitably from the very existence of an enterprise. Its research laboratories may identify a new product, or its customers may require a full range of products rather than only one. A desire for long-run survival encourages growth also, partly because large size makes it easier for an enterprise to overcome its mistakes, and partly because regular annual sales growth keeps the share price high and thus defends the enterprise from acquisition. An enterprise likes to reduce the uncertainty it has to face and by growing larger an enterprise generally gains greater control over its environment. There is also evidence to suggest that large enterprises are more profitable than small firms in a depression and less profitable in boom conditions, possibly as they have spread their interests into a variety of different product markets.

Motives in the third group are those economic motives most commonly associated with the growth of large industrial enterprises. These include the desire to increase profits, to achieve some other measure of success such as maximising revenue and to search for economies of scale. Probably a more elusive motive to trace and study is a desire for monopolistic power.

The placing of these three groups of motives in the above order – personal, organisational and economic – is deliberate, in that it helps to emphasise non-economic growth motives. While growth is usually an enterprise's goal there are different ways in which it can be achieved, and it is a function of corporate strategy to select a growth path.

Growth Strategies

The strategy of an enterprise is defined as the selection of appropriate policies to enable it to meet its long-run objective, which is usually growth. As Ansoff observes, 'objectives alone do not meet [the] need . . . [for] . . . a well defined growth direction . . . and that additional decision rules are required if the firm is to have orderly and profitable growth'.[8] The decision rules indicate the way in which growth will be undertaken and both Wrigley[9] and Edwards & Townsend[10] among others, have presented classifications of growth strategies. Each divides a broad spectrum of strategies running from increased output of the same product to diversification into very different products. The classification used below combines their ideas.

A common strategy is producing more or *similar products*. Similar products in this case mean products using the same process or selling in the same market. A second strategy involves developing the production of goods which are in *joint supply or demand*. Products developed through joint demand are exemplified by developing clothes-drying machines after an initial development in washing machines. Joint supply is simply the development of the markets for by-products of the principal output of an enterprise. A third strategy might develop from the inter-relationships of *technology and markets*. On the one hand an enterprise can exploit its existing technology to serve new markets; on the other hand, a commitment to a specific market may well cause growth by forcing an enterprise into new technologies to meet the changed needs of the market. The fourth strategy is based on *new products* manufactured by new technologies. Sometimes these new products will emerge from a research programme, in other cases they may arise fortuitously, while in yet others an enterprise may be approached by an inventor with a specific patent. These four strategies are, in essence, concerned with expanding an enterprise's markets, but not necessarily in a spatial sense. To overcome this deficiency Cannon suggests a fifth or *geographic strategy* should be added. He argues that in the past it was 'rather common practice to let geographic expansion evolve without too much deliberate consideration'[11] but that, increasingly, profit advantage could be gained from such a strategy.

At any stage in the development of these five strategies it is possible to develop a sixth strategy of *vertical integration*. Instead of widening the product range or increasing the geographic scope of its markets an enterprise can integrate backwards and make what was previously bought, or integrate forward and purchase the outlets it supplies.

Of course, as an enterprise grows so its growth strategies may change, and, as was argued in Chapter 1, whatever the particular growth strategy adopted, the general trend will be for large industrial enterprises to become more diversified in the nature of their outputs. They will tend to move gradually from being single-product enterprises towards being diversified enterprises. As the market for their single product becomes saturated, so they move to a related product; as the markets for the related products become saturated so they diversify yet further.

Growth Methods

In an individual enterprise increased size and/or increased market share resulting from these growth strategies will come mainly through internal growth or through merger, termed usually *external growth*. Some authorities divide mergers into acquisitions and combinations and although it is possible to distinguish between them as methods of growth the 'economic base for the combination of two firms is much the same as it is for simple acquisition'.[12] So following Penrose, and throughout this and all subsequent chapters, merger denotes any method of combining existing firms and the larger enterprise is regarded as 'acquiring' the smaller even if a new joint firm is established.[13] The emotive term 'takeover' is avoided, and the terms merger and acquisition are treated as synonyms.

The relative importance of the two different methods of growth (internal and external) can be assessed by their contribution both to the increase in the absolute size of enterprises and to the increase in the relative size of enterprises. Estimates of this kind are difficult to make as they depend markedly upon assumptions as to the post-merger growth of activities associated with the acquired firms. In the United Kingdom Aaronovitch & Sawyer calculated that from 1958 to 1967 acquisitions contributed to between one-quarter and one-third of the growth rate of enterprises surviving from 1957.[14] Their study concentrated on enterprises with net assets of over £5 million in 1957 and mainly operating in manufacturing and distribution. Acquisition played a more important role in the increase in concentration. An overview of the relative importance of the two methods of growth to this increase is provided by Utton and by Hannah & Kay. Utton estimated that mergers were responsible for about half the increase between 1954 and 1965, while Hannah and Kay go further and argue that 'mergers have been the major cause of the rise in concentration in Britain'.[15] The British experience may not be typical because of its limited legal restrictions on merger, and internal growth may be much more important in other developed economies.

For an individual enterprise there is both a choice in strategy and a choice in method of growth. The principal choices open to an enterprise are illustrated in Figure 4.1. The strategic choices are here limited to two, as 'the product line offered by the company in the market place serves as a convenient way to define . . . the field of action in which the company is prepared to compete'.[16] Vertical integration could be an elaboration of either strategy. Having decided on one strategy rather than another, a choice has to be made as to the method by which this is to be achieved; that is, through merger (external growth) or through internal growth. An external growth policy inevitably means that new elements are added to an enterprise's spatial structure, whether the acquisition is to diversify or to expand the manufacture of a particular product. The complex nature of growth through merger is illustrated by corporate 'family trees'; some examples will be found in Chapter 7. If the internal growth path is selected this can be by increased utilisation of existing plants, by extension of site or sites, by the establishment of branch plants, or a combination of all three. Here again a decision has to be taken. It might be objected that Figure 4.1 hides some of the complexities of the decisions that have to be made, but it does enable the more fundamental choices open to

Figure 4.1: Principal Growth Strategies and Growth Methods in Large Enterprises

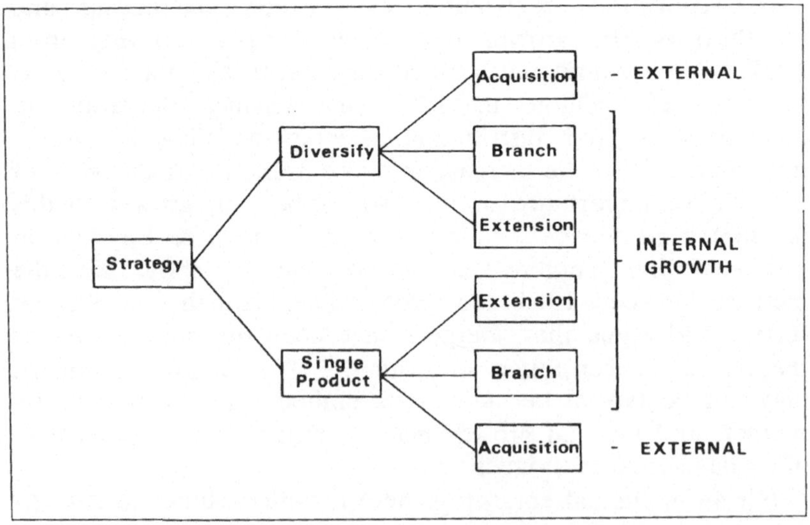

an enterprise to be conceptualised. Elaboration of strategies in a geographic context must await an understanding of these limited, but meaningful, categories.

In making a choice between the different methods of growth an obvious constraint is the financial resources available to the enterprise, but assuming they are sufficient to allow any one of the methods to be adopted other factors come into play. *In situ* developments are favoured where at least one of the plants can provide sufficient space for expansion, can offer sufficient new labour reserves if required, and is capable of expansion without infringement of planning regulations. As Broadway observes, 'with bigger companies the problem is often to decide on which of several existing sites the new facilities should be set up'.[17] Where existing sites are restricted in space, by planning requirements or by limited labour supply then other methods of growth may be taken.

Once extension is rejected, the choice is between transfers, branch plants and acquisitions. It is likely that in large industrial enterprises transfers of plants from one location to another are unusual, or at least unimportant. There is some confirmation of this from North's study of one hundred firms in the UK plastics industry. He found that firms making relocation (i.e. transfer) decisions were 'both younger and smaller than those making . . . other types of decision'.[18] Admittedly North noted that five larger firms relocated branch plants but on the whole transfers appear to be of limited significance to the large industrial enterprise. Thus for most large industrial enterprises growth, if it cannot be accommodated on existing sites, is achieved either by branch plant (internal growth) or by merger (external growth).

The principal differences between these two methods can be measured both in economic and in behavioural terms. In economic terms the attractiveness of a branch plant (internal growth) to an enterprise is that it can usually operate in a purpose-built factory, with equipment and machinery selected by the enterprise and over which it has full control. The principal difficulty is that it can take 2 to 3 years from decision to establish to reach full production levels, while training costs and learning time raise operating costs during the first few years of operation. An acquisition (external growth) is attractive primarily because of the speed with which its output can be geared to the needs of the enterprise. On acquisition the plant is working, a management control system exists, and training and setting up costs are avoided.[19] Against acquisition is principally the fact than an 'ideal' partner can be found only rarely, and even if it is, established management may not be very responsive to the acquiring enterprise's needs. Ansoff sees the distinction between the two methods simply as relating to problems of start-up costs and timing.[20]

Although these economic differences between the two modes exist, other considerations can influence the choice between them. For example, an enterprise still under family control and with sufficient capital might prefer the branch plant method, as it does not present any threat to their control by introducing new men into an enterprise through an acquisition. An enterprise run by managers may prefer acquisition. The route selected could also be a response to the kind of stress being experienced by an enterprise at the time an expansion decision has to be made. Where difficulties are caused by a very rapid expansion of the product market, acquisition may be the favoured course of action because of the rapidity with which extra production capacity can be obtained. A common problem in times of full employment is a shortage of labour and here the response would be to construct a branch plant in a labour-surplus area. To the form of control and type of stress must be added the course of action preferred by the organisation. Evidence from several large enterprises indicates that some have clearly preferred one growth method to the other. General Motors, for example, developed its multi-national operations by acquiring firms in other nations (such as Vauxhall in the United Kingdom) while Ford has usually pursued a policy of establishing branch plants.[21]

In considering the different motives, strategies and methods, the spatial implications have so far been ignored. It is with these spatial implications that the next section is concerned.

Spatial Growth of an Enterprise

The spatial growth of an enterprise is associated closely with these growth motives, growth strategies and growth methods. It is particularly important, however, to notice that growth in itself need not lead to an increase in the number of an enterprise's plants and consequently to spatial growth. Such growth could well be accompanied only by adjustments at existing plants but spatial growth is almost inevitably accompanied by the growth of an enterprise.

Motives and Spatial Growth

The spatial implications of variations in growth motives between large enterprises are difficult to identify, but some suggestions can be made. A desire for monopoly power will point an enterprise in the direction of growth through acquisition, while survival motives ensure that when an enterprise is faced with a contracting market for a single product expansion into a wider range of geographical or product markets to ensure growth is vital. Likewise, an enterprise which grows primarily to obtain a stable environment may show a propensity to make market share agreements with other enterprises (which may involve spatial allocation of markets) and to negotiate with the state to reduce the level of uncertainty in the area in which the enterprise operates. Where the motives themselves do not have many direct spatial implications, they may influence both strategies and methods of spatial growth.

Strategies and Spatial Growth

Each strategy operates upon the spatial growth of an enterprise in a variety of ways, but it will not be independent of growth motives nor, indeed, of methods. A strategy of more of the same may exhaust local resources (materials or labour) or markets and force spatial growth. Moore notes for a forest products enterprise (Weyerhauser Co.) that 'the policy of national . . . spread was one forced by the limited potentials of the Pacific North-West',[22] while Le Heron and Warr suggest for a food-processing enterprise (Watties) that one 'prime motivation for the adoption of an inter-regional growth strategy . . . was the anticipated prospect of declining returns in . . . [the core region]'.[23] Admittedly, these are perhaps special cases of resource-based enterprises but enterprises in other sectors could well respond to labour or land shortages.[24] A strategy of developing markets for products produced by a similar technology took Paccar from the manufacture of railway freight cars to the production of truck and logging vehicles and the increased geographic spread of its plants was partly 'to serve a geographically dispersed market'.[25]

The more general implications of a diversification policy are described by Hamilton, who argues that in a diversifying enterprise 'the emergent pattern of plant locations . . . is likely to differ significantly from a corporation whose management is bent on growth via a larger control of the market for a fairly narrow range of products'.[26] The direction of this significant difference is not made clear, but certainly it might be expected that diversification would lead to sudden and marked changes in an enterprise's spatial structure. Diversification, too, may influence spatial growth indirectly. An example is provided by Watties, where diversification into the canning of new products in the core region forced the enterprise to continue the development of its principal products elsewhere.[27] It is difficult to predict the characteristics of the new locations into which an enterprise will spread as these will depend on the distinctive characteristics of the products which an enterprise introduces, for these will influence inputs and outputs and hence locational requirements.

In contrast, Moore argues that a strategy of vertical integration might have some fairly distinct spatial repercussions.[28] A policy of backward integration may extend an enterprise's operations into either peripheral areas or small centres. As was argued earlier, these can be typical locations for processing functions. This argument depends upon the nature of the principal activities of an enterprise, as Watties' backward integration involved the development of plants to produce tin cans and to meet the enterprise's lacquering and lithographic requirements.[29] Similarly, forward integration can lead to more widespread activities. A good example here is MacMillan Bloedel, which integrated forwards into paper containers, and from a British Columbia base eventually operated market-centred plants in Edmonton, Calgary, Winnipeg, and Regina.[30]

The spatial growth of an enterprise can reflect the operation of more than one strategy, especially where the growth has taken place over 10 to 20 years. The example of MacMillan Bloedel can be used again. In his study of this enterprise, the largest forest product corporation in Canada, Hayter records that 'the resource and demand limitations of specific regions, the risks of geographical as well as product specialisation, and the different locational conditions associated with the various vertically linked production stages, encouraged firms to diversify geographically beyond traditional spheres of operation'.[31] Clearly, choice of strategy influences the spatial growth of an enterprise.

This discussion of the consequences of varying motives and strategies has been speculative rather than conclusive. Much stronger evidence is available as to the results of different growth methods on the spatial structure of a large industrial enterprise.

Internal and External Growth

Growth, as was shown earlier, is either internal or external, and may take different forms. Each form makes its own particular contribution to change in an enterprise's spatial structure. Clearly, branch plants and acquisitions provide an opportunity to alter the point pattern of an enterprise and allow for a marked extension of its plant space.

The literature available says very little about the spatial growth of a large industrial enterprise. There are extensive studies of the branch plant decisions[32] but only negligible material on acquisitions.[33] Synthesis of this research permits examination of the way in which spatial considerations influence the spatial growth of an enterprise. To some extent at least the direction of spatial growth may be influenced by an enterprise's linkages with other parts of the economic system. Indeed, Taylor argues that 'it is through its linkages that a firm obtains information from the environment . . . demonstrating potentialities and courses of action'.[34] It remains uncertain whether pre-existing linkages underlie some of the spatial constraints that are shown to lie behind, first, growth by branch plants, and second, growth through acquisition.

Both aggregate analyses and studies of decision-making behaviour indicate that spatial considerations, either implicitly or explicitly, influence the form of an enterprise's internal growth through the setting up of branch plants. Keeble suggests that a high proportion of movement from the South East and the West Midlands of the United Kingdom to the Assisted Areas can be explained as a function of the labour available in each Assisted Area and its *distance from the source region*.[35] Sant, using a set of smaller regions, was able to indicate that the 'main elements of locational attraction . . . [were] . . . labour availability, regional incentives and land availability and costs . . . and the ability to satisfy the *preference for short distance movement*'.[36] In each case growth patterns were constrained by a spatial element.

These studies, however, tell us little about large industrial enterprises, unless it is assumed, as it was in Chapter 3, that branch plants are set up predominantly by large industrial enterprises. It is in the more detailed studies of location decisions that the behaviour of a large industrial enterprise can be identified. A larger enterprise tends to search more widely than the smaller firm and show less tendency to accept the first feasible site. The larger enterprise, too, will be affected by the requirements of central government (Chapter 11) and, in addition, branches have to be tied into an enterprise's overall spatial structure.[37] The general pattern of considerable care in location considerations is illustrated by North, who shows that in his sample only the fairly large public companies evaluated regions before looking for a specific site. For example, one enterprise evaluated eight sub-regions to select that which satisfied the objectives of maximum financial return and minimum distribution costs.[38]

It can be argued, following the ideas of Rees, that in the spatial growth of an enterprise by the internal method two distinct phases may be recognised. The first is a search for a general area for the new plant, and this may be selected primarily on the basis of market requirements. Once this general area has been selected, a least-cost approach is adopted in the search for an adequate site within the previously identified area.[39] While the goal at the first stage could differ from that mentioned by Rees – for example, a desire to obtain government assistance rather than market potential – the recognition of spatial growth being influenced by different variables at different scales is particularly important.

The evidence for spatial considerations exerting an influence on external growth (merger behaviour) is less clear cut, although some new evidence on this is presented in Chapter 8. The only detailed studies completed are those of North and Leigh & North. In the former it was concluded that for a sample of plastics firms 'locational considerations were relatively unimportant in the search for a suitable company for takeover compared with such factors as a company's profitability, performance, management quality and market share'.[40] Later work by Leigh & North suggests that there are important variations among enterprises operating in different industries in the extent to which space influences acquisition behaviour. This research extended North's original conclusions on plastics to the whole of the chemical sector but found that in the food and clothing industries space was an important variable. In the former this was for market reasons, and in the latter to ease supervision from the acquiring enterprise's head-office.[41] Spatial considerations seem also to have been important for enterprises in the forest products industry, where one of the attractions of merger partners was seen to be the 'pooling of complementary . . . locational resources'. Mergers were the only way the enterprise could obtain 'advantageous sites'.[42]

The extent to which spatial considerations influence merger behaviour is related also to the kind of merger with which an enterprise is involved. Broadly, mergers may be classed into three types:*

(1) Horizontal merger: acquisition of a firm operating within the same industry and at the same stage of the process as the acquiring enterprise.
(2) Vertical merger: acquisition of a firm operating within the same industry, but engaged primarily in either earlier or later stages than the stage with which the acquiring enterprise is concerned.
(3) Conglomerate merger: acquisition of a firm operating in an industry which differs from that of the acquiring enterprise.

As an enterprise grows it may change first from horizontal to vertical mergers and then from vertical to conglomerate.

It seems likely that in spatial growth through merger activity spatial considerations will be more important in horizontal and vertical mergers than in a conglomerate merger. North was able to show that enterprises pursuing a policy of horizontal integration (and merger) were usually interested in particular regional markets and favoured acquiring the firm which had the

*A problem related to this kind of classification is that a very narrow definition of 'industry' results in a large number of conglomerate mergers; a wide industrial category can reduce them to almost zero.

largest share of that market. On the other hand, where an acquisition was being made as part of a policy of diversification (a conglomerate merger) the number of firms that fulfilled the acquiring enterprise's requirements were so few that the expanding enterprise could not afford to take spatial considerations into account.[43] Yet, of course, diversification strategies might change markedly the spatial structure of an enterprise by the addition of very different types of plant to the enterprise system.

The contrasting effect of the different methods of growth on an enterprise's spatial structure is illustrated by Chapman's study of the UK petro-chemical industry. Where an enterprise grew by internal growth, petro-chemical capacity was located in close proximity to an enterprise's refineries, which supplied the petro-chemical plants with their raw materials. Conversely, where external growth through acquisition took place this proximity was less important. Shell, for example, acquired and developed a major petro-chemical complex at Carrington, some 37 kms distant from its closest refinery.[44] The more general point made by Keeble is that 'choice of a new location by acquisition is by definition markedly circumscribed by the existing spatial distribution of the industry concerned',[45] whereas the branch plant methods permit the introduction of entirely new types of site. These contrasts are indicative of the important influence of alternative growth paths on an enterprise's spatial structure.

Comparison only of acquisition and branch plant routes perhaps over-simplifies the alternatives open to a growing enterprise. Another possibility, and a quite common one, is to set up a joint company with another enterprise. This was the policy adopted primarily by British Petroleum in the petro-chemical industry,[46] and by three UK brewing enterprises when they began the manufacture of lager.[47] The sites of such enterprises will be influenced not only by a single enterprise's spatial structure, but also by the inter-relationships of that structure with the structures of the enterprises co-operating in the joint operation.

What is more, although some enterprises appear to favour a particular method of growth, others may adopt a mix of methods, varying them as they grow or using different methods at the same point in time. MacMillan Bloedel's inter-regional growth in Canada was achieved through acquisitions, and greenfield investment,[48] while Weyerhauser generally made an entry into new products or processes by relatively small acquisitions. Entry by this means did not unduly upset the existing market structure, and at the same time enabled the enterprise to learn the technology. Once such experience had been gained, the enterprise changed either to internal growth through major new investment or external growth through major acquisitions.[49] Change of growth methods is well illustrated also in Taylor's analysis of Birmid-Qualcast, which 'until 1960 . . . grew mainly by building new works . . . [subsequently] . . . takeovers replace[d] the establishment of new works . . . as the main mode of expansion'.[50]

While subjective impressions seem to demonstrate that spatial growth is an important aspect of spatial evolution by large industrial enterprises, there are few aggregate data and few published case studies analysing the spatial growth of a specific enterprise. Rees plots the location and date of establishment of the US plants of Proctor & Gamble,[51] but with no distinction between methods of growth. Such a distinction is made in Taylor's depiction of the growth of Birmid-Qualcast[52] but the most striking examples so far published are those by Jansen.[53] One instance he describes in his study of the growth of large enterprises in the Netherlands is illustrated in Figure 4.2. From a core region in the south, Philips has spread its operations to most of the country's Provinces. Some further examples of spatial growth are provided in Chapter 8.

In most enterprises the core region is explicable by the location of the original manufacturing facilities of the enterprise, whether founded by Piggott (Paccar) in Seattle or by Dunlop or Cadbury in the West Midlands, as Figures 2.3 and 2.4 showed. Spatial growth from a core region is depicted by Paccar Inc. which until 1962 had its plants still confined west of the Mississippi and only after 1967 were there plants in the eastern United States.[54] Similarly, MacMillan Bloedel was restricted primarily to south-west British Columbia until the 1960s.

In his study of this enterprise Hayter tried to explain the general form its inter-regional growth took. This was influenced by prior trading connections and a philosophy of locating at or near tide-water for all but the enterprise's market-oriented paper-converting facilities. This general pattern was modified by

Figure 4.2: Spatial Evolution: Growth: Philips, Netherlands, 1950–71

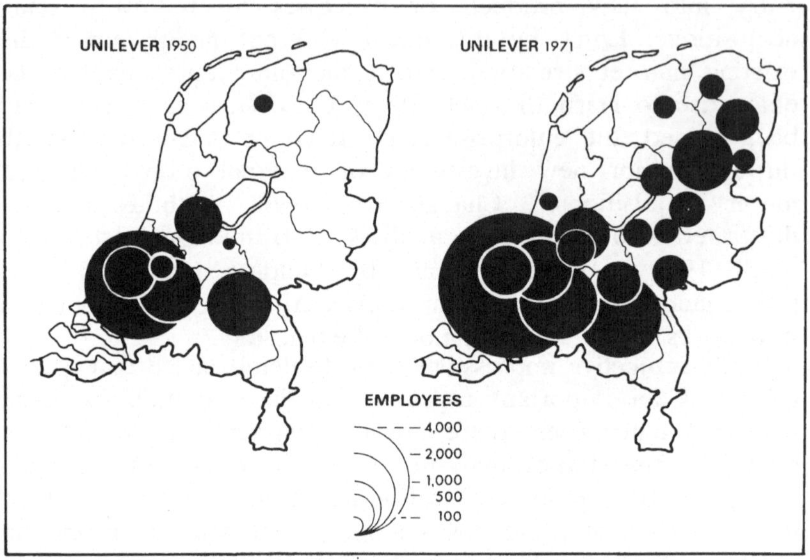

Source: A.C.M. Jansen, 'Enkele aspekten van het ruimtelijk gedrag van grote industriële concerns in Nederland, 1950–1971', *Tijdschrift voor Economische en Sociale Geograffie*, 63, 1972, p. 419.

a general desire to avoid politically sensitive regions, which in the Canadian context meant Quebec.[55]

Detailed histories of individual enterprises enable illustrations to be given of certain points, and they demonstrate why certain unique patterns emerge in the specific enterprise, but more general patterns of the spatial growth of groups of large industrial enterprises may be brought together in models of the spatial evolution of an enterprise. These models are examined in Chapter 6.

Thus far, it has been possible to examine general ideas relating to enterprise growth and some of the spatial repercussions of motives, strategies and methods of growth. Yet, as new locations are added to an enterprise's spatial structure, so adjustments have to be made to the plants and linkages it already owns both to integrate the new concerns into the enterprise and to fit the old elements into the new structure. Adjustments, too, may be forced on an enterprise when faced with a decline in a demand for one or more of its products. The next chapter begins with the second important element in spatial evolution: locational adjustment.

Notes

1. G.P.F. Steed, 'Locational Implications of Corporate Organisation of Industry', *Canadian Geographer*, 15, 1971, p. 56.
2. G. Krumme, 'Notes on Locational Adjustment Patterns in Industrial Geography', *Geografiska Annaler*, 51B, 1969, pp. 15-19.
3. J. Argenti, *Corporate Planning*, 1968, London, p. 13.
4. D.E. Hussey, *Introduction to Corporate Planning*, 1971, London, p. 11.
5. J. Rees, 'Decision-Making, the Growth of the Firm and the Business Environment' in F.E.I. Hamilton (ed.), *Spatial Perspectives on Industrial Organisation and Decision Making*, 1974, London, p. 199.
6. R. Hayter, 'Corporate Strategies and Industrial Change in the Canadian Forest Products Industries', *Geographical Review*, 66, 1976, p. 210.
7. W.H. Starbuck, 'Organisational Growth and Development', in W.H. Starbuck (ed.), *Organisational Growth and Development*, 1971, Harmondsworth, pp. 13-32.
8. H.I. Ansoff, *Corporate Strategy*, 1968, Harmondsworth, p. 94.
9. L. Wrigley in D.F. Channon, *The Strategy and Structure of British Enterprise*, 1973, London, pp. 10-12.
10. R.S. Edwards and H. Townsend, *Business Enterprise: its Growth and Organisation*, 1958, London, pp. 44-62.
11. J.T. Cannon, *Business Strategy and Policy*, 1968, New York, p. 219.
12. E. Penrose, *The Growth of the Firm*, 1959, Oxford, p. 172.
13. Department of Trade and Industry, *A Survey of Mergers, 1958-68*, 1970, London, p. 3.
14. S. Aaronovitch and M.C. Sawyer, 'Mergers, Growth and Concentration', *Oxford Economic Papers*, 27, 1975, p. 151.
15. M.A. Utton, 'The Effect of Mergers on Concentration: UK Manufacturing Industry, 1954-65', *Journal of Industrial Economics*, 20, 1971-72, p. 50, and L. Hannah and J.A. Kay, *Concentration in Modern Industry*, 1977, London, p. 4.
16. B.R. Scott, *Stages of Corporate Development*, Harvard Business School, mimeographed, 1971, p. 8.
17. F. Broadway, *Management Problems of Expansion*, 1966, London, p. 72.
18. D.J. North, 'The Process of Location Change in Different Manufacturing Organisations', in Hamilton (ed.), *Spatial Perspectives*, pp. 225-6.
19. Hussey, *Corporate Planning*, p. 95.
20. Ansoff, *Corporate Strategy*, p. 167.
21. F.E.I. Hamilton, 'A View of Spatial Behaviour, Industrial Organisations and Decision Making' in Hamilton (ed.), *Spatial Perspectives*, pp. 15-16.
22. C.W. Moore, 'Industrial Development Linkage Paths', *Tijdschrift voor Economische en Sociale Geografie*, 64, 1973, p. 104.
23. R.B. Le Heron and E.C.R. Warr, 'Corporate Organisation, Corporate Strategy, and Agribusiness Development in New Zealand', *New Zealand Geographer*, 32, 1976, p. 12.
24. D.E. Keeble, 'Industrial Decentralization and the Metropolis: the North-West London Case', *Transactions of the Institute of British Geographers*, 44, 1968, pp. 3-13.

25. Moore, 'Linkage Paths', p. 98.
26. Hamilton, 'A View of Spatial Behaviour', p. 14.
27. Le Heron and Warr, 'Corporate Organisation', p. 11.
28. C.W. Moore, 'Industrial Linkage Development Paths in Growth Poles: a Research Methodology', *Environment and Planning A*, 4, 1972, p. 265.
29. Le Heron and Warr, 'Corporate Organisation', p. 12.
30. Hayter, 'Corporate Strategies and Industrial Change', p. 227.
31. Ibid., p. 217.
32. Examples are provided by P.M. Townroe, *Industrial Location Decisions: a Study in Management Behaviour*, 1971, Birmingham; M.J.M. Cooper, *The Industrial Location Decision-Making Process*, 1975, Birmingham.
33. North, 'The Process of Location Change'; R. Leigh and D.J. North, 'Acquisition in British Industries: Implications for Regional Development', in F.E.I. Hamilton (ed.), *Contemporary Industrialisation, Spatial Analysis and Regional Development*, 1978, London.
34. M.J. Taylor, 'Organisational Growth, Spatial Interaction and Location Decision Making', *Regional Studies*, 9, 1975, p. 313.
35. D.E. Keeble, 'Employment Mobility in Britain' in M. Chisholm and G. Manners (eds), *Spatial Policy Problems of the British Economy*, 1971, Cambridge, pp. 57-60.
36. M. Sant, *Industrial Movement and Regional Development: the British Case*, 1975, London, p. 151.
37. Cooper, *The Industrial Location Decision-Making Process*, pp. 84-9.
38. North, 'The Process of Location Change', pp. 234-6.
39. J. Rees, 'The Industrial Corporation and Location Decision Analysis', *Area*, 4, 1972, pp. 199-205.
40. North, 'The Process of Location Change', p. 241.
41. Leigh and North, 'Acquisition in British Industries'. I am grateful to the authors of this paper for permitting me to see the manuscript prior to publication.
42. Hayter, 'Corporate Strategies and Industrial Change', pp. 219-20.
43. North, 'The Process of Location Change', p. 241.
44. K. Chapman, 'Corporate Systems in the United Kingdom Petro-Chemical Industry', *Annals of the Association of American Geographers*, 64, 1974, pp. 134-6.
45. D.E. Keeble, *Industrial Location and Planning in the United Kingdom*, 1976, London, p. 126.
46. Chapman, 'Corporate Systems', p. 132.
47. H.D. Watts, 'Lager Brewing in Britain', *Geography*, 60, 1975, pp. 139-45.
48. Hayter, 'Corporate Strategies and Industrial Change', p. 227.
49. Moore, 'Linkage Paths', p. 102.
50. Taylor, 'Organisational Growth, Spatial Interaction', pp. 317-18.
51. Rees, in Hamilton (ed.), *Spatial Perspectives*, p. 201.
52. Taylor, 'Organisational Growth, Spatial Interaction', p. 318.
53. A.C.M. Jansen, 'Enkele aspekten van het ruimtelijk gedrag van grote industriële concerns in Nederland, 1950-71', *Tijdschrift voor Economische en Sociale Geografie*, 63, 1972, pp. 411-25.
54. Moore, 'Industrial Development Linkage Paths', p. 97.
55. Hayter, 'Corporate Strategies and Industrial Change', pp. 225-6.

5 THE SPATIAL EVOLUTION OF AN ENTERPRISE: ADJUSTMENT AND INTERACTION

This chapter continues the discussion of the spatial evolution of an enterprise begun in the preceding one. Attention is focused on two elements: locational adjustment and the spatial outcomes of interaction between enterprises. It will be remembered that in Chapter 1 it was argued that the latter was one of the distinguishing features of large enterprise behaviour.

Locational Adjustment

Locational adjustment is defined here to include reorganisations where the number of plants of an enterprise remains the same or is reduced, while their capacities, products or linkages are changed. Large enterprises deliberately and consciously adapt their operations to fit changed conditions. It is to be contrasted with the adoption process where the individual small firm grows partly as a result of particularly favourable economic circumstances.[1] The degree of planning behind locational adjustments varies just as markedly as it does in spatial growth. At one end of the scale are adjustments made quite quickly in response to major and sudden external stress. Second are adjustments which, although quite marked in their effects, reflect a whole series of mainly programmed decisions taken over a period of time. Third are adjustments arising after some major stress imposed upon an enterprise, either externally (for example, by a fall in demand) or internally (for example, by an acquisition facing an enterprise with the need to integrate the new activities with its existing spatial structure). Adjustments in the third group are usually based on non-programmed decisions and are implemented after a thorough review of an enterprise's operations: this kind of adjustment is often called *rationalisation*. While rationalisation may be associated with reduction of an enterprise's capacity, it is more usually part of an exercise to *increase* capacity through a better utilisation of an enterprise's resources. It is not always possible to draw clear lines bounding these three categories, but they do provide a useful starting point for any discussion of locational adjustment. Further, distinguishing the concept of spatial rationalisation indicates that it ought to be looked at more closely.

The precise meaning of 'rationalisation' has been debated since at least 1932.[2] It can imply making a pattern more rational – usually by a decrease in production costs – but its relatively wide use in everyday situations means that it is used sometimes as a synonym for reorganisation. Of course, reorganisation of a spatial pattern is not necessarily a rational one. Rationalisation tends also to be associated in the public mind with plant closures, but such closures can be paralleled by investment elsewhere. Even where a reorganisation is accepted as rational it raises the question, 'In what sense is it rational?'[3] Is it for a nation or an industry or an individual enterprise that it is rational? If it is rational for an enterprise, is it rational now or rational at some future date or rational at some future perceived output level? These questions have not been answered satisfactorily.

In Chapter 2 the discussion of the spatial structure of an enterprise covered both the characteristics of its plants and their linkage patterns. If any adjustment has to be made to an enterprise's spatial structure it might be expected to involve changes in linkages and/or changes in plant numbers, size or product mix. In this section a brief discussion of the evidence on linkage changes precedes more general evidence relating to adjustments in plant characteristics.

Linkages

Adjustments of both material and information links might be expected to occur following a period of rapid spatial growth. The establishment of a branch plant outside a pre-existing plant space could induce a re-allocation of markets among an enterprise's plants, and thus change the pattern of plant-market linkages. After a merger, acquired plants might be expected, where possible, to re-orient their links to become integrated into the acquiring enterprise. Ideas in this area are still highly speculative, but some attempts have been made to assess the extent to which changes do occur.

Clearly the setting up of a branch plant must involve the development of new linkages to provide it with inputs and markets. The main interest lies in whether the plant uses new suppliers or serves new markets or whether the enterprise's existing suppliers adjust their links to serve the new plant and the enterprise allocates some of its existing markets to the new branch. There is little evidence relating directly to the large industrial enterprise, but similar enquiries for other firms suggest the kind of results that might be expected. Moseley & Townroe's study of linkage adjustment after movement (they included branches and transfers) indicated clearly the 'unimportance of local linkages to the majority of migrant companies'.[4] Lever's work, in contrast, suggests that the degree of re-orientation of links may be influenced by the distance a branch plant has moved. In Scotland he discovered that plants with head-offices in, for example, the North West tended to get rather more of their material inputs from that area than would be expected, whereas those with a South East base had tended to break their links with it and to seek new ones in the vicinity of the plant. He concludes that 'linkages can be "inherited" by branch plants from parent companies. Beyond a certain critical distance, however, branch plants are forced to find alternative supplies either in their own region or . . . close to it'.[5]

Linkage adjustments following acquisition have been examined rather more closely. Cadden's analysis of the West Canadian flour-milling plants suggests that inclusion of plants within a multi-plant enterprise will increase the overall complexity of plant to market linkages, and may considerably extend the linkages of any one plant.[6] The latter effect is achieved when a plant formerly serving a local market is incorporated into a larger enterprise and is called upon to serve the demands of markets where an enterprise's other plants were not sufficient to meet their own demands in full. The conclusions do not consider economies-of-scale, and are based on hypothetical rather than actual flows. Nevertheless, the evidence seems strong enough to accept that in an industry with marked outbound shipping costs, some form of adjustment of material linkages might occur if plants are absorbed into a large industrial enterprise.

This finding is supported by Hayter's study of the MacMillan Bloedel forest products enterprise. On merging with the Powell River Co., plants that had belonged formerly to the latter began to obtain their timber inputs from the Vancouver Island sites of MacMillan Bloedel. Similarly, the Powell company's higher-quality logs were diverted to Macmillan Bloedel sawmill and plywood plants; in return the latter sent wood chips back to the

Powell paper-manufacturing plants.[7]

The linkage changes examined by Cadden and Hayter involved either long distances or relatively bulky, low-value products, which probably explains their findings that adjustments of material linkage patterns may occur. The results of Leigh & North are in marked contrast.[8] They studied 141 acquisitions of small firms by larger enterprises in four UK industries between 1969 and 1974 and looked for examples of post-merger adjustment of material linkage patterns. There is some doubt as to whether their post-acquisition period of two to four years was long enough for important changes to occur, but changes in supplies or markets could be implemented quite rapidly. In practice their results show that changes in material linkages were a rare occurrence, only 18 per cent of the acquired firms had any of their material linkages changed. Since these findings contrast with those of Cadden and Hayter, possibly because of the different spatial scale of the work in the United Kingdom, the extent to which large industrial enterprises adjust their material linkages after spatial growth must remain uncertain, and caution should be exercised in extending conclusions from one set of enterprises to another.

Adjustments of information links are to be expected because of the tendency for administrative functions to be separated from other activities as an enterprise increases in size. This is confirmed by Leigh & North's work, although the caveat noted earlier should be kept in mind. In their sample 'nearly 85 per cent . . . of the established [service] links of the acquired firms were severed and transferred to the acquiring groups suppliers', [9] so that, for example, links with local banks, accountants and law firms were changed to links with banks, accountants and law firms associated with the larger enterprise. Most of these changes took place immediately on merger. On this evidence, despite its limited nature, modification of information linkages appears to be an important facet of adjustment behaviour.

Plants

Linkage adjustments can be made without major capital investment. In contrast, adjustments to plants are generally part of a wider investment strategy. Once the need to reorganise its pattern of production is recognised, a large industrial enterprise has to choose from a wide range of options which Hayter sees as part of 'a sequential and frequently highly integrated chain of on-site and inter-site . . . adjustments within corporate activity patterns'.[10] Since various actions are possible and since complex interlocking relationships are involved, there will be variations between enterprises in their adjustment paths, in timing and form. As Krumme & Hayter argue, it is 'unreasonable to expect that firms are equally adaptable'.[11]

Most discussions have been focused upon the rationalisation process, but equally important are the more subtle and gradual changes resulting from the accumulation of numerous small adjustments. The pioneering study in this area was Steed's analysis of on-site adjustments at Harland & Wolff's shipyard in Belfast.[12] Not only will site adjustments change the product mix but in multi-plant enterprises they may also change the relative importance of the different plants within an enterprise's spatial structure. An example is shown in Figure 5.1. Watts described how between 1936 and 1971 the plants of the British Sugar Corporation almost doubled their overall capacity, but the figure shows that the plants did not share the increase equally.[13] The plants that show the greatest relative gains were those which were smallest at the beginning of the period, and those which were adapted to produce a wider range of products. In other enterprises there may be the occasional closure of a plant, the sale of a plant to another enterprise or the gradual contraction of operations on selected sites. These changes in products and plant size within an existing plant space must by typical of many large enterprises, but since these changes are gradual they have not attracted as much attention as the rationalisation process.

An important early study of plant rationalisation was Fleming & Krumme's examination of the Royal Hoesch Union, a co-operative agreement of three large steel enterprises in the EEC. The principal objective was to expand crude and semi-finished steel production on a coastal site and to concentrate finished steel inland near the larger centres of consumption: the coastal site could take advantage of low assembly costs and the inland sites of proximity to markets. In addition, 'a number of subsidiary firms which have been operating too inefficiently or which do not fit the new locational structure of the concern . . . have been liquidated with production programmes transferred to other concern members'.[14] At the time Fleming & Krumme reported, however, there had been little time for the new group

Figure 5.1: Spatial Evolution: Locational Adjustment: British Sugar Corporation, 1936–71

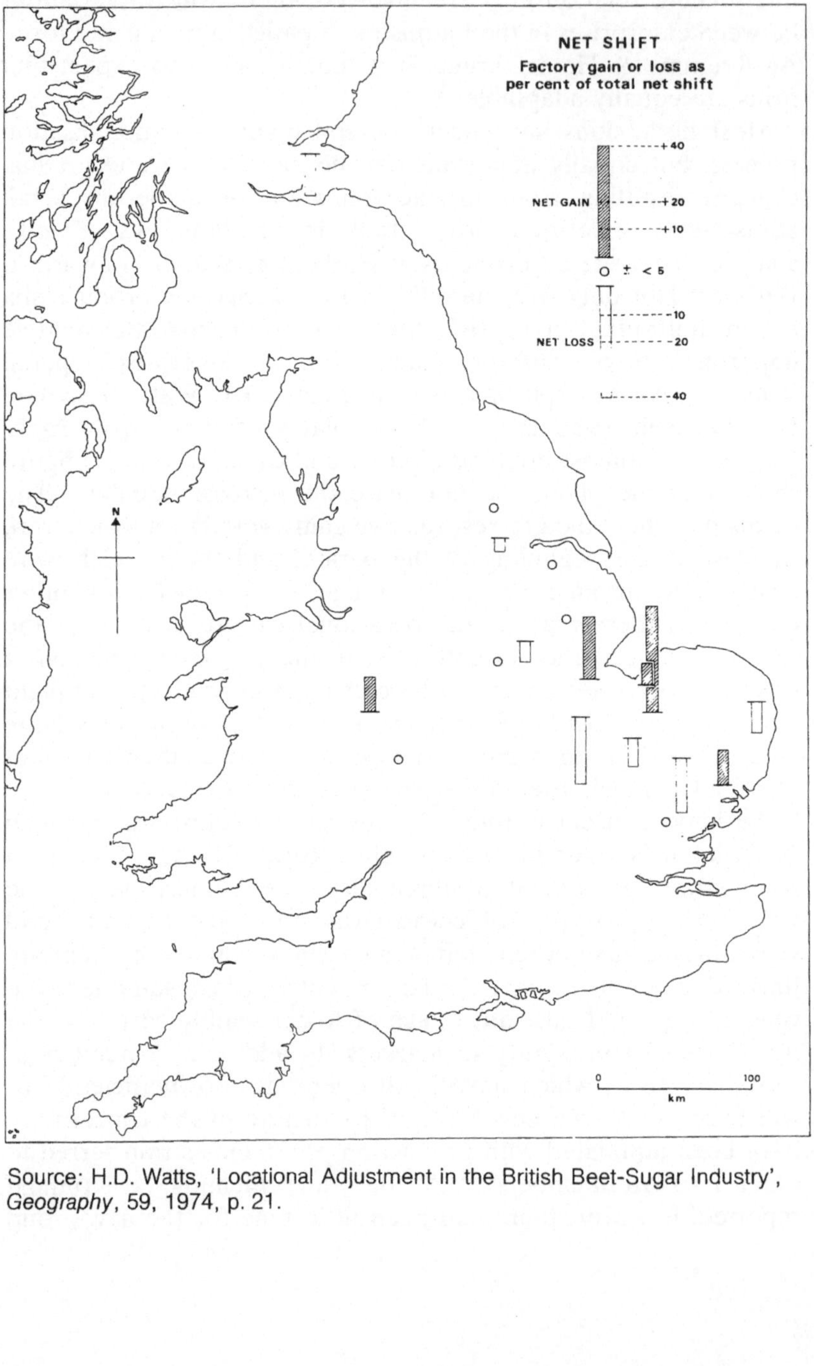

Source: H.D. Watts, 'Locational Adjustment in the British Beet-Sugar Industry', *Geography*, 59, 1974, p. 21.

to rationalise its production patterns: the study was, in a sense, premature. It is useful in drawing attention to rationalisation processes, particularly the switching of products between plants, but it is based mainly on expected rather than actual effects.

Other studies of rationalisation have tended to look, as did Fleming & Krumme, at post-merger change, particularly rationalisation following horizontal mergers. Examples are provided by Hayter who notes that 'several facilities were closed down'[15] and Le Heron & Warr who describe 'the consolidation of many processing plants'.[16] This illustrates the point that horizontal mergers offer more scope for rationalisation than do the other two types.

A move away from the case-study approach was made by Newbould.[17] His study was of 38 acquiring enterprises, and 17 (45 per cent) had closed a plant, head-office or administrative unit following an acquisition. This is reasonably high, as most enterprises were examined between eight and thirty months after acquisition. Newbould looked primarily at closures; in contrast Scherer examined in detail 36 large enterprises 'to determine whether mergers were followed by substantial rationalisation actions, in the sense that a significant fraction of acquired plants were modernised and enlarged, or closed down to permit the expansion of other facilities'. The terms 'substantial rationalisation' and 'significant fraction' give no real indication of the amount of post-merger adjustment, but he was able to claim 'substantial rationalisation' in about half of the thirty-six cases examined,[18] proportions very similar to those of Newbould, who noted that slightly more than half his cases closed over 5 per cent of their capacity.

Neither Newbould nor Scherer, however, was able to compare the relative frequency of expansions, closures, and product changes in the rationalisation process. This particular point was explored by Leigh & North.[19] In their sample they traced 130 post-acquisition adjustments to production plants. Expansion of plants occurred in 62 cases and a change of product in 21. Forty-seven acquisitions resulted in plant closures, and since some were multi-plant closures 61 factories were closed altogether. Perhaps the most interesting aspects of these results is that rationalisation following merger is as likely to result in the expansion of a plant's output as in its closure. This finding is at variance with earlier but less detailed studies, which have suggested a strong link between rationalisation and closure; much less emphasis was previously placed on the expansionary elements of rationalisation procedures.

These studies all focus on post-merger rationalisation and thus look at only one part of the process; rationalisation to cope with the repercussions of a period of rapid internal growth have been scarcely touched upon, nor has rationalisation within an enterprise as a result of technical change. It is important to remember the special nature of the findings reported above, yet when placed with Fleming & Krumme's study they help to suggest a typology of rationalisation behaviour.

Rationalisation Policy

Rationalisation policies can be viewed in the context of either the plant or the whole enterprise. For an existing plant three broad categories may be usefully distinguished:

(1) change in the number of functions;
(2) increase in plant size;
(3) decrease in plant size (including closure).

Change in the number of functions is usually accompanied by either category (2) or category (3).

A plant within a large industrial enterprise, however, must be viewed not in isolation but in relation to other plants in a corporate system, as a change in one plant may have implications throughout that system. This particular point was stressed in Chapman's study of large enterprises in the UK petro-chemical industry; he showed that 'any major project at one manufacturing centre is evaluated in terms of its effect upon the position of other existing centres and also in terms of the operational efficiency of the [enterprise] as a whole'.[20]

Since this wider relationship is of critical importance, it is useful to model three types of rationalisation policy, as in Figure 5.2 where three basic policies are depicted.

Policy One: Specialisation. In this first solution (Figure 5.2B) each function is concentrated on one site. This may involve the concentration of head-office activities on a site no longer needed for production, or simply a switch from multi-product to single-product sites. The concentration of functions permits

Figure 5.2: Some Spatial Rationalisation Policies.
A: Pre-rationalisation; B: Specialisation; C: Partial Disinvestment; D: Greenfield Site

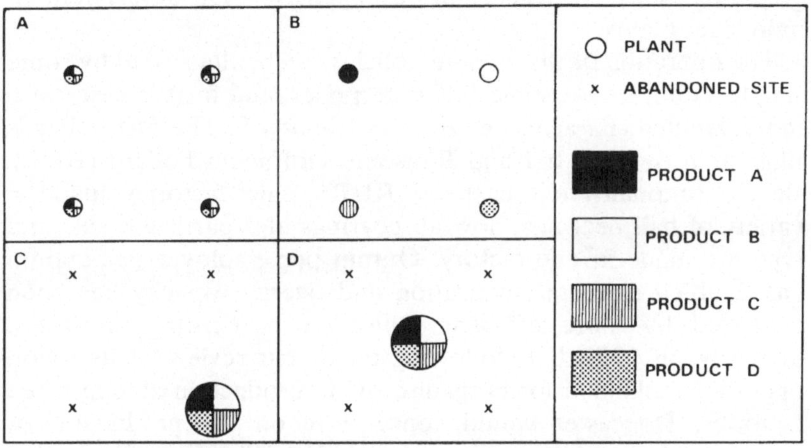

Source: H.D. Watts, 'Spatial Rationalization in Multi-Plant Enterprises', *Geoforum*, 17, 1974, p. 73.

realisation of economies-of-scale, and as Steed observes 'the assignment of products to plants provides a great deal of spatial flexibility for a corporation'.[21]

Policy Two: Concentration and Partial Disinvestment. This aims at concentrating production on fewer sites (Figure 5.2C). Production economies-of-scale can be complemented by savings in services and links between plants. The policy requires the closure of certain plants, but in favourable circumstances the sale or lease of the site might provide valuable capital for the rationalisation scheme. Indeed, site value may be one of the most critical factors favouring the closure of a particular plant.

Policy Three: Complete Disinvestment and Greenfield Site. This concentrates all production capacity on a greenfield site (Figure 5.2D). It releases older sites for alternative uses and has the added advantage that construction of the new plant can proceed without disturbing the production of existing units. Valtz believed that this is often the easiest solution to the rationalisation problem; he argues 'it is much easier to determine the cost of building a new plant than it is to appraise the cost of rationalising among even two or three plants'.[22] This view would probably be disputed in an inflationary situation which would accentuate the uncertainties inherent in a greenfield investment. At the best of times, greenfield sites are usually more expensive than adjustment of individual plants.

The operation of these three policies can be illustrated by some simple examples for some UK enterprises, and further cases of a more detailed character are given in Chapter 9. The first policy is illustrated by both ICI and Ransome Hoffmann Pollard (RHP). Before rationalisation each of RHP's nine factories made a variety of ball bearings; now all bearings of a particular size and type are made in one factory. Output per employee per annum has doubled since rationalisation and overall capacity has been increased by more efficient utilisation of existing machines. Similarly, in 1972 ICI, following an urgent review of its nylon operations, planned to reorganise nylon production among three factories. Doncaster would concentrate on the production of carpet and industrial yarns together with textile staple fibres, and factories at Pontypool and Gloucester on the production of nylon textile yarns. The importance of this policy is seen also in aggregate data from the United States, where over the period 1960 to 1965 in 494 large American corporations 'most of the plants which survived the five-year period did so by shifting their production emphasis, frequently from one industrial category to another'.[23]

Illustrations of the second policy are provided by GEC's rationalisation of its plants making telephone exchange equipment, and by Charrington's adjustment of its malting activities in Scotland. GEC's policy led to the closure of its Woolwich plant employing 5,500 workers, which at the time had the dubious honour of being the largest single works closure in Britain.[24] The plant was manufacturing electro-mechanical exchange equipment which was being phased out. The factory was over 100 years old and would have been difficult to adapt for modern production methods; the products it made were being replaced by electronic equipment and what demand remained could be met by other plants in the group in Coventry, Scotland and the North East. In the other example, Charrington's concentrated all their Scottish malting into one plant at Alloa. This expanded unit employed 17 men and had a potential output of 100,000 quarters per annum. It replaced 80 men in 8 plants operating a 25 per cent smaller capacity. The firm estimated that expanding on an old site cost £300,000 compared with the £850,000 it would have cost to build a completely new plant with associated storage facilities.

The third policy is illustrated by the Lyons group rationalisation of its cake and pastry operations. In 1972 much of this production was at the Cadby Hall site in London; the rationalisation scheme envisaged the redevelopment of this site for offices and a hotel once production had been moved elsewhere. It was decided to concentrate cake and pastry production on a greenfield site at Barnsley (South Yorkshire) and cease manufacturing these products in London, Smethwick and Hove. It was still intended to serve Scotland from a separate plant.

Inter-Enterprise Contrasts in Rationalisation

The rationalisation policies and the examples outlined above indicate some of the possible choices open to a large industrial enterprise faced with rationalisation. To understand why a particular choice is made it is necessary to investigate some of the factors which might influence the selection of a particular option. Some will be a result of external pressures upon an enterprise such as the behaviour of rival enterprises (discussed in the final section of this chapter) and the actions of government (discussed in the final chapter), but here attention is focused upon characteristics of the enterprise itself. While variations in policy will be caused by the differing financial resources available to different enterprises, within any given budget rationalisation policies will reflect, in part, the possibilities inherent in existing sites, the spatial structure and the organisational structure.

Utilisation of Existing Sites

Rationalisation policies which change the point pattern of an enterprise are the last rather than the first stage of a rationalisation scheme, simply because they are expensive and disruptive. They tend to be made only after other economies have been exhausted. Rawstron showed that the Central Electricity Generating Board turned to locational savings only when it seemed that the economies of increased thermal efficiency were exhausted.[25] Similarly, Watts noted that it was only in the 1970s that the British Sugar Corporation considered an overall rationalisation policy involving plant closure; there had been other means of reducing costs in the 1960s. Massive re-equipment schemes in the 1950s and 1960s were accompanied by economies in the use of labour and fuel. From 1950 to 1960 factory labour per ton of beet was halved and coal consumption was cut by one-sixth. These trends continued in the next decade and between 1958/9 and 1967/8 the labour needed to process a tonne of beet decreased by a third. Only then, with these costs reduced, was spatial rationalisation considered.[26] Thus, where there remains scope for changes within the existing plants rationalisation and closure, like spatial growth, is unlikely to occur. A further constraint militating against disinvestment is that it is a decision which is unpopular to make; as Katz observes, 'disinvestment decisions . . . are among the most difficult and emotionally loaded issues that must be faced'.[27] An enterprise may be willing to take it only if the economic case is unanswerable and no alternative course of action is possible.

There is an important exception to these generalisations and that is where alternative non-industrial uses of a site appear to offer higher returns. This is particularly important, for example, during booms in demand for office and commercial property, where industrial sites can be sold for office development, and the cash raised by the operation can be used to develop other parts of the enterprise. Some examples of this policy are illustrated in Chapter 9.

Spatial Structure

The assessment of the future roles of particular sites within the spatial structure of an enterprise will reflect their relative position and standing within the enterprise. One obvious criterion is the relative efficiency (either perceived or actual) and it does not seem unreasonable to assume that the most efficient plants in an enterprise will be retained in any rationalisation programme. These may be, for example, the largest plants with their lower average costs, the best-practice plants (Chapter 2) or the most modern ones.

The durability of equipment is clearly a relevant factor and it is a variable which appears to be particularly important in the cases described in Chapter 9. Modern plants may be worth retaining even if they do not fit well into a new spatial structure. British Leyland when it was set up inherited four recently commissioned engine plants. Fewer sites ultimately will be used but, as the enterprise commented, 'you cannot just close down new multi-million pound plants'.[28] Similarly, in the early 1970s British Aluminium planned to concentrate all its alumina production at Burntisland and to close its Newport works. The principal reason for the Newport closure was the fact that the plant was obsolete. Presumably non-investment in the plant over a period of years committed the enterprise to closing it. Of course, the recent closure of a modern textile plant at Skelmersdale (cf. p.278) suggests that modernity is no guarantee of survival, it only makes it more likely. Age of plant can be measured not only in absolute terms, but also in relation to the other sites in the enterprise.

Another measure of a plant's status is its spatial context within the enterprise. It might be expected that the sites on the periphery of an enterprise's plant space would be more likely to close than those in the core region. Similarly, plants displaying a low degree of material linkages with other parts of an enterprise might also show a greater propensity to close, whereas those with two-way input and output links with other plants in the system would survive.

Organisational Structure

It seems possible too that rationalisation, like other behaviour, is affected by the different organisational structures discussed in Chapter 2. Rationalisation requires an appropriate structure for it to be implemented. An enterprise should be able to view its manufacturing operations as a whole or, at least, the activities relating to one product group. Broadly, this could involve a move from a multi-divisional structure subdivided areally to one where each division is based on a product. In the former, an overview of total capacity and need for change is unlikely to emerge; problems will be seen in regional compartments and if rationalisation does occur it will be within a regional framework. With product-based divisions an overview of national production patterns will emerge more readily and adjustment over the whole system may be planned carefully.

The importance of organisational structure is well illustrated by enterprises in the railway engineering and steel industries. A full account of the former rationalisation scheme has been given by Cook,[29] but the point of interest in this context is that the rationalisation scheme depended upon changes in the organisational structure. The enterprise concerned was Britain's nationalised railway industry, whose railway engineering operations were moved out of a series of regional divisions into a product division of their own. The regional divisions with their interests in provision of rail services had tended to ignore the engineering plants and some managers of the plants felt that their plants were last on the list of investment priorities. Until this structural reorganisation took place there was little co-ordination of engineering plant policy among divisions. This was a hangover from the pre-nationalisation (1948) period, and the fact that after nationalisation 'little attention was given to the nature of integration or to how it was to be achieved. There seems to have been some feeling that nationalisation would do it automatically'.[30] The setting up of a Workshops Division in 1962 marked a major structural change. The fundamental nature of this change is spelt out by Cook, who argues 'it is important to recognise that [the engineering plants] were then for the first time looked at as a single business and that for the first time their capacity was looked at from a national rather than a regional point of view'. Thus the structure was adjusted to permit a review of engineering operations, which was followed by the implementation of a rationalisation scheme (Figure 5.3) similar to that in Policies One and Two, where product rationalisation was accompanied by investment in selected sites.

Similarly Heal shows how the initial structure of the nationalised British steel industry, based upon regional divisions, had 'tended to preserve . . . [the] . . . vestigial company and regional jealousies' and it was only the organisation into product divisions that had 'obliterated the old company boundaries'[31] in 1970. At the end of 1972 the rationalisation plan was produced. It follows Policy Two outlined earlier with concentration on existing sites. Although the phasing of this rationalisation has been modified, it provides another example of a rationalisation scheme emerging after a change in an enterprise's organisational structure.

This discussion has illustrated a number of variables which may cause differences between enterprises in rationalisation policies. Three important ones seem to be the potentialities of existing sites and an enterprise's spatial structure (these two could be included under the less satisfactory concept of inertia), and particular stress has been placed on the role of an enterprise's

Figure 5.3: Spatial Rationalisation: Workshops Division of the British Railways Board. A: Plants in 1962; B: Post-rationalisation Pattern

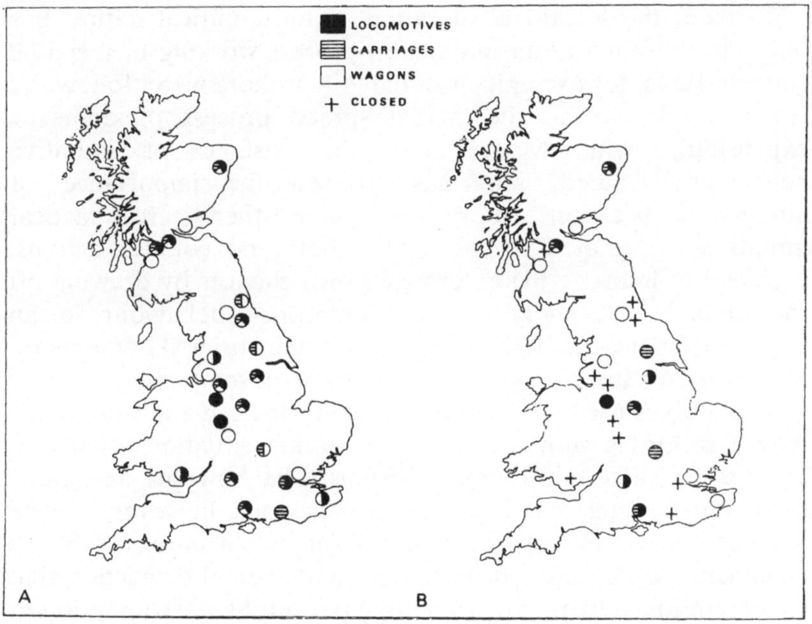

Source: based on data in P.L. Cook, *Railway Workshops: the Problem of Contraction*, 1964, Cambridge.

organisational structure. The effect of these variables is, of course, influenced and modified by cost constraints.

Up to this point the evolution of a large industrial enterprise has been treated in isolation from other enterprises operating in the same industry, yet it was argued in the introduction that one of the unique features of the large industrial enterprise was that its behaviour was often influenced strongly by the action of other enterprises. The next section is devoted to this interaction process, which may influence both spatial growth and locational adjustment.

The Inter-Action Process

It was shown in Chapter 2 that many large industrial enterprises operate in oligopolistic environments, where their spatial growth and locational adjustment are influenced by the behaviour of other enterprises. It is the aim of this section to examine the interaction process and its influence on the spatial patterns of an enterprise's plants. Unfortunately lack of data means that it is not possible to consider linkages in this context.

To date, the locational literature of an empirical nature has only offered hints of an interaction process working in a spatial context. Rees, for example, postulated that there were 'follow the leader tendencies in the spatial spread process of domestic expansion',[32] while Moore noted the existence of 'imitative behaviour'.[33] Steed, too, has stressed the importance of interaction between enterprises where there are 'tactical initiatives, calculated reactions by others and counter actions, designed to improve the enterprise's own chances by drawing off the others'.[34] A study of large enterprise behaviour in an oligopolistic environment allows these rather brief statements on the nature of the interaction process to be developed.

Oligopoly is used to describe a market situation and usually the main concern is with the way that market situation affects an enterprise's price and output decisions. The concepts developed for understanding price and output behaviour, however, can be adapted for use in a spatial context. This is not unreasonable as Needham has argued that there is a 'fundamental conviction that concentration is likely to play a large part in the determination of business behaviour'[35] and that behaviour influences spatial patterns.

'Fewness is an important characteristic of the economic scene' since, where a few enterprises exist in an industry, 'decision-making units shape their policies in view of how they mutually react to each other's moves'.[36] The outcomes of such interactions can affect both the point pattern and the plant size characteristics of an industry. Williams & Scott stress that in investment decisions enterprises are 'influenced by what competitors are doing or might do'.[37] A small example will illustrate this link between interaction and spatial patterns in a wider context.

The soap and detergent sector had a five-enterprise concentration ratio of between 80 and 85 per cent in 1963 and the major part of the market was shared between Unilever and Procter & Gamble. From 1960 to 1965 a rationalisation of Unilever's production activities in soap and detergents was undertaken. Increasingly these products were concentrated at Port Sunlight, releasing capacity at Leeds, Warrington and Silvertown (London) for other purposes. There was, then, a major change in the geography of soap and detergent production as a result of this rationalisation scheme. Part of the stimulus to change was technical but 'the other was the changing nature of competition in the soap market. As the major competitive struggle became one between Unilever and a single major rival (Procter & Gamble) unhindered by a history of multi-company relationship . . . the need to streamline Unilever's own operations was plain'.[38] This kind of behaviour is just one illustration of the way in which an interaction process reveals itself in space.

Exploration of the interaction process in location theory was summarised by Greenhut under the general heading of locational interdependence.[39] Although the work of Hotelling figures in most basic textbooks together with some recent developments such as that by Devletoglou,[40] Gannon was probably right when he argued that 'little has been added in a substantive way since'.[41] A further restriction on the general validity of the approaches developed by Hotelling is that although they are conceptually elegant there has been little, if any, empirical verification of either the process or the pattern they produce. Similarly, game theory, while offering some interesting insights into possible behaviour tells us little of how enterprises actually do behave. In sum, these theoretical approaches to interaction processes in industrial location literature have offered very little in relation to the real world outcomes of inter-organisational relationships.

As a result, the following discussion of the interaction process is put forward very tentatively. Scherer notes that in these small group situations 'virtually anything can happen'.[42] Some help might be expected from the field of organisational behaviour but this has had a 'predominantly intra-organisational focus' and 'few explicit models of inter-organisational relations have thus far been developed'.[43] Notwithstanding the inherent difficulties in approaching this topic some thoughts on the interaction process are presented below.

An examination of the interaction process suggests that if the interest is in the spatial outcomes of the process, space may itself operate in different ways upon that process. In the first case, the spatial outcome may be the result of an essentially aspatial conflict. A hypothetical example would be two enterprises competing for a particular contract which was essential to their survival. The enterprise obtaining the contract would retain its production sites, the enterprise losing the contract would cease business and its production facilities would be shut down. Whichever enterprise won would determine which production sites survived.

In the second case, space can be an essential part of the conflict. Here enterprises may interact either to gain access to a share of a specific market, or of a particular input, particularly in the latter case for agricultural or forest products. A hypothetical example of this type of conflict is provided by enterprises in a baking industry competing for retail outlets in specific urban areas. Where a certain minimum number of outlets is obtained it becomes feasible to build a production unit. Thus, in this case not only is there a spatial outcome, but space itself is an important element in the interaction process. Of course, this distinction is similar to that made between implicit and explicit spatial decisions in Chapter 1.

Attractive as the dichotomous classification may be, it is increasingly difficult to keep spatial considerations out of enterprise interaction. This is seen when one enterprise is located in an Assisted Area, and another in a non-Assisted Area. The former may enjoy cost advantages as a result of government subsidies which allow it to quote a lower price than its non-Assisted Area rival. Thus, space may influence price and, consequently, ability to obtain an order.

Here the centre of interest is those interaction processes where space is an important influence on inter-organisational relationships. This is not an indication that this is the most important sub-group of interaction processes; indeed the others may be more common, but it presents problems which appear to have implications for industrial location patterns. It can be argued, further, that the general features displayed in this process will be reflected in a modified form in the essentially aspatial interaction situations.

Spatial Interaction

In approaching the study of enterprises in a small group situation it seems particularly important to distinguish between an enterprise's *role* in the group, and its *behaviour* while it occupies that role. An analogy might be an informal meeting of three or four persons when one member takes on the *role* of guiding the discussion, while the *behaviour* in that role may be either dictatorial, setting out the guidelines for discussion, or participative, encouraging each member to make a contribution to the formulation of the main heads of discussion. This analogy may not be particularly appropriate as it equates organisations with individuals, but it does clarify the distinction between 'role' and 'behaviour', a distinction around which this discussion is built.

It is the roles that are considered first. Each member of an oligopoly in deciding upon its policy must take into account its expectations of its competitors' behaviour, and it is an enterprise's attitude to its competitors that assists in the definition of its role. Gadreau suggests that among the roles which enterprises take up two – 'leader' and 'satellite' – are particularly important.[44] If an enterprise adopts the attitude that whatever behaviour it undertakes other enterprises will follow suit, then it fits within the leader role. While if an enterprise assumes its rival's policy cannot be changed and adapts to that policy in what it sees as the most appropriate manner then it occupies the satellite role. Of course, these roles need not be fixed: challenges to the leader role may be made, and a more exhaustive categorisation of enterprise roles would be possible, but this dichotomisation of roles is a useful one with which to work.

The significance of recognising 'leader' and 'satellite' enterprises is that the leader may well have a major influence on the spatial outcome of the interaction process. A leader pursuing a vigorous policy of both vertical and horizontal integration could result in satellite enterprises following suit; likewise, a policy of rationalisation of production facilities begun by the leader might result in similar policies being forced upon the satellite enterprises. Although the leader may influence the broad pattern of spatial change, the detail of the spatial outcome of the interaction process will reflect the behaviour of the individual enterprises.

Chamberlain argues that in selecting its most appropriate form of behaviour an enterprise 'must consider not only what [its] competitor is doing now, but also what he will be forced to do in the light of the change which he himself is contemplating'.[45] Studies of interaction suggest a three-fold classification of enterprise behaviour: passive, competitive and co-operative.[46]

Fellner has indicated that co-operative behaviour can be subdivided into behaviour resulting from explicit agreements (collusion) and that resulting from implicit agreements, otherwise termed 'spontaneous co-ordination'.[47] It is the former category that is explored here.

Passive behaviour is, by definition, unlikely to be characteristic of the leading enterprise, but some satellites could react in a passive manner. Faced with action by other enterprises the passive enterprise either fails to adjust its policy or may withdraw from the conflict. Growth of mass production encouraged by the leader could lead to a decision to concentrate on one small sector of the market – either a particular geographic area or a specific product. This, in the long run, may remove the enterprise from the small group dominating the industry, and it probably increases the chances of acquisition by the leader at a later stage.

Co-operative behaviour of an explicit nature, or collusion, depends upon the existence of at least some communication links between the enterprises. These can vary in strength from casual encounters through trade associations to the holding of equities in each other's activities. Initiative for collusion could come from either leader or satellite, although the former would have more bargaining power in drawing up any agreement. Such agreements with direct spatial outcomes can include market-sharing arrangements, with different enterprises operating plants in different areas, or co-operation in contraction and expansion of plant capacity. These agreements, provided no new entrants appeared, could ensure the emergence of a rational (from the industry viewpoint) production pattern. The stimulus for such agreements is that they help to reduce the uncertainty associated with an enterprise's external environment.

Most interest perhaps centres upon competitive interaction within the small group as each enterprise seeks to maintain or improve its position. There seems to be a number of policies an enterprise could adopt when competing for space, of which five are set out below. Some of these policies are illustrated in detail in Chapters 8 and 9.

(1) Where locations for plants are difficult to find, an enterprise could follow an offensive policy and obtain options on particularly favoured sites in order to constrain the choice open to the opposition. This does raise the possibility of reaction by

competitors adopting a defensive policy of selecting site options to control the growth of the leader.

(2) If an enterprise adopts an innovative role by introducing new technologies or products within an existing industrial group, then it may be able to select the most appropriate sites before competition becomes intense.

(3) If there is a danger of new entrants challenging existing enterprises, early warning of such schemes allows the enterprises to attempt to acquire or absorb the new concern before any major growth occurs.

(4) Attempt to influence other decision makers to decide in your favour, particularly official groups. This is not to argue that government is corrupt, but that through informal contacts an enterprise's viewpoint can be expressed.

(5) Try to obtain allies outside the industrial sector; an individual enterprise's bargaining power can be strengthened by liaison with powerful groups such as regional development organisations or local trade unions.

These policies are not presented as a guide for a successful competitive strategy and they certainly raise questions as to whether they are acceptable to society as a whole. Competition of this sort does exist and ought to be investigated.

The listing of strategies is not exhaustive and they could be employed singly or in combination. Further, Williamson suggests that in inter-organisational relationships there is a recurrent cycle of collusion and conflict.[48] When the economic environment deteriorates one enterprise is likely to break away from a collusive agreement, especially where the declining demand for a product means that gains can be made only at the expense of rivals.

This discussion of the interaction process has ignored internal and external constraints on enterprise behaviour. Internally, since most actions require time and have a clear cost an enterprise's options will be constrained by the time it is prepared to devote to the interaction, by the cost of such actions and by the period within which a decision has to be made. An enterprise on the verge of bankruptcy has little time or resources for elaborate interaction policies. Explanation of variations between enterprises in their policies might be found in an examination of the internal constraints operating upon a particular enterprise. The external constraints have been summarised succinctly by Phillips, who has argued that 'in a world of organisations, the pressure to be a good citizen as well as the fear of the policeman, may have significant effects on what a group will or will not do'.[49] In other words, within the range of options open to an enterprise it should not be seen to do too well and break established norms, nor should it come into conflict with government policies on regions, monopolies and mergers.

Few published accounts look at the interaction process in any detail, and with one exception, described briefly below, they tend to examine the process in an historical context. This is partly a function of availability of records in a particularly sensitive area of business activities.

Examples of interaction over fifty years ago are provided by Aduddel & Cain and Cromar. The former study of the North American meat-packing industry came to the conclusion that part of the reason for US meat packers' failure to move their processing plants westwards from Chicago reflected collusion among the principal enterprises. What is more, they were dividing the meat-packing business among themselves and allocating to themselves shares of particular supply areas. Further, they also followed policy (1) described earlier and gained control of the most desirable stockyard sites and were thus able to control entry to the yards as well as to the business.[50] Similarly, Cromar's study of the collusive agreement known as the 'Limitation of the Vend' in the Tyneside coal industry indicates how this agreement influenced the spatial pattern of mining developments.[51]

A contemporary example is provided by Watts's examination of the development of the UK aluminium-smelting industry. Government economic experts had suggested that the country could support two new smelters, and it was expected that two enterprises (British Aluminium and Rio Tinto Zinc) would build them. Examination of publicly available evidence suggests that Alcan, by following policy (5), was able to obtain permission to construct an additional smelter. By gaining the support of coal-mining interests it made it extremely difficult for a government to refuse to allow it to proceed, although it clearly upset the viability of the other two plants. The spatial outcome of this particular interaction was that the United Kingdom gained three instead of two plants, and one was located on a coalfield utilising electricity generated by a coal-fired power station. The other two used nuclear power drawn from the national electricity transmission system.[52]

The very limited nature of the empirical evidence of the interaction process resulting from inter-organisational relations indicates an obvious gap in knowledge about the spatial behaviour of large industrial enterprises. For this reason it forms one of the key themes in the case analyses in Chapters 7 through 9.

Conclusion

These two chapters have looked at the spatial evolution of large industrial enterprises separating out two main elements, spatial growth and locational adjustment, each of which may be influenced by the interaction process.

From the point of view of an individual enterprise the motives for growth arise from the personal, organisational and economic characteristics of an enterprise, and to achieve that growth the strategy can vary from expansion of a single product to complete diversification. The methods of spatial growth are branch plants and acquisitions, and each mode has its own spatial expression, influenced by the motives and strategies of an enterprise.

The spatial growth is accompanied by locational adjustment. The exact form this adjustment takes still needs careful measurement. Changes in material and information linkages have been shown to occur, mainly in the post-merger situation. Adjustment of activities at plants has been related to three different rationalisation policies, such rationalisation policies including plant expansion as well as plant closure. Inter-enterprise differences in rationalisation behaviour seem to mirror the potentialities of existing sites, the spatial structure of an enterprise and its organisational structure. The interaction process creates leader and satellite roles, and the behaviour of large industrial enterprises in these roles can be summarised as falling within one of three categories; competitive, collusive and passive.

The next chapter tries to bring many of these ideas together by looking at attempts to model the evolution of an enterprise.

Notes

1. R.L. White and H.D. Watts, 'The Spatial Evolution of an Industry: the Example of Broiler Growing', *Transactions of the Institute of British Geographers*, New Series, 2, 1977, pp. 175-91.
2. R.A. Brady, 'The Meaning of Rationalization: an Analysis of the Literature', *Quarterly Journal of Economics*, 46, 1932, pp. 526-40.
3. D. Fleming and G. Krumme, 'The Royal Hoesch Union: Case Analysis of Adjustment Patterns in the European Steel Industry', *Tijdschrift voor Economische en Sociale Geografie*, 59, 1968, pp. 177-8.

4. M.J. Moseley and P.M. Townroe, 'Linkage adjustment following industrial movement', *Tijdschrift voor Economische en Sociale Geografie*, 64, 1973, p. 144.
5. W.F. Lever, 'Manufacturing Linkages and the Search for Suppliers and Markets', in F.E.I. Hamilton (ed.), *Spatial Perspectives on Industrial Organisation and Decision Making*, 1974, London, p. 326.
6. P.G. Cadden, 'Multi-Plant Firms and Commodity Flows: the Case of the Western Canadian Flour Milling Industry', in B.M. Barr (ed.), *Western Canadian Research in Geography: the Lethbridge Papers*, 1975, Vancouver.
7. R. Hayter, 'Corporate Strategies and Industrial Change in the Canadian Forest Products Industries', *Geographical Review*, 66, 1976, p. 220.
8. R. Leigh and D.J. North, 'Acquisition in British Industries: Implications for Regional Development', in F.E.I. Hamilton (ed.), *Contemporary Industrialisation*, 1978, London. I am indebted to the authors for allowing me to see this paper before publication.
9. Ibid.
10. Hayter, 'Corporate Strategies and Industrial Change', p. 212.
11. G. Krumme and R. Hayter, 'Implications of Corporate Strategies and Product Cycle Adjustments for Regional Employment Change', in L. Collins and D.F. Walker (eds.), *Locational Dynamics of Manufacturing Activity*, 1975, London, p. 327.
12. G.P.F. Steed, 'The Changing Milieu of a Firm', *Annals of the Association of American Geographers*, 58, 1968, pp. 506-25.
13. H.D. Watts, 'Locational Adjustment in the British Beet-Sugar Industry', *Geography*, 59, 1974, pp. 10–23.
14. Fleming and Krumme, 'The Changing Milieu', p. 197.
15. Hayter, 'Corporate Strategies and Industrial Change', p. 220.
16. R.B. Le Heron and E.C.R. Warr, 'Corporate Organisation, Corporate Strategy, and Agribusiness Development in New Zealand', *New Zealand Geographer*, 32, 1976, p. 12.
17. G.D. Newbould, *Management and Merger Activity*, 1971, Liverpool, pp. 164-5.
18. F.M. Scherer et al., *The Economics of Multi-Plant Operation: an International Comparisons Study*, 1975, Harvard, p. 167.
19. Leigh and North, 'Acquisition in British Industries'.
20. K. Chapman, 'Agglomeration and Linkage in the United Kingdom Petro-Chemical Industry', *Transactions of the Institute of British Geographers*, 60, 1973, p. 63.
21. G.P.F. Steed, 'Forms of Corporate-Environmental Adaption', *Tijdschrift voor Economische en Sociale Geografie*, 62, 1971, p. 92.
22. R.C. Valtz, 'The Case of the Multi-Plant Manufacturer', *Harvard Business Review*, March/April 1964, p. 176.
23. G.P.F. Steed, 'Plant Adaptation, Firm Environments and Location Analysis', *Professional Geographer*, 23, 1971, p. 324.
24. W.W. Daniel, *Whatever Happened to the Workers in Woolwich?*, P.E.P. Broadsheet, No. 537, July 1972, p. 1.
25. E.M. Rawstron, 'Changes in the Geography of Electricity Production in Great Britain', *Geography*, 40, 1955, p. 93.
26. Watts, 'British Beet-Sugar Industry', pp. 17-20.
27. R. Katz, *Management of the Total Enterprise*, 1970, Englewood Cliffs, p. 242.
28. H.D. Watts, 'Spatial Rationalisation in Multi-Plant Enterprises', *Geoforum*, 17, 1974, pp. 69–76.
29. P.L. Cook, *Railway Workshops: the Problem of Contraction*, 1964, Cambridge.

30. A.W. Thomson and L.C. Hunter, *The Nationalised Transport Industries*, 1973, London, p. 131.
31. D.W. Heal, 'Ownership, Control and Location Decisions: the Case of the British Steel Industry Since 1945', in Hamilton (ed.), *Spatial Perspectives*, pp. 276-7.
32. J. Rees, 'Oligopoly, Investment and the Spatial Growth of Multi-National Enterprise', in F.E.I. Hamilton (ed.), *The Organisation of Spatial Industrial Systems*, IGU Working Group (Novosibirsk) on Industrial Geography, 1976, London, p. 190.
33. C.W. Moore, Industrial Linkage Development Paths in Growth Poles: a Research Methodology', *Environment and Planning A*, 4, 1972, p. 264.
34. G.P.F. Steed, 'Plant Adaptation, Firm Environments and Locational Analysis', *Professional Geographer*, 23, 1971, p. 326.
35. D. Needham, *Economic Analysis and Industrial Structure*, 1969, London, p. 83.
36. W. Fellner, *Competition Among the Few*, 1949, New York, p. xi.
37. B.R. Williams and W.P. Scott, *Investment Proposals and Decisions*, 1965, London, p. 14.
38. C. Wilson, *Unilever 1945-65*, 1968, London, pp. 157-8.
39. M.L. Greenhut, *Plant Location in Theory and Practise*, Chapel Hill, 1956, pp. 37-83.
40. H. Hotelling, 'Stability in Competition', *Economic Journal*, 39, 1929, pp. 41-57; and N.E. Devletoglou, 'A Dissenting View of Duopoly and Spatial Competition', *Economica*, 32, 1965, pp. 146-60.
41. C.A. Gannon, 'Consumer Demand, Conjectural Inter-Dependence and Locational Equilibria in Simple Spatial Duopoly', *Papers and Proceedings of the Regional Science Association*, 28, 1972, p. 83.
42. F.M. Scherer, *Industrial Market Structure and Economic Performance*, 1970, Chicago, p. 171.
43. W.M. Evan, *Inter-Organisational Relations*, 1976, Harmondsworth, pp. 11 and 15.
44. M. Gadreau, 'Location and Oligopoly Location of Production Units When Location Decisions are Interdependent', *Regional and Urban Economics*, 2, 1972, pp. 175-217.
45. E.H. Chamberlain, *The Theory of Monopolistic Competition*, 1956, Harvard, p. 47.
46. F.M. Scherer et al., *The Economics of Multi-Plant Operation: an International Comparisons Study*, 1975, Harvard, p. 144.
47. Fellner, *Competition Among the Few*, p. 11.
48. O.E. Williamson, 'A Dynamic Theory of Interfirm Behaviour', *Quarterly Journal of Economics*, 79, 1965, pp. 579-607.
49. A. Phillips, 'A Theory of Inter-Firm Organization', *Quarterly Journal of Economics*, 74, 1960, p. 610.
50. R. Aduddell and L. Cain, 'Location and Collusion in the Meat Packing Industry', in L. Cain and P. Uselding, *Business Enterprise and Economic Change*, 1973, Kent, Ohio, pp. 85-117.
51. P. Cromar, 'The Coal Industry on Tyneside 1771-1800: Oligopoly and Spatial Change', *Economic Geography*, 53, 1977, pp. 79-94.
52. H.D. Watts, 'The Location of Aluminium Reduction Plant in the United Kingdom', *Tijdschrift voor Economische en Sociale Geografie*, 61, 1970, pp. 148-56.

6 MODELS OF THE SPATIAL EVOLUTION OF AN ENTERPRISE

The previous two chapters by general discussion and reference to particular cases have illustrated some of the many varied influences guiding the spatial evolution of an enterprise, as well as some of the forms that evolution can take. The purpose of the present chapter is to review models of both the growth and the associated spatial evolution of an enterprise. These models give an opportunity to integrate some of the material that has gone before, and they provide the first steps towards a general model of the spatial evolution of a large industrial enterprise against which the patterns of an individual enterprise might be compared. The chapter is in three parts. The first examines metamorphosis models, the second illustrates two attempts to model the spatial evolution of an enterprise and the third presents a new model of spatial growth and locational adjustment in enterprises where a major problem is posed by the need to balance distribution costs against economies-of-scale.

Metamorphosis Models

The different motives, different strategies and different methods of growth interact with one another in various ways as an enterprise evolves, and as it grows it often becomes concerned with an increasingly oligopolistic environment. Various models of the growth of an enterprise have been proposed but the main interest in the geographical literature (for example, Steed,[1] Hayter,[2] and Le Heron & Warr[3]) has been in what Starbuck[4] terms metamorphosis models. The essential characteristics of the metamorphosis model is that the nature of an enterprise changes as it grows, and the change from one state to another tends to be abrupt. Growth is seen not as a steady progression but as a series of steps, each step marking the end of a specific stage of development. Growth at each stage sets up a series of stresses within an enterprise, and only if these stresses are resolved can growth continue. Dicken has set out this problem formally.[5] He argues that any deviation of observed from expected results (for example less output or unmet demand) results in an enterprise experiencing stress. Some forms of stress will occur regularly and programmed decisions will be made to deal with them. If, however, a particular stress reaches the *stress tolerance threshold* different procedures will have to be adopted, as the stress cannot be dealt with (tolerated) by standard procedures. Once this threshold is reached a non-programmed decision will have to be made by defining the problem carefully and finding the solution to it. If a solution is not found growth may stop. The stresses faced by an enterprise as it grows vary in magnitude, and periods of major stress mark the change from one stage of growth to another.

The stages through which an enterprise passes are discussed by a number of authorities (for example, Whyte,[6] Cannon,[7] and Scott[8]) although there is disagreement concerning the number of stages in the sequence and their characteristics: Cannon specifies five stages,[9] Scott[10] only three. Although the discussion is about stages of stepped growth, these steps may not be obvious in the development of any one enterprise. Some enterprises will move easily from one stage to another and the transition may be difficult to identify; indeed some may omit one phase in its entirety. At the other extreme certain enterprises may never succeed in reaching their next stage.

The most widely discussed metamorphosis model is that proposed by Chandler,[11] and its essential features are described below. After initial small-scale operations there are four stages.

Stage I. The first stage of growth involves the accumulation of resources, generally in relation to a single product or group of related products. It sees the rapid build-up of an enterprise from a small beginning and profits provide funds for further expansion. The expertise of the enterprise increases as it learns through experience. This expertise provides the basis for yet more growth. In this stage most decisions are taken by the owner who often constructs a large, unwieldy organisation.

Stage II. Chandler's second phase sees the rationalisation of the use of resources. Of necessity it involves developing methods for managing rationally the large organisation that has been built up. Techniques for manufacturing and selling are further developed, there may be both forward and backward integration, and schemes for the co-ordination of functions within the enterprise are set up. This co-ordination may be achieved by the setting up of a functional organisation structure.

Stage III. By the end of the second stage, imitators have begun to catch up with and challenge the first enterprise. It begins to respond to its competitors and a third phase, typified by renewed growth, takes place. Some of the further growth is developed from strengths built up earlier, other growth is stimulated by a strategy of diversification into new products and into new markets. Growth, typically, may be by acquisition and the enterprise attempts to control its operations through the holding-company structure.

Stage IV. The final phase was viewed by Chandler as another phase of rationalisation, rationalising the use of expanding resources, attempting to co-ordinate the increasingly diverse interests of the enterprise and trying to bring them under control; this last objective often being achieved through the setting up of a multi-divisional structure.

Broadly, Chandler sees the four phases of growth in a pattern of growth and then rationalisation, growth and then rationalisation. This can be related back to growth of a single and related-product enterprise, followed by rationalisation; and then growth of a diversified enterprise and then rationalisation. The change from one stage to another inevitably presents a challenge and a major stress. Whether or not an enterprise can overcome this challenge will influence its growth, and possibly its chances of survival. The difficulties of meeting or coping with the change from one condition to another must not be under-played. As Edwards & Townsend have observed, 'the qualities possessed by the builders of firms are not necessarily those best suited to sustaining firms once they have grown'.[12] Convincing the owner-entrepreneur of this may not be easy. Moore suggests that an enterprise needs first a promotor or activity generator, second a consolidator and third an administrator or manager,[13] but this sequence does not fit neatly into the four-stage model.

During the growth of an enterprise through these four stages it can be assumed to take on the special characteristics of a large industrial enterprise, which were set out in Chapter 1. Instead of operating one plant it begins to operate several; in the third phase it may well operate several plants in each of several industries. The declining role of the owner-entrepreneur removes the influence of the family, and control passes to the executives from those who own the shares. Periods of rationalisation see the introduction of formal organisation structures, or the replacement of one established structure by another, particularly a change from the functional to the multi-divisional structure. While size continues to increase, interaction with other enterprises begins and the state may initiate a policy of monitoring the enterprise's decisions. Finally, attention is turned to new markets overseas, which again presents new crises, new challenges and a particular kind of stress. In different enterprises these changes may come in a different order – for example, multi-national operations might pre-date organisational change, and a number of quite small concerns do have overseas subsidiaries or branches.

Chandler's four-stage model has little explicit spatial content and there have been difficulties in adapting it into a spatial context. Tentatively, Taylor established two stages in the growth of some iron-foundry firms in the United Kingdom. Threshold sizes appeared to separate firms with from 1 to 50 employees from those with 91 to 500 employees. The first group were characterised by privately owned single-plant firms, the latter with publicly owned multi-plant enterprises. Possibly, and very cautiously, these stages might be equated with Chandler's Stage I and Stage II, but this is not done by Taylor. The Stage II firms are shown by Taylor to have fewer local linkages and are moving towards wider market areas and setting the scene for spatial growth. It can be inferred that in moving from Stage I to Stage II 'the location decisions of firms . . . will become less parochial and geographically more dispersed'.[14]

An attempt to make a more direct link between Chandler's ideas and the geographical study of a large industrial enterprise is made by Le Heron & Warr. They argue that a Stage I enterprise reacts to its environment, in their example the food-processing plant locating and developing in relation to patterns determined by the farming system. In subsequent stages the enterprise adopts a more complex strategy and manipulates the environment, often locating plants to stimulate the growth of a crop.[15]

Hymer is rather more successful in placing the stages of growth into a spatial context. Adapting his ideas to the terminology used here, at Stage I all decision making is undertaken by the owner-entrepreneur. At Stage II, the day-to-day programmed decisions become separated from the higher-level decisions while at Stage III the major non-programmed decisions are concentrated in a group head-office.[16] The increasing separation of the two types of decision making as the enterprise evolves results in the location of some of the decision-making units, particularly those concerned with non-programmed decisions, at separate sites. This, of course, relates back to the aggregate data on the location of head-office functions examined in Chapter 2.

Despite these links between aspatial models of growth and consideration of spatial evolution, the two elements do not fit easily together. As Hayter rightly observes, 'the range of factors influencing the spatial morphology of corporate systems, and the wide variations in the extent to which equally large firms are geographically diffuse prevents ready association between "stages" of growth and the spatial scope of corporate operations'.[17] Models of spatial evolution have thus developed in an autonomous manner.

Models of Spatial Evolution

Two attempts have been made to build up a general model of the spatial evolution of an enterprise. Taylor concentrates upon the spatial growth aspects of evolution, while McNee does pay at least some attention to the adjustments that take place as the enterprise evolves; like Taylor, however, his principal interest is spatial growth. Currently, Håkanson is developing a more sophisticated theory of the spatial evolution of large industrial enterprises.[18] A summary of the essential characteristics of Taylor's and McNee's models is presented below with attention focused on McNee's as, despite its deficiencies, it has attracted more interest.

An Idealised Sequence of Corporate Expansion[19]

The spatial growth of an enterprise as envisaged by Taylor is shown in Figure 6.1. The diagram depicts a four-region nation; three regions contain urban industrial agglomerations (A), and three contain secondary urban centres (B). The enterprise begins (P_1) in the agglomeration in Region 2, where perhaps the initial choice of centre is influenced by the entrepreneur's home town. After a successful period the enterprise selects the branch plant method of expansion and opens a second plant (P_2) in the same

Figure 6.1: Taylor's 'Idealised Sequence of Corporate Expansion'

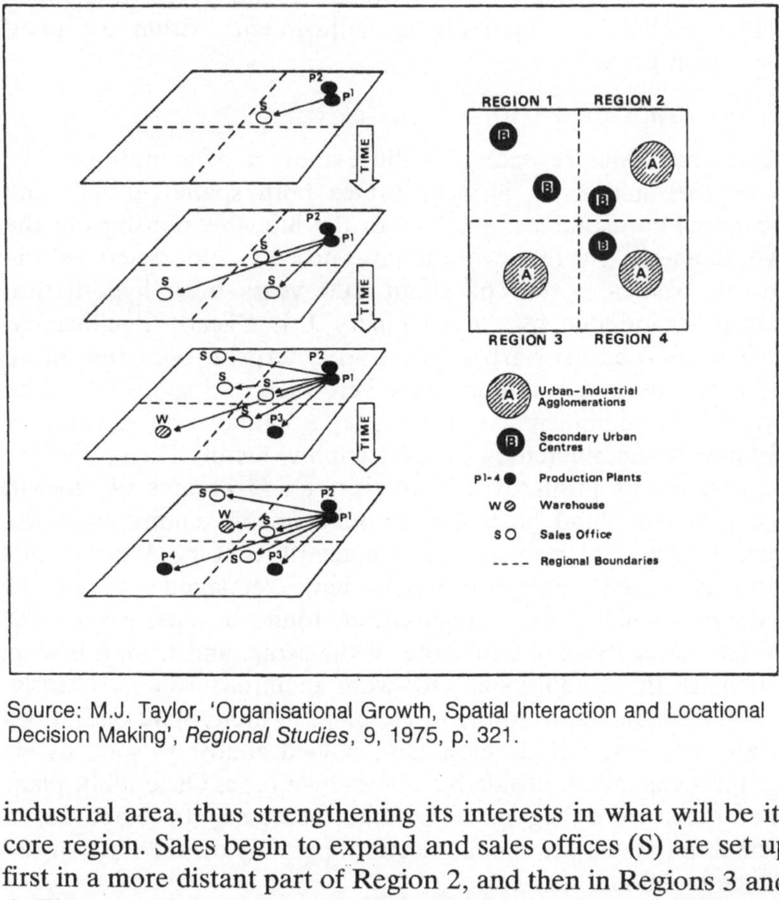

Source: M.J. Taylor, 'Organisational Growth, Spatial Interaction and Locational Decision Making', *Regional Studies*, 9, 1975, p. 321.

industrial area, thus strengthening its interests in what will be its core region. Sales begin to expand and sales offices (S) are set up first in a more distant part of Region 2, and then in Regions 3 and 4. This growth is then confirmed, this time by the acquisition of the plant (P_3) of a competitor in Region 4. At the same time a depot or warehouse is added to the sales office in Region 3. With growth continuing, a branch plant (P_4) is set up in Region 3, and depot operations are begun in Region 1. The model follows through Taylor's idea that changes in the plant space reflect earlier changes in the market area of the firm, and the firm's plant to market linkages.

Taylor sees the move from one phase to another as crossing a threshold to development, and recognises that for many firms growth will stop at any one stage. He does not explicitly include any of the organisational variables discussed earlier within the sequence. Implicitly he seems to be dealing with a single-product firm, and so perhaps models Stages I and II of Chandler's sequence. Further, there are no adjustments within the plant space as it grows.

International Gismo[20]

In contrast, McNee examines the evolution of a multi-product enterprise, and since it incorporates both spatial growth and locational adjustment it emphasises the inter-relationships of the two elements in the evolutionary process. He describes the growth over a period of about 100 years of a hypothetical enterprise founded by the imaginary J. J. Gismo. Significantly, McNee used as his starting point an enterprise operating in an industry where distribution costs were high and space would be particularly significant; indeed, for a bakery the friction of distance is accentuated by the perishability factor. The motive for expansion was primarily the entrepreneur's dreams of 'growth and grandeur', and he began to build up his empire from the small bakery set up in the late nineteenth century. Without this motivation the enterprise would have remained one of the numerous small baking organisations found in most towns. The initial strategy was one of more of the same, and from a base in Cincinatti three additional sites were acquired in Ohio. Clearly, J. J. Gismo moved from the single-plant to multi-plant operations at an early stage of development, indeed almost as soon as his interests expanded outside his home-town base. Once multi-plant operations were begun, it became necessary to elaborate a formalised system of communication, possibly on the lines of the classic functional structure.

From the initial baking enterprise growth continued, nót only by expansion of baking operations, but also through a conscious policy of backward integration into raw material supplies (grain milling) and equipment supplies (bread-slicing machinery). The method of growth was primarily by acquisition. Milling operations were begun when a small grain-handling firm in Chicago was taken over, and expansion into machinery dated from the acquisition of a Pittsburgh firm producing bread-slicing machines. These changes influenced the area within which the enterprise operated, and its plant space was widened considerably. The enterprise spread eastwards, through its metal interest, to Pittsburgh, Buffalo and the Upper Ohio Valley towns; north-westwards to Indiana, Illinois and Wisconsin through grain-producing interests, and in 'nearly all directions' by what was now a regional system of bakeries. At this stage, it becomes meaningful to talk of a core region from Pittsburgh to Decatur (Illinois) and from Cincinatti to Toledo. In this core region activities were held together through a tightly knit complex of flows of information and materials.

The enterprise is still run by the founder but the devolution of power through a new administrative structure has begun. The enterprise changes to a multi-divisional structure based on products; McNee sees these as a Central Division (baking), a Grain Products Division and a Metal Products Division. These new divisions recognise that the enterprise is moving steadily away from its original single-product character. It seems that by now the 1920s or 1930s have been reached.

This first stage ends with the death of the founder. McNee sees this point as the one at which control of the enterprise can pass from family to managers as the share capital is dispersed to a variety of different financial institutions. From this stage on managerial rather than family interests affect the spatial evolution of the enterprise. The change in control, and a merger with a New York metal firm (called by McNee the Gadget Corporation) inevitably alters the vital features of the enterprise.

At this stage, the enterprise faces major problems of locational adjustment in order to integrate the activities of Gismo and Gadget into Gismo-Gadget. Rationalisation schemes are implemented. The structure is adjusted to fit the needs of the new enterprise. Plants are closed or expanded, new sites are developed and linkages between supplier and plants, plants and plants and plants and markets are modified. There are changes too in the degree of functional separation within the enterprise as the head-office is moved from Cincinatti to New York. The core region of the enterprise now encompasses the whole of the US Manufacturing Belt, with the plant space including the greater part of the United States. There are a few minor overseas operations but the full expansion in this area is yet to come.

The final phase takes Gismo – as International Gismo – into major international markets. Power is delegated increasingly to divisions, while the head-office function becomes one of broad strategic planning. The enterprise has been consolidated into a system which works and works well. Once this stage is reached the total enterprise has a secure future; even if financial disaster threatens to overwhelm it, its social significance is such that either its associated enterprises or the government will attempt to save its operations, if not the form of the institution itself.

This account summarises the evolution of International Gismo from J. J. Gismo via Gismo-Gadget, but it appears that the Gismo model is rather unsatisfactory and three criticisms may be made, not the least being the very weak development of the spatial component. Space appears to be an afterthought rather than a critical part of the sequence. Significantly perhaps no map or diagram of spatial change is presented. This may reflect the decision to choose what became a metal products enterprise, for plants in this industry tend to have a wide locational tolerance and thus space might be of limited significance. A closer concern with the food sector in which the enterprise originated might have prevented this, but it would have restricted the generality of the model.

Second, the sequence seems to have been developed in isolation from the non-spatial models of the growth of an enterprise, especially the metamorphosis models outlined earlier. It is difficult to relate McNee's model to motives, strategies and methods of growth, and to Chandler's four stages.

Third, in both Taylor's and McNee's approaches there seems to be an implicit assumption that outward growth will be very similar to the pattern postulated in models of spatial diffusion. It does not seem unreasonable to challenge this assumption and suggest spatial growth may show a pattern more similar to that produced by the hierarchical diffusion process, that is expansion not from core region to adjacent region but from core region to the largest city in the national city system. If a parallel is drawn with Watts's study of market areas, the enterprise may follow first a spatial growth pattern and then a hierarchical one.[21]

To be fair, neither McNee nor Taylor would claim to have presented final or sophisticated models of the evolution of an enterprise in space, and both would admit their models have been derived inductively from studies of individual enterprises. Perhaps if further models are to be developed it is necessary to proceed deductively and to test a more carefully structured model against the empirical evidence.

A Model of Spatial Evolution

This new model develops from the ideas presented in Chapters 4 and 5. It takes up the theme of spatial growth and locational adjustment and tries to include the interaction process. It is, however, concerned primarily with single-product enterprises, and is particularly relevant to enterprises with relatively high distribution costs where their products are distributed in small lots to a multiplicity of purchasers and where advantages accrue to an enterprise by increasing the size of its production units. Thus, it is particularly relevant to enterprises operating in industries such as baking, soft drinks, concrete products, cement, bricks, and services such as laundries. Indeed, it was developed in the preliminary stages of the study of the brewing enterprises discussed in the case analyses. It is also relevant to the evolution of enterprises processing agricultural products (for example, Watties) and forest products (for example, Weyerhauser and MacMillan Bloedel). It is stressed that it is *not* seen as a general model applicable to all industries, although some of the tendencies it identifies should be found, in less marked form, in industries where distribution costs are less important. In these industries, information and uncertainty about distant areas, rather than distribution cost, may restrict the expansion of an enterprise's plant space and influence its locational adjustment patterns.

Since this model is focused upon industries with high distribution costs, its plant space will be related closely to its market area. The discussion is thus framed in terms of market area extension (broadly, growth of an enterprise's plant space) and adjustment of production facilities after growth. The emphasis is placed on spatial growth which is explored through the presentation of an 'ideal-typical' development sequence. The ideal-typical sequence has been an important way of dealing with time-space problems in economic geography.[22] As a method, it is now less common but the restricted knowledge of large enterprise behaviour makes it still appropriate in this context. The method allows consideration of the inter-relationship among variables that may have important effects upon the spatial pattern under investigation. Further, and more importantly, it may clarify hypotheses for testing at a later stage in the investigation.

There is little precedent for this approach in industrial

geography. Admittedly Hamilton illustrates the emergence of a modern industrial location pattern, but this drew heavily on the ideas contained in a paper by Taaffe, Morrill and Gould.[23] An independent line was taken in Wilson's outline of the evolution of mining industry,[24] a model more elaborately developed in Hay.[25] The closest parallel to this work is the sequence proposed by Taylor which was described earlier in this chapter.[26] The major difference between Taylor's work and that described below is that here an attempt is made to set the large enterprise both in its industrial context and in the context of other large enterprises in the same industry. Taylor, too, included other functions besides manufacturing, whereas attention in this instance focuses on the manufacturing plants.

The model is presented in two parts. The first illustrates a relatively straightforward development sequence; the second attempts to include some potential interaction effects resulting from inter-enterprise relationships. An earlier version of the first part of the model has been discussed elsewhere.[27]

A Development Sequence

To simplify the model it is assumed that concern is with single-product firms, that growth takes place by acquisition, that demand is constant throughout the period reviewed, that each enterprise and plant is a spatial monopolist and that interest is in only one large industrial enterprise. The last two assumptions are later dropped.

The development sequence is summarised in Figure 6.2, which takes as its starting point an adaptation of the economic landscape proposed by Lösch.[28] The logic of such a landscape has been explored in detail by Beavon,[29] but any idealised landscape would form an adequate beginning for the exercise. This economic landscape is used to provide a 'differentiated and bounded space economy'[30] within which enterprise behaviour can be examined.

Twenty-five towns of various sizes are located in the area under consideration (Figure 6.2A) and one, marked (M), is a major metropolitan centre. One function (industry X) is common to all the towns, and this industry's products are extremely sensitive to the friction of distance and are distributed over very limited market areas. This friction may represent either consumer resistance to payment of a delivery charge, or a firm's concern to

Figure 6.2: A Model of Market Area Change and Spatial Rationalisation. A: Mergers; B: Market Areas and Plant Locations

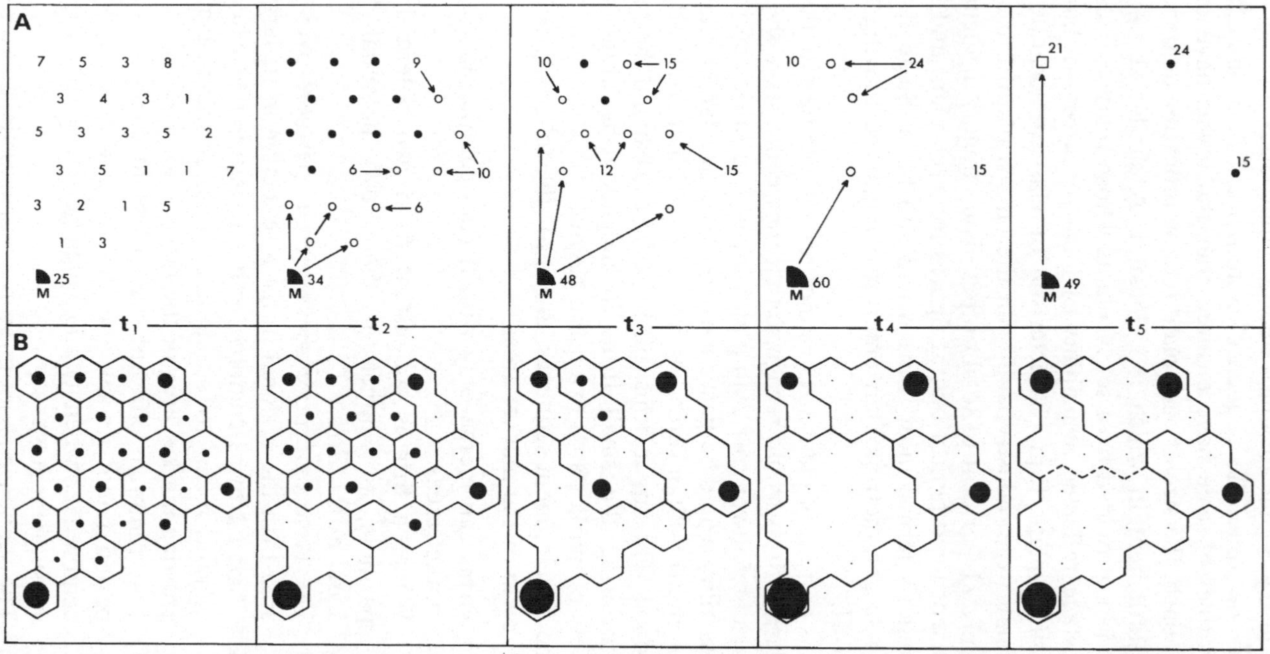

Source: modified from H.D. Watts, 'Market Areas and Spatial Rationalization: the British Brewing Industry After 1945', *Tijdschrift voor Economische en Sociale Geografie*, 68, 1977, p. 226.

minimise its distribution costs. It is the market areas of the plants in industry X that are illustrated in Figure 6.2B.

At the time the sequence commences, it is assumed that economies-of-scale have ensured that the towns have only one plant each, the size of each plant mainly reflecting demand within the settlement in which it is located. A similar starting point would be provided by a set of plants whose relative sizes at this first stage reflected availability of local resources. In both cases the single-plant firm characteristic of classical location theory dominates the industry, and even the largest plant/firm accounts for only 21 per cent of total output. The integers in Figure 6.2A represent hypothetical output figures for each plant and firm. In Chandler's terms, most firms would still be in Stage I, but the much larger metropolitan enterprise might be moving towards Stage II.

This pattern of plant sizes cannot reflect a static situation, since the larger firms would recognise that they could serve the smaller centres at a lower cost than plants located in those centres. Such a possibility would be particularly obvious to a larger plant based in a metropolitan area or an area with particularly good resources. The larger firms (plants) begin to expand their markets by acquiring the small firms in neighbouring areas and the process of market area extension begins.

The development sequence allows for the following features in the growth of the market areas:

(1) Firms can merge only with firms operating in contiguous market areas.
(2) Where a firm is equidistant from two potential merger partners, the larger of these two potential partners acquires the firm.
(3) The large enterprise seeks merger partners over a wider area than the regional firms, a reflection of its larger size.
(4) Regional firms combine with one another to extend their market areas to strengthen their position against the growing market area of the large enterprise.
(5) The minimum efficient scale of plant changes during the period under review and thus only very small firms are acquired between t_1 and t_2; larger firms are acquired in subsequent stages.
(6) The sequence is not entirely deterministic, and a stochastic element is introduced when a firm has a choice of merger

partners but each potential partner has the same economic characteristics. In these cases the partner is selected randomly.

These six rules guide the pattern of market area extension and the spatial growth of the enterprise; the pattern of adjustment within the extended market area is guided by a further two.

(1) A larger plant takes on the production of a smaller plant or plants following the merger. In the sequence, expansion of the acquiring plant and closure of the acquired plant is immediate, but in practice it might be expected that in the large enterprise the acquired firms will be absorbed at first, within a holding company structure, and then this will be modified to a multi-divisional one. Once this change is made, rationalisation of the plant may follow. Rationalisation may be delayed until the structural change is complete. In Chandler's terms the enterprise may rapidly reach Stage III with an unco-ordinated and diversified (geographically) market area, and rationalisation will await the arrival of new structures in Stage IV.

(2) Closure does not occur if the merger partners are a sufficient distance apart as the saving from expanding the acquiring plant to meet the new demand will not offset the increased distribution costs to the new market. In these cases, both plants are retained. Once these more distant merger partners are sought, the plant economies-of-scale argument for growth applies no more, but growth continues to be stimulated by some of the motives discussed in the first part of Chapter 4.

The effect of these changes on an industry during the spatial evolution of a large industrial enterprise is illustrated in Figure 6.2, which shows one *probable* outcome if the above rules are adopted. No interval scale is put on the time sequence, where t_1 represents market areas, plant distribution and plant size at the beginning of the sequence. By t_2 the first round of mergers and closures is complete. It might be objected that the distribution of plants at t_2 leaves plants non-centrally located within their market areas, but the fixed capital invested on site will eliminate any tendency to set up new plants. Stages t_3 and t_4 present a simple development of the t_1/t_2 change. The large enterprise acquires more distant producers, and major regional centres of the industry develop in the more remote parts of the area. At t_4 the area has been divided into four market areas, and the large enterprise controls 51 per cent of the market, compared with the 20 per cent of the largest rival.

An element new to the system emerges at t_5; the smallest surviving regional firm is purchased by the large enterprise, but the plant is not closed. The reasons for this were outlined above. The enterprise expands its new unit's capacity, and to reduce its distribution costs, allocates some of the area supplied by the metropolitan plant to the expanded plant. The boundary between the markets of the two plants of the multi-plant firm is indicated by the pecked line. This must, of course, be a slow adjustment or capacity in the larger of the two plants would be under-utilised. Instead a long term policy to focus investment on the acquired plant would lead to the situation envisaged by the model. At the end of the sequence almost 60 per cent of capacity is controlled by one enterprise.

This sequence presents a 'model' of changes in market areas, and the associated changes in the pattern of production units. Of course, the rules could produce outcomes which differ from those in the figure, but it is reasonably certain that most outcomes would, in their overall characteristics, reflect the patterns shown. The limitations of the model follow from some of its assumptions: it deals with only one large enterprise; it considers only spatial monopolists; it holds demand constant, and growth is only by acquisition. Further, it is relevant only to those industries where distribution costs impose restrictions on the extent of market areas, where there are distinct economies-of-scale in the production process and where these two costs form the dominant elements in the location problem. Nevertheless it is a model attractive both in its formal characteristics and in its inherent simplicity; more importantly it suggests several important hypotheses relating to enterprises, market areas and plants. The predictions which arise from the sequence, of course, come from the underlying rules upon which the model is based, and do not derive from the working of the model itself. Nevertheless, the model does allow the derivation of the spatial pattern of an industry during the spatial evolution of a large industrial enterprise.

Examination of the model shows the following features relating to enterprises and market areas.

(1) The number of firms operating in the industry is reduced.
(2) The large enterprise increases in importance at the expense of the small firms.
(3) Mergers take place over longer distances as time progresses.
(4) Multi-plant enterprises characterise the later stages of development.

Concerning the plants, ideas arise which can form the basis of hypotheses:

(1) The number of plants operating in the industry is reduced.
(2) The mean size of plant increases, and the plant size frequency distribution shows a positive shift.
(3) Plants within large settlements (or based on larger resources) are more likely to survive than smaller plants.
(4) Plants remote from the metropolitan centre (or principal resource area) are more likely to survive than those close to it.
(5) Regional firms will show a higher propensity to close acquired plants than does the large enterprise.

These expected outcomes tell something of the possible results of spatial growth and of the subsequent locational adjustment.

Incorporating the Interaction Process

This basic model has illustrated features which might be involved in the growth of a large industrial enterprise selecting the single-product external growth path. This growth has, however, been solely that of a single large enterprise; yet in earlier chapters interaction between enterprises has been stressed. The remainder of this chapter explores some possible spatial patterns that might evolve through inter-enterprise relationships. To handle this interaction it is useful to drop from the sequence the reactions of the regional enterprises and to focus on the behaviour of the large industrial enterprises in isolation. Some of these possible behaviour patterns are explored in the relationships between two initially equal-sized enterprises based in a metropolitan area or upon natural resources.

Figure 6.3 shows three possible outcomes of the interaction process, the general features of each outcome being a function of the strategies of the different enterprises. The strategies considered are those outlined in Chapter 5, that is co-operative, competitive and passive.

Figure 6.3: Potential Outcomes of the Interaction Process: Spatial Monopolists

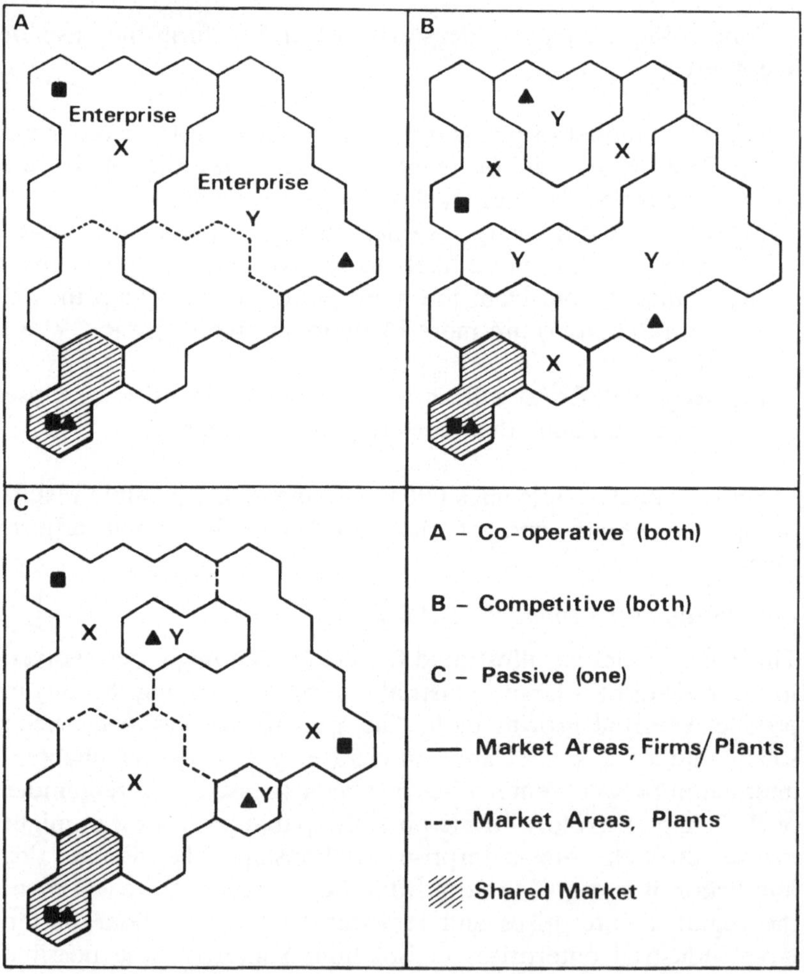

Source: based on H.D. Watts, 'Inter-Organisational Relations and the Location of Industry', *Regional Studies*, 12, 1978, p.219.

The co-operative strategy will produce some kind of agreement over market shares, which may or may not be translated directly into space. Markets could, of course, be divided by types of product, or by specified shares in each area, but Figure 6.3A assumes a simple allocation of territory between the two enterprises, each having a monopoly in its own area; obviously other divisions of the space could be made, but clear territories help to reduce distribution costs, and the number of plants in the overall system is minimised. Evidence of such agreements is difficult to trace, but one such division of the markets in the UK sugar industry has been recorded.[31]

The competitive strategy produces more complex patterns. It can result in the inter-digitation of the market areas of the different firms (Figure 6.3B), though some contiguity constraint is still likely to ensure that a remarkably broken market does not exist. Once control of a certain market is obtained building upon the newly acquired base can be attempted. The pattern of the plants fits less well into a pattern which tends towards minimising production and distribution costs; instead plants might tend to remain in each market area (thus enterprise Y has three), and on average the plants are slightly smaller than those which would obtain under a co-operative strategy. The net result is that more plants survive, partly because of the fragmented market areas of the competing firms.

A passive policy by one enterprise can lead to the situation depicted in Figure 6.3C. The distribution pattern of the very largest plants is similar to that of the co-operative strategy, except that the two large provincial plants are controlled by the one enterprise. But superimposed upon this pattern are small plants operated by the second enterprise; plants like this may have been acquired through initiatives from the smaller firms themselves. When opportunity offers, plants are acquired, but no active growth policy is pursued. In sum, the total pattern comprises a series of major plants associated with a dominant enterprise, and a few small plants under the passive enterprise's control.

In these cases the differing forms of the interaction process obviously have spatial outcomes which vary both in plant sizes and plant locations. These are, admittedly, only some hypothetical outcomes of the interaction process in particular situations.

A development of the competitive situation is shown in Figure

6.4. Here the assumption of a spatial monopoly in each market area has been removed and most settlements have some two plants, with each a potential partner for one of the metropolitan-based enterprises. Since each enterprise will acquire plants of different sizes, sometimes in the same town, the end product of each enterprise's behaviour will differ. The overall selection of merger partners may well mirror a stochastic process.

Figure 6.4: Potential Outcomes of the Interaction Process: Spatial Duopolists

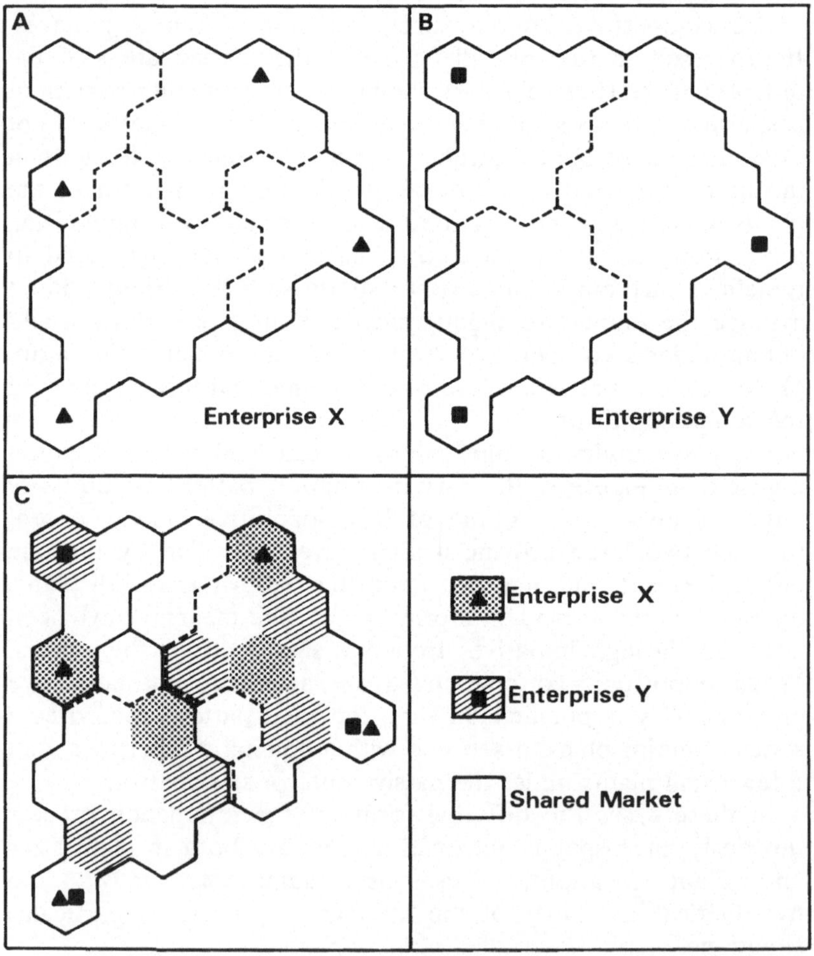

With such a high degree of chance, the one certain feature that can be reported is that the pattern of market areas and plants of the two enterprises will differ. One such possible comparison is provided by Figure 6.4. Figure 6.4C demonstrates that the degree of control by each enterprise will vary throughout the market area. Certain parts of the area are monopolised by one enterprise either because these parts were supplied by one plant or because the enterprise has acquired all the plants formerly operating in that area. In other parts the market is shared between them. The plants tend to be located either in an area where the enterprise has a monopoly, or where the market is shared jointly with the other enterprise. With different plant locations and market shares the allocation of areas to plants is inevitably rather different from enterprise to enterprise.

In this kind of situation it is possible also to explore the leader and satellite roles discussed earlier. The leader will, *ceteris paribus*, have first choice of merger partners among the smaller firms, and might therefore select those firms which fit best into its spatial framework. The satellite enterprise may be able to acquire only what the leader does not want, or rejects as unsuitable. The leader might develop a rather more ordered pattern of plants than that produced by the satellite.

The further development of these models might have been appropriate for a simulation exercise. This was not attempted, partly because of data difficulties and partly because of the validation problems.[32] Nevertheless the adoption of an ideal-typical sequence has a valuable pay-off in that some of the fundamental elements in the spatial evolution of a certain group of large industrial enterprises are clarified.

Conclusion

This chapter has tried to bring together some of the ideas relating to the evolution of an enterprise. Initially, attention was focused on the aspatial metamorphosis growth models and the difficulties of applying them in a spatial setting were described. A critical outline of the existing models of the spatial evolution of an enterprise preceded the presentation of a more elaborate model of spatial evolution in enterprises operating in industries with high distribution costs and marked economies-of-scale. This not only put the large industrial enterprise into its total industry setting, but also examined the behaviour patterns of rival enterprises.

None of these models of spatial evolution has, as yet, been tested against reality. It is not suggested that the evidence from an appropriate industry will fit exactly the predictions of the model proposed here, for each industry will have its own distinctive balance between processing costs (economies-of-scale) and distribution costs. Nevertheless, the general tendencies should be apparent in data collected from a number of large industrial enterprises operating within an industry where balance between production and distribution costs is a major concern. This is one of the themes picked out in the cases that follow.

Notes

1. G.P.F. Steed, 'Locational Implications of Corporate Organisation of Industry', *Canadian Geographer*, 15, 1971, p. 55.
2. R. Hayter, 'Corporate Strategies and Industrial Change in the Canadian Forest Products Industries', *Geographical Review*, 66, 1976, pp. 210-12.
3. R.B. Le Heron and E.C.R. Warr, 'Corporate Organisation, Corporate Strategy, and Agribusiness Development in New Zealand', *New Zealand Geographer*, 32, 1976, p. 3.
4. W.H. Starbuck, 'Organisational Growth and Development' in W.H. Starbuck (ed.), *Organisational Growth and Development*, 1971, Harmondsworth, pp. 11-142.
5. P. Dicken, 'Some Aspects of Decision-Making in Organisations', *Economic Geography*, 47, pp. 432-3.
6. W.F. Whyte, *Men at Work*, 1961, Homewood, pp. 82-8.
7. J.T. Cannon, *Business Strategy and Policy*, 1968, New York, pp. 524-8.
8. B.R. Scott, *Stages of Corporate Development, Part I*, Harvard Business School, mimeographed, 4-371-294, BP 998, 1971, p. 7.
9. Cannon, *Business Strategy*, pp. 524-8.
10. Scott, *Corporate Development*, p. 7.
11. A.D. Chandler, *Strategy and Structure*, 1962, Cambridge, Mass.
12. R.S. Edwards and H. Townsend, *Business Enterprise: Its Growth and Organisation*, 1967, London, p. 34.
13. D.G. Moore, 'Managerial Strategies', in W.L. Warner and N.H. Martin, *Industrial Man*, 1959, New York, pp. 221-2.
14. M.J. Taylor, 'Organisational Growth, Spatial Interaction and Locational Decision Making', *Regional Studies*, 9, 1975, pp. 314-17.
15. Le Heron and Warr, 'Corporate Organisation', pp. 13-15.
16. S. Hymer, 'The Multi-National Corporation and the Law of Uneven Development', in J.N. Bhagwati (ed.), *Economics and World Order*, 1972, London, pp. 122-4.
17. Hayter, 'Corporate Strategies and Industrial Change', p. 211.
18. L. Håkanson, *Location and Growth of the Firm: Towards a Theory of Corporate Growth and Location Change*, Ekonomiska Forskningsinstitutet, 1977, Stockholm.
19. Taylor, 'Organisational Growth', pp. 321-2.
20. R.B. McNee, 'A Systems Approach to Understanding the Geographic Behaviour of Organisations, Especially Large Corporations', in F.E.I. Hamilton

(ed.), *Spatial Perspectives on Industrial Organisation and Decision-Making*, 1974, London, pp. 51-9.

21. H.D. Watts, 'The Market Area of a Firm', in L. Collins and D.F. Walker, *Locational Dynamics of Manufacturing Activity*, 1975, London, pp. 366-73.

22. E.J. Taaffe, R. Morrill and P. Gould, 'Transport Expansion in Under-Developed Countries', *Geographical Review*, 53, 1963, pp. 503-29; P.J. Rimmer, 'The Search for Spatial Regularities in the Development of Australian Seaports', *Geografiska Annaler*, 49B, 1967, pp. 42-54.

23. F.E.I. Hamilton, 'Models of Industrial Location', in R.J. Chorley and P. Haggett, *Socio-Economic Models in Geography*, 1968, London, p. 399; Taaffe, et al., 'Transport Expansion', pp. 503-29.

24. M.G.A. Wilson, 'Changing Patterns of Pit Locations on the New South Wales Coalfield', *Annals of the Association of American Geographers*, 58, 1968, pp. 78–90.

25. A. Hay, 'A Simple Location Theory for Mining Activity', *Geography*, 61, 1976, pp. 65-76.

26. Taylor, 'Organisational Growth', pp. 314-17.

27. H.D. Watts, 'Market Areas and Spatial Rationalization: the British Brewing Industry After 1945', *Tijdschrift voor Economische en Sociale Geografie*, 68, 1977, pp. 225-7.

28. A. Lösch, *The Economics of Location*, 1954, New Haven, p. 128.

29. K. Beavon, *Central Place Theory: a Re-interpretation*, 1977, London, especially pp. 80-102.

30. G.B. Norcliffe, 'A Theory of Manufacturing Places', in Collins and Walker, *Locational Dynamics*, p. 37.

31. H.D. Watts, 'Locational Adjustment in the British Beet Sugar Industry', *Geography*, 59, 1974, p. 16.

32. R.L. Schultz and E.M. Sullivan, 'Developments in Simulation in Social Science', in H. Guetzkow, et al., *Simulation in Social and Administrative Science*, Englewood Cliffs, 1972, p. 37.

Part Three

CASE ANALYSES: ENTERPRISES IN THE UK BREWING INDUSTRY

7 BREWING ENTERPRISES: SPATIAL STRUCTURES

This analysis of aggregate data and case studies of enterprises in the UK brewing industry attempts to bring together ideas presented in the earlier chapters. This chapter describes some of the practical difficulties of studying enterprise behaviour in the brewing industry, examines the spatial structure of the industry in 1976 and considers the aspatial changes that have taken place. Chapter 8 looks at the spatial growth of the large enterprises from 1951 to 1976, while Chapter 9 focuses upon adjustment by the enterprises of production capacity.

Enterprises in the UK Brewing Industry

In 1976, the seven largest brewing enterprises in the United Kingdom controlled 56 brewing plants, with total sales of 32.6 million barrels.[1] A barrel represents 164 litres. In total, the enterprises provided 87.4 per cent of all beer sales, and the ten-firm concentration ratio had risen from 40.8 per cent in 1957 to 87.2 per cent in 1969.[2]

Not surprisingly, such changes, together with the high level of concentration, have attracted considerable public attention. This is seen in the work of economists such as Cockerill,[3] Mark,[4] and Hawkins & Radcliffe,[5] in the reports of government agencies, like the National Board for Prices and Incomes,[6] the Monopolies Commission[7] and the Departmental Committee on Liquor Licensing,[8] and in the activities of a consumer association – the Campaign for Real Ale.[9] The following chapters adopt a spatial perspective in examining the development of large industrial enterprises in the brewing industry. More specifically, they explore the spatial behaviour of these large enterprises in the light of the hypotheses suggested by the model of the spatial evolution of an enterprise discussed in Chapter 6. No comprehensive geography of the brewing industry is attempted, and the focus upon the larger enterprise entails the omission of detailed discussion of smaller firms. Further, attention is focused upon an enterprise's sites rather than upon its linkages.

The last chapter argued that the proposed model was appropriate for enterprises operating within a particular group of industries, that is those with high distribution costs and marked economies-of-scale. In this analysis enterprises have been selected from only one industry. Although there is some loss of generality by looking at enterprises within a single sector, the influences of technological and organisational differences between industries are controlled.

There were several reasons for selecting the brewing industry. Its largest enterprises for most of the 1960s were among the UK's 100 largest manufacturing enterprises; they are *relatively* large, too, since the industry has a highly oligopolistic market structure, while both absolutely and relatively the major enterprises have grown rapidly over the last twenty-five years.

Additionally, the industry is a relatively self-contained manufacturing sector, with few interests outside brewing and the activities associated closely with it. It exports little, and has to meet only very limited competition from imports. Further, it recognises that one of its central problems is to produce a plant location scheme that minimises the sum of production and distribution costs. Nowadays material inputs are of little locational significance, although favourable water supplies may have encouraged local concentrations of activity in the past.

The introductory section of this chapter examines the major data sources, the constraints imposed by the characteristics of the industry and some methodological problems presented in analysing the data. Together they impose quite severe restrictions upon the way in which the spatial behaviour of large industrial enterprises can be approached, and they illustrate some of the general difficulties of studying that behaviour.

Sources

The brewing enterprises in the United Kingdom are very reluctant to reveal the detailed information required for this kind of study, one obvious omission in the following pages being data on plant capacity or employment. Other possible sources were the Brewers' Society (a trade association), which had no publicly available data set,[10] and the Customs and Excise authorities, whose data, even of an historical nature,[11] were confidential. Recourse had to be made to the less reliable sources discussed below.

(1) The *Brewers Almanack*[12] provided (until it ceased publication in 1971) an almost complete listing of brewing sites. It was published *during* the year to which it referred. The principal omissions were plants operated by the larger enterprises and there was sometimes considerable delay in removing closed plants from the list. Occasionally, office, rather than plant, locations were recorded. These deficiencies meant it had to be rejected as a source of plant closure data, but it provided a basic working list of plants. A modern listing of plants is found in the *Good Beer Guide.*[13]

(2) The *Brewery Manual*,[14] while not recording all breweries, included financial information on many firms and considerable detail on merger activity. This source was a useful compilation (unfortunately incomplete) of merger data.

(3) The *Stock Exchange Official Year Book*[15] provided details of subsidiary companies, capital employed, number of retail outlets owned and controlled, head-office locations and sometimes lists of plants. It covered only the more important firms.

(4) *Annual Reports*. The larger enterprises record their principal developments each year in a Chairman's Statement appended to their Annual Report. This provided cross-checks on the *Manual* and *Almanack* and often gave details of plant closures and expansions. Apart from the self-congratulatory nature of most statements, the main difficulty is that reports refer to financial years ending in different months. A reference to 'this year' usually refers to parts of two calendar years, and so the exact year of an event remains uncertain. As a general policy, all events are dated here by the year in which the financial year ended. Occasionally, maps of plants were published in these annual reports but they were liable to contain errors.

(5) The *Brewers Guardian* appeared to be the most useful trade journal for the 1950s and 1960s, although the *Brewing Review* covered similar ground. In addition to providing general background material the *Brewers Guardian* reported plant closures, expansions and mergers but not on any consistent basis.

(6) *Investor's Chronicle.* For many years this weekly periodical produced a *Drink* or *Brewing* supplement. A lengthy review of the year's events was accompanied by a wide range

of data on the industry (not always reliable) in tabular and cartographic form.

These six principal sources were supplemented from miscellaneous newspaper, trade and journal sources. Detailed histories have been written about three of the enterprises,[16] but these tend to concentrate on their early history. The only comprehensive published work on the industry is by Vaizey.[17]

The nature of the source materials should indicate that the data are open to error but, subjectively, it seems that this means that many expansion, closure or merger dates should be read as plus or minus one year. Other errors may have entered the data set. It has not always proved possible to trace detailed local changes, as the emphasis has been on trying to tease out the national pattern. The intrinsic interest of the product may mean that some readers are better informed about local changes than the writer. One particular source of error does deserve mention. Cessation of brewing at a particular site often meant that it was retained as a distribution depot or packaging plant and so could give the outsider the erroneous impression that the brewery was still operating. Consequently the number of plant closures may sometimes have been under-estimated.

These documentary sources were supplemented by one-hour interviews with those responsible for corporate strategy at the time the most important changes were taking place.[18] The interviews were used primarily to clarify points raised by the documentary sources, and to discuss the general patterns of change. Clearly, in dealing with very large organisations and with changes over a twenty-five-year period interviews with one or two decision makers could not indicate what was really happening within an organisation, and the fallibilities of human memory precluded detailed discussion of any but the most recent events.

Industry Characteristics

The output of the brewing industry is differentiated by various brand names but broadly *draught* and *packaged* beers can be distinguished.[19] Packaged beer is the beer sold in cans and bottles, while draught beer, dispensed from bulk containers, is subdivided into cask, keg and tank beer.[20] Table 7.1 shows the relative importance of these different types. The important distinction is between cask conditioned (living) beer and brewery

Table 7.1: Beer Sales by Type of Beer, 1951, 1962, 1976

	1951[a]	1962[b]	1976[c]
		Per Cent of Sales	
Draught			
Cask	46.0	60.0	14.0
Keg and Tank	—	4.0	63.0
Packaged	54.0	36.0	23.0

Notes:
a. J. Vaizey, *The Brewing Industry 1886–1951*, 1960, London, p. 68.
b. Estimates based on A. Cockerill, 'The Merger Movement in the Brewing Industry', *Journal of Industrial Affairs*, 4, 1976, p. 12.
c. Price Commission, *Beer Prices and Margins*, 1977, London, p. 2.

conditioned (sterile) beer. The type of container can be the same, but popular usage calls the former 'cask' beer and the latter 'keg' beer. Cask beers (the traditional British beers) have a limited life,[21] whereas the keg beers, which are filtered and usually pasteurised in the brewery, have, in the short run, little tendency to deteriorate, and allow the manufacturer a closer control over the quality of the product sold to the consumer. Not surprisingly keg beers command a higher price. In 1967 a barrel of keg from one plant cost £25.60, a barrel of cask beer £18.80.[22]

The relative importance of these different types of beer has changed markedly over the last 25 years. Table 7.1 shows an important decline in the relative importance of the packaged beers, but, more strikingly, within the draught beer category, cask beers show a major decline and now account for only 14 per cent of sales, compared with around 60 per cent in 1962. The significance of this change is explored later. Lager in these figures is treated either as a packaged beer (when sold in bottles and cans) or as a keg beer (when sold from bulk containers). The growth of lager consumption has accentuated the trend towards keg beers shown in the table.

Beer can be sold in the United Kingdom only through licensed outlets and registered clubs. Table 7.2 estimates the proportion of sales going to different types of outlet in 1951 and 1976. The brewing firms own or lease about three-quarters of the public houses, and this is the '*tied*' trade;[23] the remaining sales, to non-tied houses and clubs, is the '*free*' trade. A repercussion of the licensing system is that since new licences are limited in number an enterprise can increase its markets for beer either by acquiring

Table 7.2: Sales Outlets in the Brewing Industry, 1951 and 1976

	1951[a]	1976[b]
	Per Cent of Sales	
Off-sales (Specialist shops and grocers)	12	12
Public Houses	73	66
Tied	70	53
Free	3	13
Clubs	10	22
Other	5	

Notes:
a. J. Vaizey, *The Brewing Industry, 1886–1951*, 1960, London, p. 69.
b. Estimates based on data in Price Commission, *Beer Prices and Margins*, 1977, London, p. 4.

another firm, which will gain it access to more tied houses (external growth), or by extending its free trade to clubs and free houses (internal growth). The latter course is eased if the firm's beers are known already in an area through its tied houses. So whether interested primarily in the free or the tied trade, external growth by acquisition has been characteristic of most of the enterprises in the brewing industry.

One further important industry characteristic deserves mention. It is sometimes argued, particularly by those closely involved with the industry, that much of its behaviour can be explained by inter-personal relationships, family ties and long-established trading connections. Admittedly such links can be found underlying most of the acquisitions in the industry, but equally, numerous links of this type did not result in mergers. It is argued here that these links facilitated acquisition rather than caused it. Further, as Cook & Cohen observe in relation to the brewing industry, there 'have been so many [mergers] that . . . generalisations can be made which ignore the effects of outstanding personalities with peculiar individual characteristics'.[24]

In the following discussion it is important that the distinctions between draught and packaged beer, cask and keg beer and the free and tied trade are understood.

Methodological Problems

An attraction of the brewing industry is that, in general, tied outlets and growth by acquisition provide useful surrogates for the growth of market areas and plant space.

The market area of an enterprise is treated as being reflected in the distribution of its tied outlets. The reason for this is that for most firms details of the location or general area of its tied estate are available. For this study it means that enterprises with limited tied estates have to be excluded from most of the discussion, as do changes in an enterprise's free trade.

The specific interest in the tied estate has a corollary. Tied outlets do not give a reasonable indication of the market for packaged beers since many of them go to the free trade or through the tied outlets of other brewers. So, for most of the discussion, packaged beers are excluded; indeed the growth of the market area for packaged beers would form a study in itself. In the account that follows, the centre of interest is *the market area of draught beers – 'cask' and 'keg' – sold through tied outlets.* On average, 70 per cent of brewery sales were through tied houses in 1951,[25] but this had dropped to only 51 per cent for the largest enterprises by 1976.[26]

The discussion focuses upon the *beer production sites*. Within the market area it thus excludes maltings, packaging operations and distribution depots, unless they are included within a production complex. A brief discussion of distribution systems is given in Riley.[27] The breweries provide a reasonably homogeneous group of sites which may be compared between enterprises.

The growth patterns of these enterprises are so complex that to identify the *core enterprise*, the original firm from which the enterprise has grown, some rather arbitrary rule has to be adopted. The most obvious would be to follow the name of the present enterprise, but this causes difficulty with the double-barrelled (*sic*) names. Instead, merger patterns were traced back from the present large enterprises, treating the larger enterprise as the acquirer at each merger. Obviously various measures of size were possible, but capital employed was used, as this was available for all the critical cases. A major difficulty with this measure is that it includes a valuation of the tied estate, and whereas some firms re-valued that estate every year others did not. So capital employed is not a consistent measure of relative size. A further difficulty arising from the acquisition data was that, in a very few cases (under ten) plants were acquired without tied outlets, or vice versa. In each instance the firm was linked to the enterprise which acquired its outlets, although a case could be made for tracing the link through to the enterprise which acquired the plant.

It is fairly clear from this description of data sources, industry characteristics and methodological problems that, to no small extent, they dictated what was investigated. For example, data problems made it impossible to replicate Horowitz's work on the US brewing industry,[28] nor could the work develop along the lines of Lewis on the UK paper industry.[29] Nevertheless, the results seem to be sufficiently encouraging to vindicate this attempt to look at the spatial behaviour of large industrial enterprises in the UK brewing industry over the last twenty-five years.

Spatial Structure of Brewing Enterprises, 1976

Chapter 1 argued that there is an important distinction between enterprises operating in the industrial system, and firms operating in the market system. The brewing industry illustrates this dichotomy well, and there is little difficulty in drawing the line between the two groups. The smallest of the large enterprises had a turnover four times larger than that of the largest market system firm.

Figure 7.1 illustrates the plants operated by the market system firms (excluding post-1951 new entrants). This pattern is characteristic of a market system economy. Five firms operate 2 plants, one 3 and one 4, but the system is dominated by sixty-five small single-plant firms. Barriers to entry into this system are low, and there have been new entrants to it over the last five years (for example, Pollard's at Reddish), together with the deaths of some long-established brewing operations (for example, Gray's of Chelmsford). The spacing of the plants indicates limited competition among the firms in their tied trade, and the dispersed plant pattern is very similar to that predicted in Lösch's discussion of market areas and plant location.[30] These firms sell about 70 per cent of their output to tied outlets within a restricted geographical area.[31] The market system firms are, however, relatively unimportant, supplying only 12.6 per cent of beer sold in 1976,[32] the greater part of the market being supplied by the large enterprises of the industrial system.

Table 7.3 lists these seven large industrial enterprises. Two of them are subsidiaries of larger organisations; Courage is the

Figure 7.1: Market System Firms (excluding post-1951 new entrants) in the United Kingdom Brewing Industry, 1976

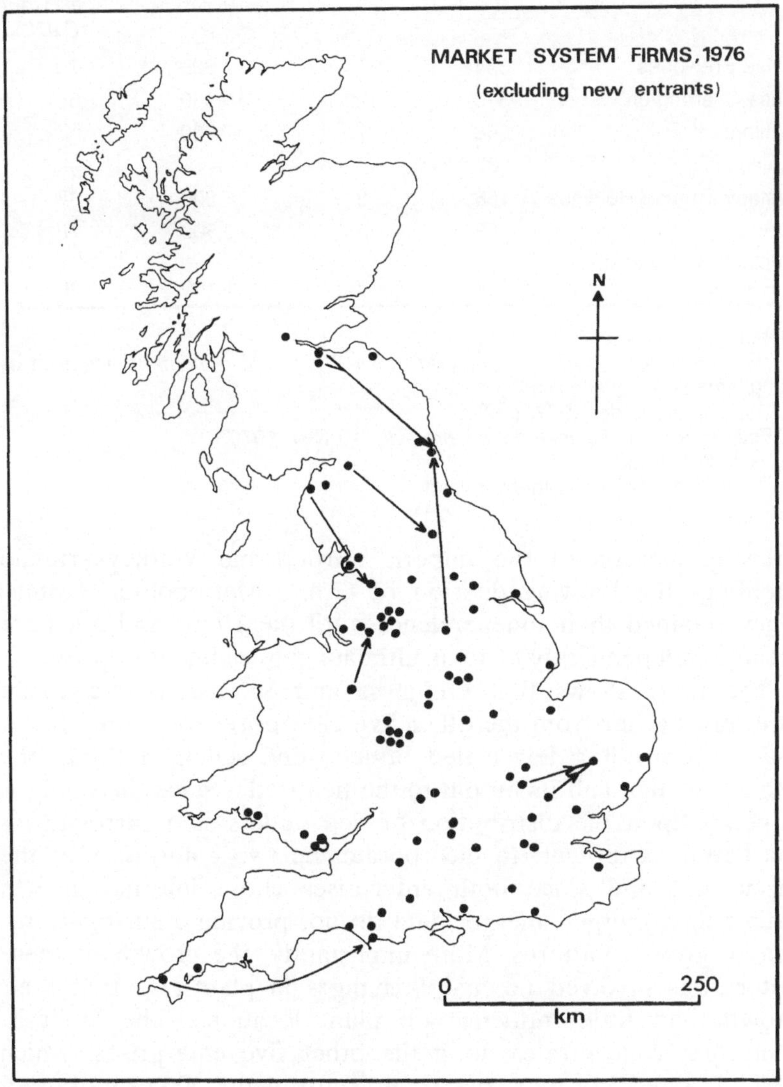

Source: Campaign for Real Ale, *The Good Beer Guide, 1977*, 1977, St Albans.

Table 7.3: The Seven Largest Enterprises in the Brewing Industry, 1970s

Enterprise	Turnover[a] (£ mill) (1971–2)	Breweries (1976)	Tied Outlets[b] (approximate, 1976)	Tied as Per Cent all Trade[c] (1970)
Allied Breweries	384	7	7,600	70
Bass-Charrington	343	12[e]	10,000	65
Whitbread	198	17	7,700	63
Guinness	182	1	—	—
Watney-Truman Holdings	158[d]	8	7,000	67
Courage	153	6	5,800	75
Scottish & Newcastle Breweries	134	3	1,100	36

Notes:
a. *The Times 1000*, 1971–2; last year before Watney and Courage acquired by conglomerates.
b. *Good Beer Guide*, 1977, p. 255.
c. Estimates for 1970, *Investor's Chronicle*, 13 Nov. 1970.
d. excludes Trumans.
e. includes a plant in Northern Ireland.

brewing division of the Imperial Group and Watney-Truman Holdings the brewing division of Grand Metropolitan Hotels. They retained their independence until the 1970s and are here treated independently of their ultimate controlling enterprise.

The table shows that Guinness and Scottish & Newcastle Breweries differ from the other five enterprises, operating fewer plants, controlling fewer tied outlets, one selling nothing, the other less than half its output to the tied trade. Since this analysis depends upon the distribution of tied outlets as a surrogate of markets it is difficult to incorporate the two enterprises in the discussion, and since both enterprises chose internal growth rather than merger, merger data do not provide a surrogate for spatial growth patterns. More importantly, the growth of these enterprises involved no major changes in plants, so that their growth had little influence on plant locations. The analysis, therefore, concentrates upon the other five enterprises, which each operated 5 or more plants and controlled 5,000 or more tied outlets in 1976.

In the five enterprises the number of tied outlets ranges from 5,800 to 10,000, but all send over 60 per cent of output to these outlets; in three of the five over two-thirds of the output is so tied. The figures indicate that the exclusion of the free trade from most of the discussion is not unduly restrictive. Nevertheless, as Table 7.2 showed, the proportion of sales to the tied trade has been falling.

An immediate contrast between these five enterprises and the smaller firms is that they are multi-plant enterprises, operating between 6 and 17 brewing sites each. Not surprisingly, they are also multi-regional, and all have plants in at least five of the British planning regions. This again contrasts with the predominantly regional market system firms. All five depict the characteristic functional specialisation of large industrial enterprises, with at least some head-office functions in the South East, although Bass-Charrington has recently transferred many head-office activities to one of its major production areas. Watney-Truman's head-office functions are located on a production site. The other three enterprises utilise former brewery sites, thus hinting at some reorganisation of functions. Only Bass-Charrington's chairman's office occupies a site not previously used by the industry.

Figure 7.2 illustrates the distribution of the 56 plants of the industrial system. One region (Yorkshire & Humberside) possesses the plants of all five enterprises, whereas the East Midlands and East Anglia have only one plant each. The overall pattern reflects the contrasting but complementary patterns of the large enterprises. Bass-Charrington and Allied dominate the West Midland area, Courage, Watney-Truman and Whitbread being poorly represented there.

The plants cannot be classified along any of the parameters discussed in Chapter 2, but an important distinction is between greenfield development and adaption of pre-existing sites. Whitbread controls major greenfield sites at Salmesbury and Luton, and has a third under construction at Magor (near Newport, South Wales); Bass-Charrington's major new complex is at Runcorn, while Courage is building a new plant at Reading. In contrast, Watney-Truman and Allied have focused upon the redevelopment of existing sites, which were well placed to serve national markets.

The remaining plants in Figure 7.2 are those of Guinness, Scottish & Newcastle and Harp Lager (a consortium of Guinness, Scottish & Newcastle Breweries and Courage). The one entirely

Figure 7.2: Industrial System Enterprises and Plants in the United Kingdom Brewing Industry, 1976

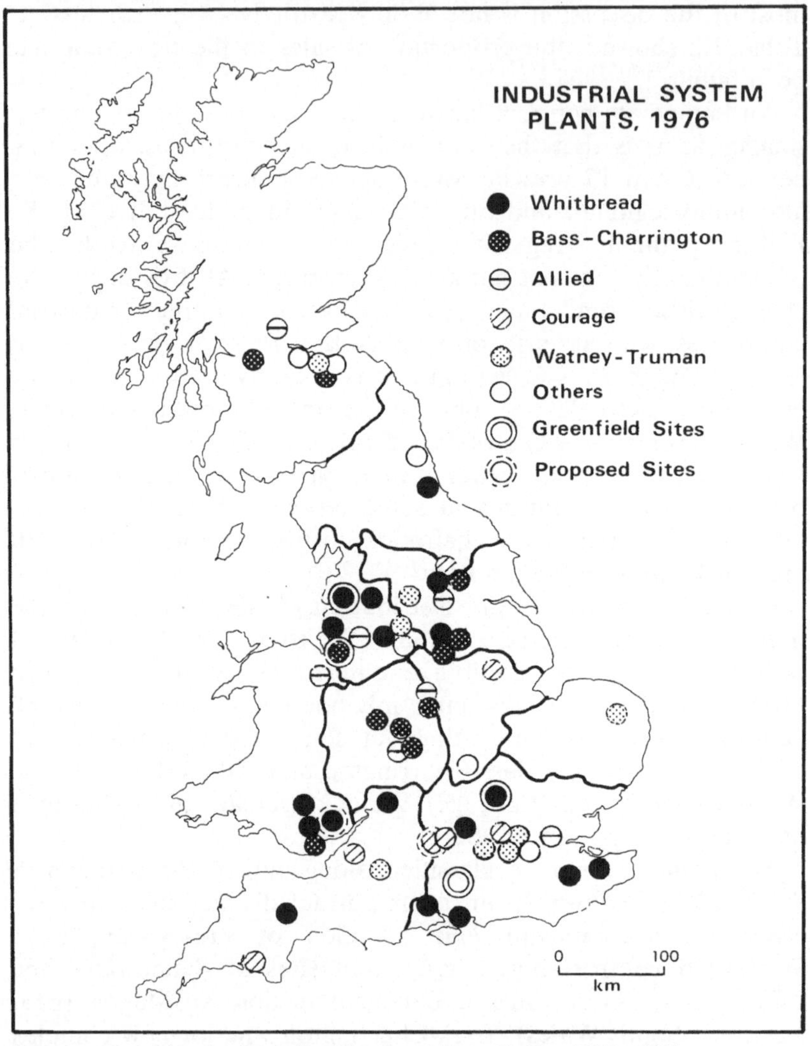

Source: Campaign for Real Ale, *The Good Beer Guide, 1977*, 1977, St Albans.

new operation is that of Carlsberg at Northampton. This is the only foreign brewing enterprise to establish its own production site in the United Kingdom since 1951. Its central single plant differs from the multi-plant operations of the big five, but its site was tied to that of a plant no longer required by Watney-Mann, who originally had a 49 per cent share in the Carlsberg operation.

The plants shown in the figure account for 87.4 per cent of UK beer output, and the pattern reflects primarily the spatial evolution of the five large enterprises, which control 49 of the sites. This spatial evolution was influenced by industry-wide changes, which are examined in the final part of this chapter.

Growth and Change, 1951 to 1976

1951 was chosen as the starting point for tracing the growth of the large industrial enterprises because the special circumstances of the immediate post-war period were less marked by then, and it was also the point at which Vaizey[33] concluded his history of the industry.

The growth strategy of virtually all firms after 1951 was to expand their beer sales, although some did diversify slightly into related products, such as wines, spirits and soft drinks. Few of them took any major steps outside their traditional sphere of operations, and so followed the single-product or, at most, related-product growth path. This focus upon brewing activities brought growth mainly by acquisition of other firms and their tied houses. Its importance is illustrated by Hannah & Kay, who suggest that in the rise of 46.4 percentage points in the ten-firm concentration ratio in the drinks industry between 1957 and 1969, only one of those points resulted from internal growth.[34] The very conservative and inbred nature of the industry dictated a strategy of more of the same, which in turn indicated acquisition as the principal method of growth because of the tied house system.

Table 7.4 summarises the components of change in the

Table 7.4: Number of Firms in the Brewing Industry, 1951 and 1976

	Frequency	Per Cent of Sample
Independent Firms, 1951[a]	329	
No Information after 1951	19	
Independent Firms in Sample	310	
Ceased Brewing without Acquisition	22	7.1
Acquired by others	209	67.4
Operating in 1976	79	25.5

Note:
a. Listed in *Brewers Almanack*, 1951. May exclude some small-scale brewing operations. Data adjusted to include subsidiaries with their parent firms.

industry as a whole. The number of independent firms fell by 80 per cent between 1951 and 1976, from 329 to 79. Twenty-two ceased brewing without being acquired, but a few of them retained their tied outlets, which they supplied by purchasing beer from other firms.[35] 209 acquisitions produced most of the change.

Figure 7.3, based on the 204 acquisitions for which data were available, illustrates the temporal pattern of this merger activity. A distinct peak in 1960 is separated from smaller peaks by troughs in 1958 and 1964. The principal impression is of considerable structural change in the industry. Department of Industry data show that the drinks industry (brewing plus soft drinks and spirits) saw a greater percentage decline in the number of firms between 1958 and 1968 than any other of the seventeen categories of manufacturing industry, and only the electrical engineering industry acquired assets of greater total value.[36]

How this merger activity contributed towards the growth of large industrial enterprises in the brewing industry is illustrated by data for two of those enterprises, summarised in Figure 7.4. In the dendograms each horizontal line represents an independent firm in 1951, the thicker line representing the core enterprise.

Figure 7.3: Mergers in the United Kingdom Brewing Industry, 1952–76

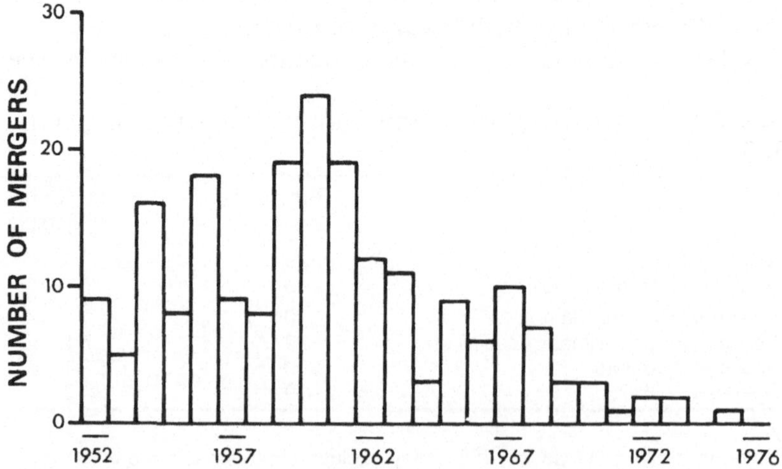

Source: various, but mainly *Brewery Manual*, 1951 to date.

Figure 7.4: Dendograms Illustrating Growth of Two Large Enterprises. A: Courage; B: Watney-Truman (Courage diagram excludes one firm)

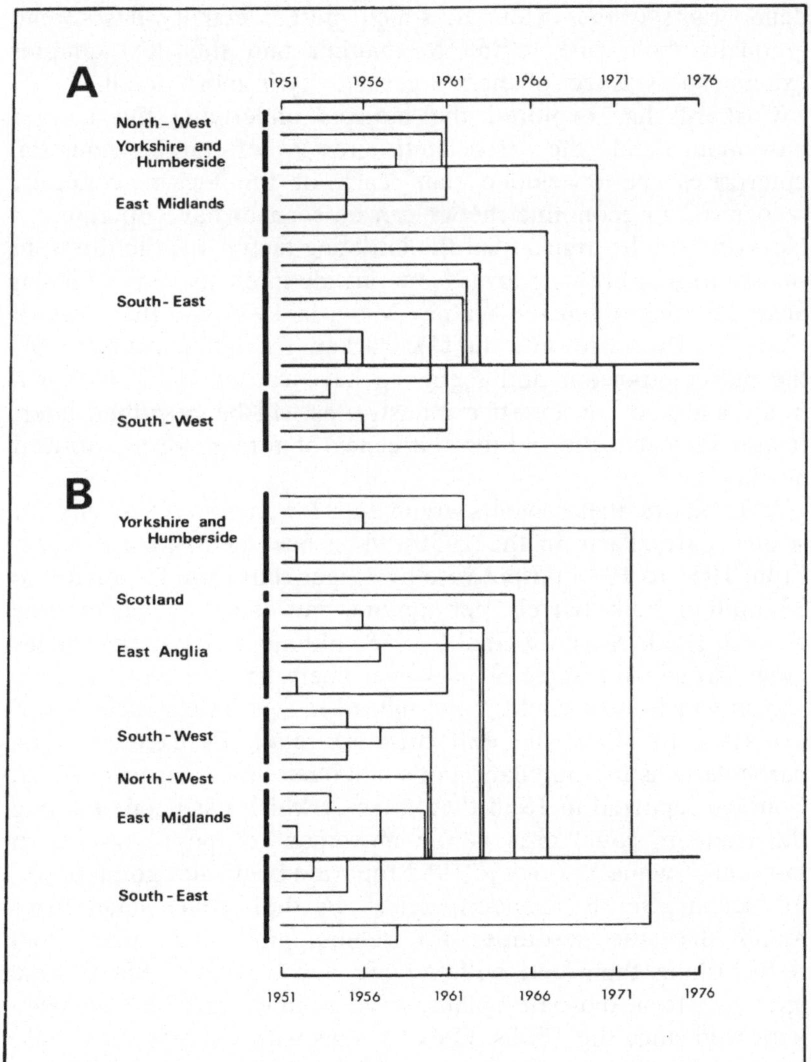

Source: mainly *Courage, Brewers Almanacks, Brewery Manuals*.

The vertical lines record merger activity within the acquired firms, as well as acquisitions made by the core enterprise. Similar diagrams could be constructed for the other enterprises in the industry, and most large enterprises have corporate 'family trees' of this type. The most distinctive feature of these two dendograms is the extent to which merger activity has spread gradually from one region to another and the next chapter examines this aspect of the merger activity in more detail.

Cockerill has explored the motives underlying the merger movement and the associated growth of large industrial enterprises; he concluded that 'each of the factors generally recognised in economic theory can be seen to have operated'.[37] Nevertheless, he argues that the initiating factor was the threat to the security of brewing firms from outside interests – in particular Sears Holdings's bid for Watney-Mann in 1959 and the entry of Canadian Breweries into the UK market. The latter was probably the more important and seems to have caused panic within a traditional and conservative industry, as will be described later. It also indicates the indirect influence of foreign firms, noticed in Chapter 3.

Yet, before these events arguments for merger were already strong, particularly in the 1950s when beer demand was static. From 1951 to 1976 output rose by 48 per cent from 25 million to 37 million bulk barrels per annum, but this rise began only around 1960. So until about 1958, although some enterprises grew through the sales of packaged beers, merger was the only way in which most could grow; indeed in several instances it was necessary to allow the enterprise to retain its existing sales, particularly as the population of some inner city areas was falling. Courage reported in 1955 that 'a factor which has been affecting the trade in [our] area is the movement of population from London',[38] while Watney in 1952 reported beer sales going down, 'particularly in the London area'.[39] Further, some small firms found that the resources for re-equipping their plant and re-furbishing their tied outlets were beyond them. Many were operating from out-dated plant, serving outlets that had not been improved since the 1930s. Only by links with a larger firm could plant and outlets be modernised. In this early period, too, production economies-of-scale may have been important, but they were of limited significance in the 1960s when, as will be seen, they could justify only major regional firms.

The emergence of the very large enterprises demands attention to firm (rather than plant) economies-of-scale. The enterprises claim that 'there was a growing demand for a draught beer [keg] that was nationally available' and this was followed by a 'remarkable growth in the consumption of lager'.[40] These new products required not only massive new capital investment but also nationally co-ordinated advertising activity, which only the resources of a large enterprise could meet. These arguments dodge a major issue – whether this demand was stimulated by the enterprises or whether, as they argue, they developed to meet it. Significantly, it is estimated that the five enterprises were spending £6 million per annum on advertising in 1971,[41] and the major growth in keg and lager sales came after rather than before the merger activity.

A purely personal and subjective view is that the principal motive for the growth of these enterprises in the late 1950s and the 1960s was the desire to obtain a national system of tied outlets for themselves and thus to stimulate the free trade demand for their products. Once the process of market area growth began, the enterprises interacted with one another until their competitive behaviour ensured that they controlled almost the whole market. Only by growth could the long-run survival of the enterprise be assured. Indeed, in the interviews with those responsible for corporate strategy, the need to secure outlets was always the first-mentioned motive for merger activity.

The growth of these enterprises from 1951 to 1976 can be associated with Chandler's Stages III and IV. Stages I and II saw the building of quite large concerns serving a fairly homogeneous market within a single region, often with families still managing the day-to-day operations of the firms. The 1960s saw the larger ones develop into Stage III enterprises, with multi-regional (more diversified) markets and with their behaviour influenced strongly by that of their competitors. By the late 1960s and early 1970s they were moving towards Stage IV with rationalisation of production, distribution and marketing (cf. pp. 141-2).

Conclusion

This chapter has set the scene for the study in the next two chapters of the large brewing enterprises. Clearly, the sources, the industry characteristics and the methodological problems present awkward but not insurmountable difficulties. The description of the spatial structures in 1976 indicates the kind of pattern towards which the industry moved throughout the twenty-five-year period examined. Finally, the temporal variation in merger activity illustrates the importance of acquisitions to the industry. Against this background the spatial evolution of the large industrial enterprises is explored in relation to the development sequence proposed in the last chapter.

Notes

1. Price Commission, *Beer Prices and Margins*, 1977, London, p. 8.
2. L. Hannah and J.A. Kay, *Concentration in Modern Industry*, 1977, p. 89. These figures relate to the drinks industry, which includes malting, wines, spirits and soft drinks in addition to brewing.
3. A. Cockerill, 'The Merger Movement in the Brewing Industry', *Journal of Industrial Affairs*, 1976, 4, pp. 8-17.
4. J. Mark, 'The British Brewing Industry', *Lloyds Bank Review*, 112, 1974, pp. 31-45.
5. K. Hawkins and R. Radcliffe, 'Competition in the Brewing Industry', *Journal of Industrial Economics*, 20, 1971-2, pp. 20-41.
6. National Board for Prices and Incomes, *Costs, Prices and Profits in the Brewing Industry*, 1966, London; National Board for Prices and Incomes, *Beer Prices*, 1969, London.
7. The Monopolies Commission, *Beer: a Report on the Supply of Beer*, 1969, London.
8. *Report for the Departmental Committee on Liquor Licensing* (The Erroll Report), 1972, London.
9. The Campaign for Real Ale (CAMRA), based at 34, Alma Road, St Albans, Herts.
10. Personal Communication to author from The Brewers' Society stating 'our Code of Security for statistical enquiries . . . forbids . . . the disclosure of individual figures'.
11. Personal Communication to author from Customs and Excise Authorities.
12. The Brewers Society, *Brewers Almanack*, annual to 1971.
13. Campaign for Real Ale, *The Good Beer Guide*, annual.
14. H. Darrington (compiler), *Brewery Manual*, annual.
15. *The Stock Exchange Official Year Book*, 2 volumes, annual.
16. H. Janes, *The Red Barrel: a History of Watney Mann*, 1963, London; J. Pudney, *A Draught of Contentment: the Story of the Courage Group*, 1971, London; K. Hawkins, *The Brewers' Tale: A History of the Bass-Charrington Group*. Privately published for limited circulation, 1978. I am indebted to the author and to Mr A. Elliott of Bass-Charrington for permission to consult the manuscript of this history prior to publication.
17. J. Vaizey, *The Brewing Industry, 1886–1951*, 1960, London. This work is summarised in P.L. Cook and R. Cohen, *Effects of Mergers*, 1958, London, pp. 397-422.
18. The individuals interviewed are acknowledged in the Preface to this volume.
19. Terms as used by the Price Commission, *Beer Prices and Margins*, p. 2.
20. This classification follows the Monopolies Commission, *Report on the Supply of Beer*, p. 8.
21. It has not been possible to quantify this distinction.
22. Ibid., Appendix 6.
23. Some off-licences are tied also to the brewers.

24. Cook and Cohen, *Effects of Mergers*, p. 15.
25. Vaizey, *The Brewing Industry*, p. 69.
26. Price Commission, *Beer Prices and Margins*, p. 8.
27. R.C. Riley, 'The Brewing Industry', in R.C. Riley, *Industrial Geography*, 1973, London, pp. 149-67.
28. For example, I. Horowitz and A. Horowitz, 'Structural Changes in the Brewing Industry', *Applied Economics*, 2, 1970, pp. 1-13.
29. P.W. Lewis, *A Numerical Approach to the Location of Industry*, 1969, Hull.
30. A. Lösch, *The Economics of Location*, 1954, New Haven, pp. 105-14.
31. Price Commission, *Beer Prices and Margins*, p. 8.
32. Ibid., p. 8.
33. Vaizey, *The Brewing Industry*.
34. Hannah and Kay, *Concentration in Modern Industry*, p. 89.
35. Examples are the Aylesbury Brewery Company, and Heavitree Brewery, Exeter.
36. Department of Trade and Industry, *A Survey of Mergers, 1958-68*, 1970, London, pp. 20-1.
37. Cockerill, 'The Merger Movement', p. 15.
38. Courage, *Report and Accounts*, 1955.
39. Watney, Combe & Reid, *Report and Accounts*, 1952.
40. From Cockerill, 'The Merger Movement', p. 12.
41. Anon, 'Brewing and the Beer Market, Part II', *Retail Business*, 175, 1972, p. 29.

8 BREWING ENTERPRISES: SPATIAL GROWTH

Chapter 7 discussed some basic problems facing a study of large industrial enterprises in the UK brewing industry, and described the spatial structure of those enterprises and the aspatial patterns of change. This chapter briefly describes the industry in 1951 and then has three parts. The first explores aggregate data on spatial change; the second examines case studies of spatial growth by the five core enterprises and the third considers the interaction process. These elements are all related back to the earlier discussion of the spatial evolution of an enterprise. Except where a detailed reference is given, the material is drawn primarily from the data set assembled from the sources discussed in Chapter 7, with supplementary material from the interview programme.

Industry Characteristics, 1951

The markets for cask beer in 1951 were supplied by the small single-plant firm characteristic of the market system. Figure 8.1 depicts the typical market area for the cask beer of these small firms. The graphs are based on the density of tied houses within 5 km bands; the population densities were similar within each band. The market areas extended over a radius of 20 to 25 km, with only limited sales beyond, and within the area the density of sales per unit area decreased steadily as distance from the brewery increased. It must be emphasised that within this area the plant was not a spatial monopolist, part of the demand for cask beer being met by other brewers. Similar distance decay curves have been established for other small plants, but the processes producing such curves have yet to be verified empirically. The distance decay pattern probably reflects, in part, attempts to remove competition near the plant and more intense competition from rivals in areas distant from the plant, but the brewer's high distribution costs also influenced the decline of sales with distance.

Data on the distribution costs of individual firms are difficult

Figure 8.1: Market Areas of Three Small Single-Plant Firms.
A: Webbs, Aberbeeg; B: David John, Pentre; C: Kirkstall, Leeds

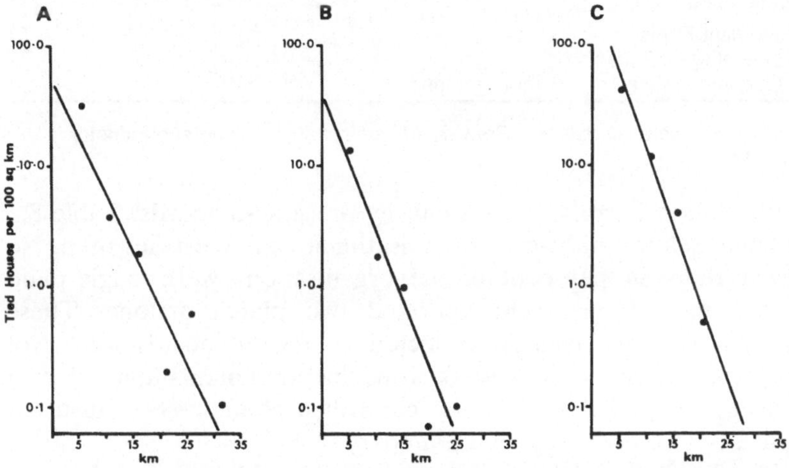

Source: H.D. Watts, 'The Market Area of a Firm', in L. Collins and D.F. Walker, *Locational Dynamics of Manufacturing Activity*, Wiley, London, 1975.

to obtain: Vaizey found that 'few small or medium brewers keep detailed . . . [distribution] . . . cost breakdowns'.[1] Data for a much later date suggest that the food and drink industries as a whole have a higher proportion of distribution costs to net output than all other industrial groups but one.[2] In the brewing industry the dominance of excise duties damps down the effects of other costs, but with these duties excluded the National Board for Prices and Incomes estimated distribution costs at 18 per cent of total brewery costs.[3]

To minimise these distribution costs sales were concentrated close to the production plant and most cask beer produced was shipped direct from the brewery to the retail outlet. The proximity of a brewing plant to its markets, in Weber's terms, reflects the input of a high proportion of a low-value ubiquitous material (water).[4] The short life of cask beer, and the fact that many brewers believed it did not travel well, accentuated the need for a brewery to be close to its market.[5] Cask beers served regional and local rather than national market areas in 1951, so the national market for cask beers was served predominantly by a network of small firms, many of which were family-influenced, if not family-controlled. The mean capacity of plant in 1951 was

Table 8.1: Firm Characteristics, 1951

Single-Plant Firms		278
Multi-Plant Firms		51
Operating > 2 plants	14	
Operating plants in 2 or more regions	19	

Source: *Brewers Almanacks, Brewery Manuals*, various trade and industry sources.

0.06 million barrels,[6] very small by present standards. Table 8.1 summarises the industry's organisational characteristics then. No fewer than 84 per cent of the organisations were single-plant firms, and 95 per cent operated two plants or one. These two-plant firms usually reflected a recent acquisition. Not surprisingly, only 6 per cent of firms operated plants in more than one region, and most of these controlled plants a short distance apart, but across a regional boundary.

The larger multi-plant firms were to provide most of the core enterprises of the larger organisations. Already by 1951 there were some enterprises twice the size (by capital employed) of any smaller firm either single or multi-plant. These enterprises were based either in a region of high population density, mainly the South East (Watney, Combe & Reid, Whitbread and Charrington are examples) and the West Midlands (Ansells and Mitchells & Butlers), or in an area with favourable resources such as Burton-upon-Trent where, originally, suitable water supplies had encouraged the growth of packaged beer output. Enterprises based here included Ind Coope & Allsopp, and Bass, with its subsidiary Worthington. While most of these enterprises depended upon tied outlets, Whitbread and Bass had built up a national distribution of their packaged beers, to supplement sales through the 1000 outlets each owned.

Despite these already large enterprises the spatial pattern of the industry in 1951 (Figure 8.2) reflected primarily the single-plant firms. This pattern is similar to that shown in the first phase of the development sequence (Figure 6.2). The changes that resulted in the emergence of a distinct set of industrial system plants are examined first through an analysis of aggregate data for the large enterprises as a group.

Aggregate Data

The development sequence envisaged a pattern of change such

Figure 8.2: Breweries in Great Britain, 1951

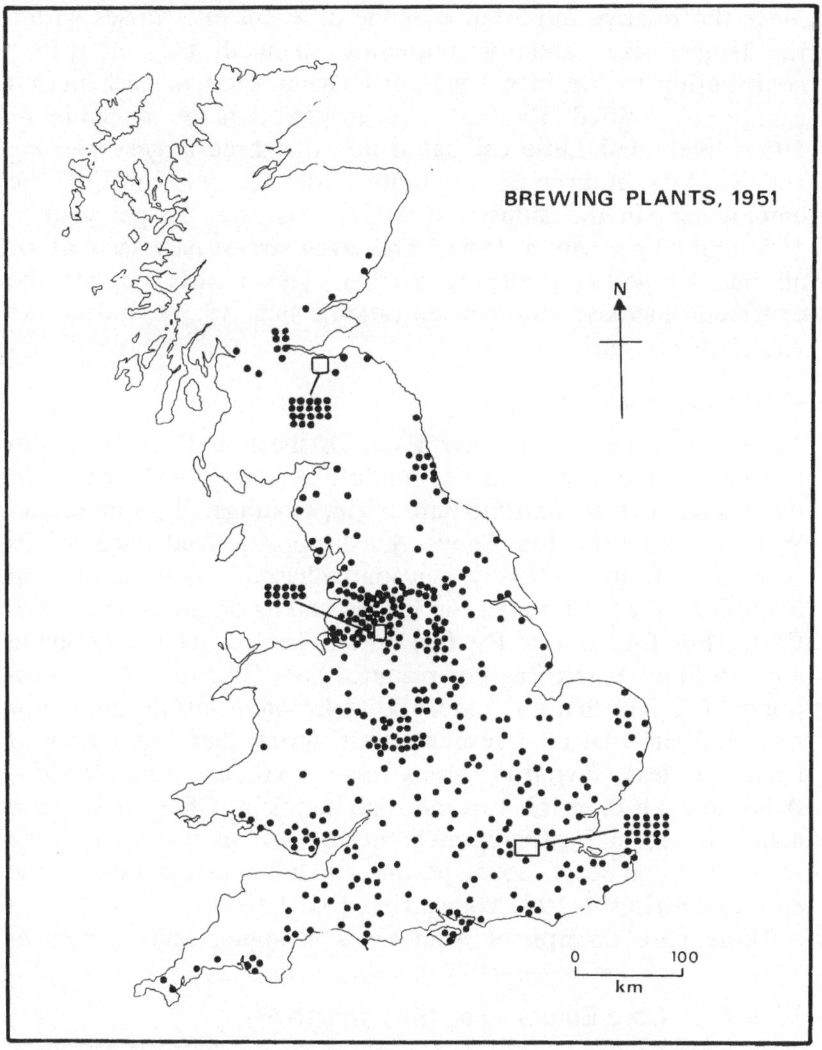

Source: *Brewers Almanack*, 1951, with some adjustments from *Brewery Manual, Stock Exchange Year Book*.

that large enterprises would come to dominate the industry, and that those large enterprises would grow out of either a resource base or a metropolitan centre. These two elements can be explored by examining changes in industrial concentration, and by identifying core enterprises and investigating their pattern in 1951.

Industrial Concentration

Since the relative importance of the different enterprises within the largest size category frequently changed, the enterprises contributing to the high levels of concentration at each period cannot be specified. The first concentration data are available for 1951. Evely and Little estimated that the three largest brewing and malting enterprises accounted for 13 per cent of the employment in the industry in 1951.[7] This was 16 per cent in 1958 and 33 per cent in 1963.[8] The seven largest now account for all but 13 per cent of the market. This clearly depicts the expected increase in concentration, but where were the enterprises based?

Core Enterprises

Table 8.2 lists the core enterprises. Of the four that grew from regional to multi-regional tied outlets between 1951 and 1976 three have a clear metropolitan origin, Courage, Whitbread and Watney. The fifth, Ind Coope & Allsopp, derived much of its strength from initially resource-based operations in Burton-on-Trent, although Ind Coope had its origins in the South East. Thus four out of the five enterprises reflect the expected metropolitan (South East) or resource base (Burton-upon-Trent) origin. The fact that one enterprise originated outside the major metropolitan area or a resource base shows that a grouping of firms in less favoured areas may challenge the leaders. Admittedly, it later joined a metropolitan firm (Charrington) and a firm based in Burton-upon-Trent (Bass), but it did so as the stronger or, at least, equal partner. A fuller description of the core enterprises in 1951 comes later (pp. 191-2).

These core enterprises, sometimes changing their names as

Table 8.2: Core Enterprises, 1951 and 1976

Core Enterprise	Tied Outlets in 1951	Present Name
Ind Coope & Allsopp	Multi-regional	Allied Breweries
Watney, Combe & Reid	South East	Watney-Truman
Barclay Perkins	South East	Courage
Whitbread	South East	Whitbread
Hammonds	Yorkshire and Humberside	Bass-Charrington

they grew, acquired directly 86 other firms and indirectly (through earlier acquisitions by the acquired firms) another 75 firms. Thus 161 independent, but often overlapping, market areas of small firms in 1951 were controlled by the five major enterprises by 1976. On average, the core enterprises acquired directly 17.2 firms each. This contrasts with the firms they acquired, which on average had acquired only 0.87 firms each, and with the firms that remained independent, which acquired only 0.54 firms each. The small number of acquisitions by the acquired firms reflects, of course, the fact that they were independent for only part of the 25 years under consideration.

Merger Distance

Whatever the location of the core, the development sequence suggested that as market area extension progressed so mergers with more distant partners would occur. This hypothesis was tested with data from a random sample of thirty mergers with core enterprises (Table 8.3). The distances between a core enterprise's head-office (at the time of the acquisition) and the acquired plant varied from ten km to 350 km, with a median distance of 180 km. A significant difference ($p < 0.05$) between the early and the later periods can be identified. The results confirm the tendency for market area extension as the enterprise grows; mergers with nearby firms in the 1950s and early 1960s were replaced by mergers with more distant firms in the late 1960s, despite the existence of some potential partners nearby.

Multi-Plant Characteristics

The change in the merger distance produced an increase in multi-plant operation, a feature characteristic of the later stages of the development sequence. This is reflected in Census of Production data. From 1958 to 1963 the mean number of plants

Table 8.3: Merger Distance and Time, 1952–76

	Less than Median Distance	More than Median Distance
Peak and earlier mergers (1952–63)	12	6
Post-peak mergers (1964–76)	4	8

$\chi^2 = 3.2$* One-tailed test n = 30

(as defined by the Census) of the three largest enterprises rose from 12 to 27, while the seven largest operated over 20. In 1968 the six largest operated on average 21 establishments each. While these Census of Production data indicate the general trend, inclusion of some non-brewing sites exaggerates the extent of multi-plant operations at their peak. Estimates of the maximum number of plants operated by an enterprise are difficult to make accurately, but on average the five core enterprises operated 15 plants in their peak years, although some of these plants were operated for only a short time and were never seen as part of a sustained multi-plant operation. Nevertheless, this clearly contrasts with a mean of 5.2 plants operated per core enterprise in 1951.

Regional Response

In addition to this growth of the multi-plant large enterprise reorganisation was taking place in the regions. While almost half (44 per cent) the mergers were with the core enterprises, 38 per cent were between other firms before merger with the larger enterprise, and 18 per cent with the smaller market system firms.

The general contrasts in the merger behaviour between the core enterprises and regional firms are brought out in

Table 8.4: Merger Distances: Regional Firms and Core Enterprises, 1952–76

a) Distance from head-office

	Less than Median Distance	More than Median Distance
Core Enterprises	6	24
Regional Firms	24	6
$\chi^2 = 21.6$***		n = 60

b) Distance from existing plant space

	Less than Median Distance	More than Median Distance
Core Enterprises	8	22
Regional Firms	20	10
$\chi^2 = 9.6$**		n = 60

Table 8.4(a), which compares the merger distances for core enterprises and other firms. The data for core enterprises are based on the random sample used earlier and those for regional firms on a random sample from other mergers. The median merger distance serves as the spatial divide. Core enterprises show a significant difference ($p < 0.001$) from regional firms in acquiring many more long-distance partners. This may partly reflect their increasing plant space, but Table 8.4(b) indicates that they differed also ($p < 0.01$) from regional firms by acquiring plants at a greater distance from their own plants. Not only were core enterprises acquiring over longer distances than regional firms, but they were also taking larger steps from their existing plants.

The aggregate evidence from the study of brewing enterprises supports the predictions of the model that the number of firms operating in the industry is reduced, the larger enterprises originate predominantly from a metropolitan core or resource base, mergers take place over longer distances, multi-plant operations increase in importance, and regional firms reorganise themselves, too. Yet, inter-enterprise variations in spatial growth have a major influence.

Inter-Enterprise Contrasts

This description of change in the industry as a whole and the reorganisation of regional firms preceding it hides the fact that not all enterprises grow in the same manner, at the same time and at the same rate. Further, not all enterprises grew from the same starting point. The remainder of this chapter focuses on contrasts in enterprise behaviour and on the identification of some possible interaction effects.

The core enterprises were part of the group of multi-plant enterprises in 1951; more significantly, four were among the largest enterprises in the industry. These four had capital employed of over £10 million, but other metropolitan firms (such as Charrington's), West Midland firms (like Mitchells & Butlers) and resource-based firms in Burton (such as Bass) rivalled them in size. There was little to distinguish them from the other large firms of the period. Similarly, Hammonds was only one of several large regional firms; other examples were Tetley in Leeds, Wilson's in Manchester and Simonds in Reading. The distinctiveness of the core enterprises came from the post-1951 evolution, rather than from special characteristics in 1951.

Within the core enterprises there were marked differences in their market areas in 1951. Table 8.2 indicated that the most extensive was that of Ind Coope & Allsopp, which controlled 3,800 licensed properties, mostly along a line from London to Liverpool, but with additional interests in the South West and around its lager brewery in North Wales. Even if its tied outlets were not found everywhere in the United Kingdom, they were sufficiently widespread to make the enterprise the first of the five core enterprises to serve an extensive multi-regional market of tied houses. The Watney, Combe & Reid area covered mainly west London, but had extended south-westwards to Alton and Southampton. It was clearly more restricted than Ind Coope & Allsopp. Barclay Perkins, based in Southwark (London), had its principal outlets in south and east London, Essex and Kent. Whitbread's 1,000 tied outlets were in London and, like Barclay, in Kent. These three enterprises were producers of cask beer for the regional market in south-east England, but the fifth core firm (Hammonds) was a regional firm, serving a predominantly Yorkshire market mainly west and north of Leeds. The contrasts within the five largest enterprises probably reflect the different stages of development when the initial cross-section was taken in 1951. Ind Coope & Allsopp were already some way through the kind of sequence proposed in the model, Barclay Perkins, Whitbread and Watney had barely begun, while Hammonds introduces an element not foreseen in the hypothetical sequence, and can be adequately explained only by consideration of the interaction process.

The following sections summarise the spatial growth of the five large enterprises. Figures 8.3 to 8.7 illustrate cartographically the growth of each enterprise's plant space and market area (in this context they are almost identical). The specific years illustrated indicate important phases in the development of each enterprise. The area served by each 1951 plant is depicted by a circle of fixed size; markets served by plants acquired and closed before 1951 are ignored. Ideally, the circles would vary to allow for variations in firm size, and allowance would be made for pre-1951 acquisitions. The data were not sufficiently full to allow either of these approaches to be adopted. The maps under-estimate the spatial extent of tied outlets acquired before 1951 and the extent of the markets served by some of the larger firms. Conversely, they over-estimate the markets supplied by the smaller rural firms. Each acquisition included at least one plant and thus extended the enterprise's plant space. So, in exploring the changes in market areas we are looking at the spatial growth of the enterprise's plant space. The figures emphasise the outward spatial growth of the enterprise's plant space and do not show acquisitions of plants within the same urban area.

To clarify the discussion each core enterprise is usually referred to by its modern name. This is preferable to using the name of the enterprise at the time a change was made, and then providing the present name in parenthesis.

Allied Breweries

Allied, unlike the other groups, effectively halted its major market area extension by the early 1960s. It began, as Figure 8.3 shows, with a head start, already having a wide, but discontinuous, spread of outlets in 1951. Initially change was slow, only a small firm in Shrewsbury (Trouncer) being acquired in 1954, but the enterprise increasingly recognised that it needed a stronger base in London, as most of its south-eastern outlets were on the conurbation periphery in Essex. Tentative attempts to link with the south London firm of Meux in the 1950s failed, but successful acquisition of Benskins' 800 outlets to the north-west of London compensated for this. Central London, however, still had only limited Allied houses. This problem was overcome in 1959 by acquiring Taylor-Walker, which had been seen as a useful potential partner for some time. Figure 8.3C illustrates the enterprise's major tied outlets before 1961.

Allied was to acquire, primarily, firms with a strong base in the major urban areas. It was not interested, though others were, in the mainly rural-based concerns: in 1956 it sold off 40 houses west of Shrewsbury which had been acquired two years earlier, and some Northamptonshire outlets of Taylor-Walker. The implications of the policy on its acquisition behaviour is clear. Both Ansells and Tetley-Walker, which joined the enterprise in 1961, met the criteria well. Tetley-Walker, with 2,800 tied outlets, served both the North West and the Yorkshire & Humberside regions, while Ansells, with about 1,500 tied outlets, served mainly the West and East Midlands and parts of South Wales (Figure 8.3D). Merger with Ansells had been talked about for some time but it was feared that an Allied bid would be countered by one from Mitchells & Butlers, the only other large

Figure 8.3: Spatial Growth by Core Enterprises: Allied Breweries, 1951–67

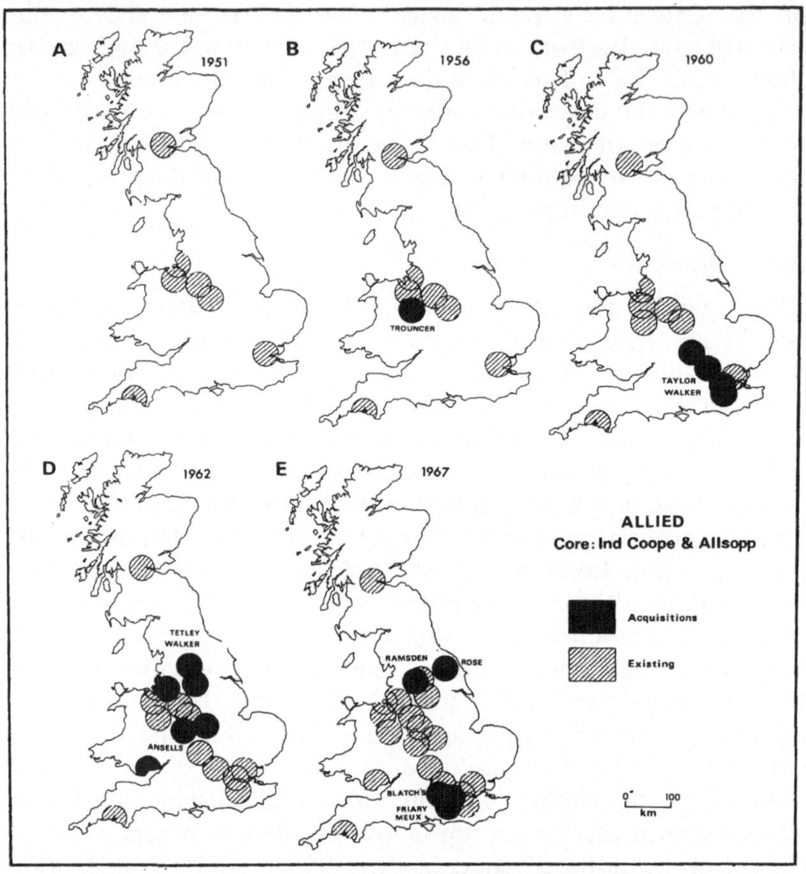

Source: Allied Breweries, *Brewery Manual* and *Stock Exchange Year Book.*

West Midlands firm. This could be prevented only if the acquisition was part of a bigger strategy, so the enterprise looked for a large firm in areas where it had few outlets and the only candidate which was both very large and with widespread outlets in the right areas was Tetley-Walker. The grouping of Tetley-Walker, Ansells, and Ind Coope & Allsopp into what was termed a 'commonwealth' considerably extended the Allied group's market area.

The concentration upon urban areas continued (Figure 8.3E).

The Tetley-Walker base in Yorkshire was strengthened by the addition of further outlets in Leeds and Ramsden's 186 houses in Halifax. An attempt to strengthen the north-west base by acquiring Boddington's in Manchester, however, failed. The south-eastern base was consolidated by adding Friary Meux with some 780 outlets, mainly in Surrey and south-west London, prior to which the enterprise's interests in southern England were 'very scattered'.[9] Some rural outlets (Rose) were acquired in Yorkshire but, while not urban, they did complement the outlets owned already in the region. These post-1961 acquisitions were useful rather than vital to market area growth; indeed by 1962 the enterprise announced that it believed its period of market area extension had come to an end as 'the broad framework that . . . [would] . . . enable . . . [them] . . . to compete effectively' had been established. It was prepared to take on new markets only 'in an area close to a production centre and where . . . [it was] . . . not well represented'.[10] In effect, concern with market area change in Allied Breweries stops in 1962; its major period of growth complete, it could turn to problems of product distribution and plant rationalisation. In 1963 it controlled 12 plants compared with 7 in 1951; this is indicative of the complementary growth of its plant space. Other enterprises were possibly less discriminating in their choice of merger partners, and no other enterprise placed such a marked emphasis on acquiring plants in major urban areas.

Watney-Truman

In contrast to Allied's extensive tied outlets in 1951, Watney's sales of draught beers were confined to south-east England, particularly west London and Hampshire (Figure 8.4), and it spent the early 1950s building up its free trade in packaged beers and consolidating its south-eastern base. To this end Tamplin's 400 outlets were acquired in 1953 and some 125 outlets in the Chichester area in 1955. The 'trade would not conflict with any of Watney's houses, and . . . would fill the gap . . . from Southampton to the Kent coast'.[11] Expansion south and west from London was probably encouraged by the location of the enterprise's principal interests in that sector of the metropolis. Consolidation was seen too in the 1958 acquisition of Mann's, which added new outlets in east London, although the prime objective was to acquire additional brewing capacity.

Figure 8.4: Spatial Growth by Core Enterprises: Watney-Truman, 1951–72

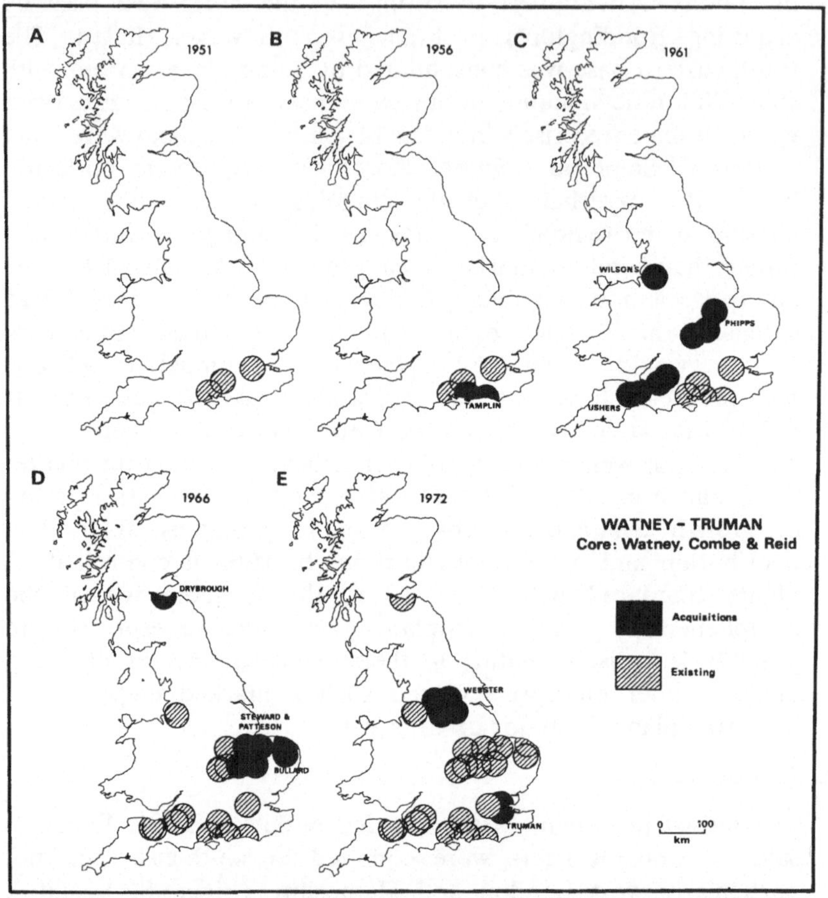

Source: Watney-Truman, *Brewery Manual, Stock Exchange Year Book* and H. Janes, *The Red Barrel: a History of Watney-Mann*, 1963, London.

It is sometimes argued that Watney's expansion of its tied outlets was in response to the takeover attempt by Sears Holdings, but in the late 1950s merger with Bass-Worthington of Burton-upon-Trent was being considered and the two enterprises agreed to work closely together for a year. Conflicts during the year, however, demonstrated that a fuller linking of the two companies was not possible. Yet in 1961 Watney's through its merger policy was the largest UK brewing enterprise; indeed it is claimed that this growth strategy was decided *before* the challenges presented by other enterprises were well established.

This growth was achieved by acquiring three major regional firms (Figure 8.4C). One was Usher's, serving a market area in central and south-west England with about 900 outlets. Phipps, in the East Midlands, served 1,200 houses in an area of 100 km around Northampton, and the most northerly, Wilson's brewery, based in Manchester, controlled 1,200 outlets at the time of the merger.[12] The three companies were acquired 'because of their geographical location . . . and were well suited to provide . . . a more economical distribution of products'.[13] Although Phipps was intended to help towards a free trade in the West Midlands, only Wilson's gave a firm hold in a major urban area.

After this big push outwards, extension continued northwards to Scotland, where Drybrough's 180 outlets were acquired, and eastwards, where acquisition of about 1,200 outlets of two Norwich firms (Steward & Patteson and Bullard) conferred a virtual monopoly. Hindsight suggests that the major Norwich acquisitions reflected growth for growth's sake, and the enterprise's monopoly position in East Anglia later created quite severe problems. A seven years' standstill followed, partly imposed by financial constraints, before the final phase of expansion, in the traditional form, in 1972. In that year, Webster of Halifax agreed that Watney-Mann should increase its partial shareholding and take full control, so gaining an additional 280 outlets in Yorkshire.

Changes for Watney's were not, however, over. Acquisition of the enterprise by Grand Metropolitan Hotels meant that from 1973 its activities were integrated with those of Truman, already owned by Grand Metropolitan. Significantly, Watney's had attempted to acquire Truman at the time it was acquired by Grand Metropolitan. This added outlets mainly in east London, Essex and Kent, and increased the enterprise's scope for rationalisation of production facilities. As Figure 8.4E shows, by 1972 the enterprise had major outlets in most of the major regions, except for Wales, the West Midlands and the Northern Region. Not surprisingly, it operated its peak number of plants (12) in 1965, some two years later than Allied.

Courage

Courage is the enterprise with perhaps the least national spread of tied outlets and plants. The main basis of the enterprise was the merger between Courage and Barclay Perkins in 1955. Both were based on the south bank of the Thames in London, but whereas Courage had spread west to Hampshire (Alton) and Surrey (Kingston), Barclay Perkins had moved towards Kent (Figure 8.5). After merger the new enterprise controlled some 2,500 outlets. This merger was stimulated primarily by Barclay Perkins's inability to provide sufficient capital to modernise its own out-dated plant, and a link with Courage enabled its beers to be brewed in the more modern Courage plant. Apart from the

Figure 8.5: Spatial Growth by Core Enterprises: Courage, 1951–72

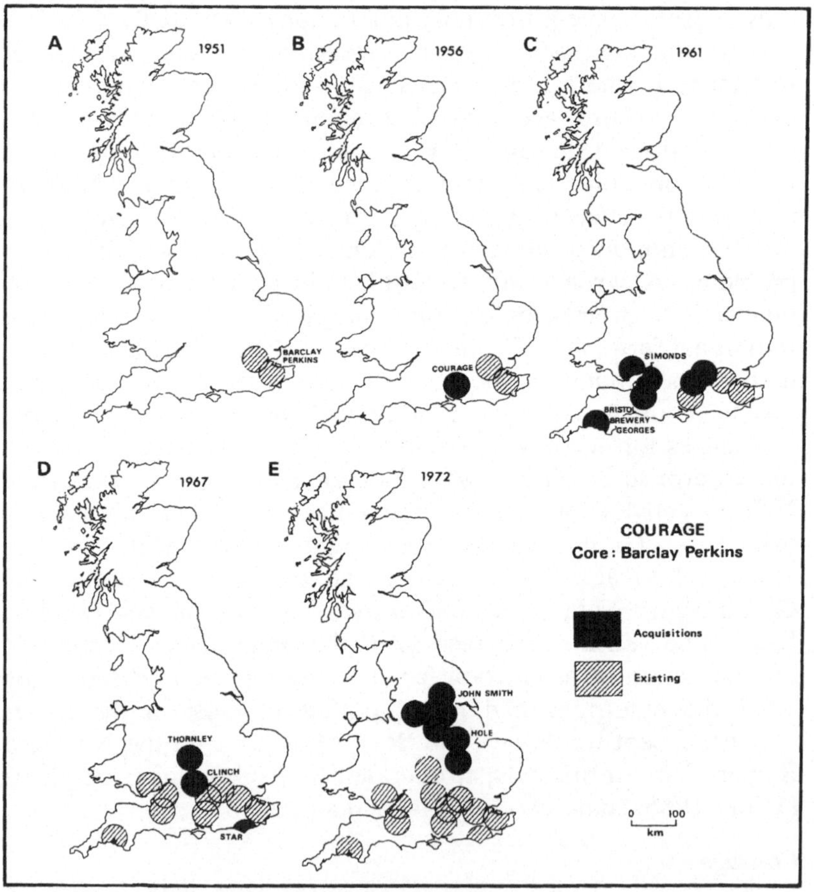

Source: Courage, *Brewery Manual, Stock Exchange Year Book* and J. Pudney, *A Draught of Contentment*, 1971, London.

acquisition of two small firms operating in 'adjacent' areas,[14] one at Bexley, controlling only 19 houses, and the other in Maidenhead, the market area changed little in the 1950s.

Caught up in the merger boom of 1960 and 1961 Courage acquired, first, Simonds of Reading, and, a year later, a Bristol firm (Figure 8.5C). Simonds had spread westwards from Reading and had acquired outlets as far west as Bridgend and Penzance, and to serve the latter operated the Tamar brewery at Devonport.[15] This addition of Simonds to the enterprise brought in 1,200 outlets, which had the attraction of adjoining the enterprise's existing market area without too much overlapping of interests. The enterprise intended thereafter to obtain tied outlets towards the Midlands and North, but was diverted from this when a northern company (United Breweries) made a bid for the Bristol firm. This challenge led Courage to acquire the Bristol firm, possibly at a rather inflated price, to enable it to maintain its hold in the South and West. Bristol Brewery Georges brought into the enterprise over 1,000 outlets, with some overlapping with the areas served by Simonds, but they also gave Courage a massive share of the tied outlets in Bristol.

Although the goal of northward expansion remained, expansion of the market area ceased temporarily. The market share in the South East was strengthened by acquiring firms in Uxbridge, Plumstead, Eastbourne and Witney, but these were predominantly small, the Eastbourne firm (Star) serving only 46 houses in the Eastbourne, Hastings and Rye areas, and the Witney firm (Clinch) 72 houses. Further consolidation in the South West came in 1971 with the acquisition of Plymouth Breweries, which had been seen as a potential acquisition for some time. By 1966 the enterprise still had primarily southern tied outlets lying south of an east-to-west line through Birmingham (Figure 8.5D).

The first successful break out of this area came with the acquisition of Hole in 1967. Although it was relatively small, it did indicate to other northern firms the kind of policy that could be expected from Courage. It was allowed to develop in its own way, and it may have influenced Smith's, the major acquisition, to join Courage in 1971. Before this acquisition, Courage had drawn up a list of potential partners in the North, but Smith's was the only serious contender. Rumour had, however, suggested links between Courage and Scottish & Newcastle. John Smith's controlled some 1,000 outlets spread widely over northern England (Figure 8.5E). Courage has had also a limited spread into other areas by exchanging outlets with other firms, notably in East Anglia and the West Midlands, areas where it is still poorly represented. Indeed, its tied outlets in the West Midlands, East Anglia, North West, Northern and Scottish areas are few. While it is much closer to national coverage than it was in the mid-1950s, it is still at an early stage of the growth depicted in the development sequence.

Bass-Charrington

The most complex of the growth patterns is presented by Bass-Charrington, which grew from a primarily regional base. The detail of this growth is introduced by a sketch of the broad framework of change. Initially, Hammonds (Bradford), Hope & Anchor (Sheffield) and Jeffrey (Edinburgh) were merged to form Northern Breweries. Subsequent expansion widened its geographical scope and then, re-named United Breweries, it merged with the London firm of Charrington to become Charrington-United. This in turn merged with a West Midlands concern, Bass, Mitchells & Butlers, to form Bass-Charrington in 1967. Behind the evolution of this organisation lay the growth-oriented policies of both Hammonds and Hope & Anchor and the subsequent interests of Canadian Breweries. A full history of this enterprise has been written by Hawkins, and this account draws upon his work.[16]

Hammonds, although originally a small town centre brewery in Bradford, had by 1951 recognised the limitations of its site and purchased more spacious plants at Huddersfield and Tadcaster. From this base in the 1950s it was actively seeking new outlets, but found no nearby firm interested, and approaches to other firms in Bradford and Leeds failed. It did gain access to Sheffield through a small firm in 1956, and so was 'able to establish [itself] in an important area'.[17] Unlike most firms of the time, it was prepared to search widely and acquired Case in Barrow, Aitchison in Edinburgh, and Westoe's 88 outlets in South Shields, some distance from its traditional trading area (Figure 8.6B).

Hope & Anchor undertook similar aggressive growth. The objective was to promote sales of its chief product, Jubilee Stout, a packaged beer. Other brewers were reluctant to sell it, and so

Figure 8.6: Spatial Growth by Core Enterprises: Bass-Charrington, 1951–71

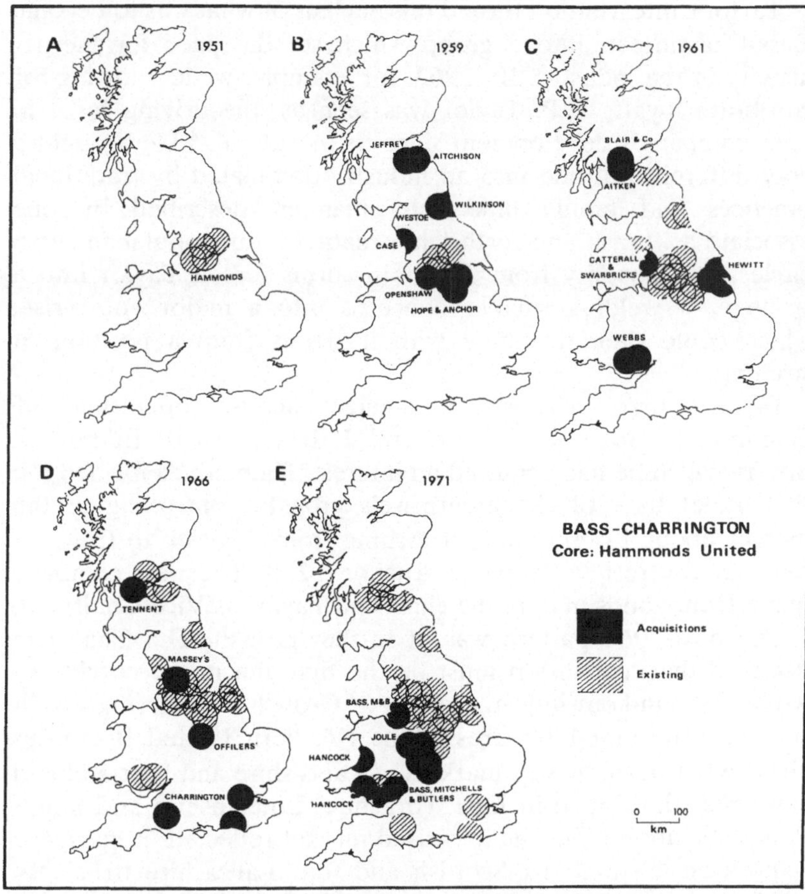

Source: Bass-Charrington, *Brewery Manual, Stock Exchange Year Book*, and K. Hawkins, *The Brewers' Tale*, privately published.

tied houses were important. Hope & Anchor initially owned only 95 outlets, but in the mid-1950s it strengthened its market in Sheffield, and like Hammonds purchased distant firms, in this case in Newcastle (Wilkinson) and Manchester (Openshaw). At the same stage it decided to begin production of stout in Canada, and to the amazement of Canadian Breweries the firm obtained both a licence to brew and a site in Canada. After much negotiation, the result of this behaviour was that E.P. Taylor of

Canadian Breweries began to take a major interest in Britain, primarily to build a national market for Carling lager.

Taylor's intervention turned this nucleus of what was to become Bass-Charrington into a group which set the pace for merger activity in the industry. By 1962, for example, while allowing for corporate loyalty E.P. Taylor was seen as 'the driving force in your company's development since its inception'.[18] He brought a very different attitude into an industry dominated by traditional practices and family links. His manner, described by one associate as 'brash and forthright', made him unpopular in some circles, and hostility from the major firms forced Taylor into a strategy of welding smaller concerns into a major enterprise, which could then negotiate with its rivals from a position of strength.

Taylor's first task was to amalgamate the operations of Hammonds, Hope & Anchor, and Jeffrey, a small Edinburgh firm in which he had acquired an interest. Hammonds formed the tied outlet base of the enterprise's growth, controlling at the merger about 1,000 outlets stretching from Alnwick to Chesterfield, in contrast to Hope & Anchor's 250. The new company had a Hammonds man in the chair and Taylor as Vice-Chairman.

The post-1960 pattern was of further growth. The Chairman declared that 'expansion must be the first aim in the conditions which surround our industry to-day'.[19] Growth would bring with it survival. The major features of the Northern/United Breweries phase were strengthened markets in Lancashire and Scotland and new areas developed in East Yorkshire, Lincolnshire and South Wales (Figure 8.6C). The increased market reflected, in part, the acquisition of some six Scottish and four Lancashire firms. By 1961 the enterprise held 20 per cent of the Scottish market, mainly by welding together the interests of the small firms. The two firms in Manchester added 350 outlets in that area, while further north the acquisition of Catterall and Swarbricks gave a strong hold on the Fylde Coast. The extension into Humberside (Hewitt) followed in the essentially northern tradition of the enterprise but it was 'an important extension to . . . [their] . . . principal trading area'[20] bringing in over 400 outlets. Expansion within West Yorkshire, however, still proved difficult, although the Melbourne brewery in Leeds was lost to Tetley only at the last minute.

Throughout this period the enterprise was trying to get into southern markets. In Wales, Hancock appeared as a possibility but Taylor's reputation prevented progress. A consolation prize was Webbs, whose tied trade was confined mainly to the coalfield. The desperate interest in the South is seen in that, while normally Taylor was not prepared to compete for a market, he did attempt to secure Bristol Brewery Georges. Courage, as was mentioned, won this battle, but they paid a high price, and there are hints that they may have been assisted by other larger firms closing ranks to keep out the newcomer to the industry. Nevertheless, within two years the initial 1,250 outlets had more than doubled to 2,850.

The merger with Charrington in 1962 brought the required southern interests, with about 2,400 outlets. Charrington was a predominantly London firm which, like others of its type, had some country interest – for example in Yeovil and Brighton. By 1962, however, it was falling behind in the building up of nationwide outlets. Watney, Courage and Allied all by now had major interests outside the metropolis, whereas Charrington did not. Its relatively weak position, plus the failure of an overseas operation, made it a logical target for Taylor, who added its tied outlets to his empire.

From 1962 to 1967 consolidation of established interest continued, with the purchase of additional tied outlets in the North West (Massey's) and South East, and of one of Scotland's major brewers, Tennent of Glasgow. Elsewhere a small step towards the Midlands was taken in purchasing the 250 outlets of Offilers' in Derby but, as Figure 8.6D shows, in the mid-1960s the major gap in the enterprise's trading area was in the West Midlands.

Entry to the Midland market required a merger either with Allied Breweries or with the still independent Bass, Mitchells & Butlers. Long drawn out negotiations with Allied failed, but with Bass, Mitchells & Butlers they succeeded. As the Chairman of the acquired firm observed, 'the merger was natural because geographically the operations dovetailed completely, our strength was predominantly in the West Midlands, whereas Charrington United was strong in the South and North'.[21] Two major tied markets outside the Bass, Mitchells & Butlers core region in the West Midlands were 500 outlets in the North West and another group in South Wales.

Subsequent growth added 1,000 outlets to the enterprise. The acquisition of Hancock gave a very firm hold in South Wales to complement the earlier absorption of Webbs; Stones increased the enterprise's market share in South Yorkshire, and Joule's 200 outlets expanded the Staffordshire market in 1970. These final changes made Bass-Charrington one of the two largest industrial brewery enterprises, with over 10,000 tied outlets, and by 1971 it was operating 20 plants. Up until 1971 spatial growth dominated its activities and it had made little attempt to adjust its production facilities.

Whitbread

Whitbread, the last of the five enterprises to be considered, had initially a different growth strategy from that of the other four; it attempted to secure national outlets by taking a substantial, but not controlling, interest in smaller firms. By the early 1950s it was already distributing packaged beers such as Mackeson Stout and Pale Ale to the national market through a system of about 40 distribution depots, and operating a brewery at Stockport and, from 1957, another at Leeds. The latter were acquired primarily to brew stout for the northern market; they had no associated tied houses and so are not shown in Figure 8.7. To ensure outlets for their packaged beers Whitbread's from 1950 were taking shares in other firms. Initially some 10 to 12 per cent of the shares were acquired, later 25 to 30 per cent. From 1955, the press noted that 'Whitbread's have accelerated their policy of making trading agreements with other companies'[22] and their trade investments rose from £0.4 million in 1951, to £2.1 million in 1957.[23] Once Whitbread's willingness to supply capital in exchange for sale of their beers and a seat on the board became known, initiative came normally from smaller firms. Whitbread claim that they 'had never taken an interest in any concern whose management had not invited . . . [them] . . . to intervene' and 'many companies approached . . . [them] . . . with a view to association'.[24] The development of this 'umbrella' was not unique to Whitbread's, but Whitbread's used it far more extensively than the others, and it gave the enterprise a strong base upon which to build once its method of growth became acquisition. By 1961, its umbrella sheltered some seventeen firms controlling over 10,000 public houses.[25] Figure 8.7B indicates the extent of this umbrella in 1958. The majority of these firms, and later additions to the 'umbrella', were subsequently acquired by Whitbread.

Focusing upon the umbrella policy meant few tied houses were

Figure 8.7: Spatial Growth by Core Enterprises: Whitbread, 1951–71

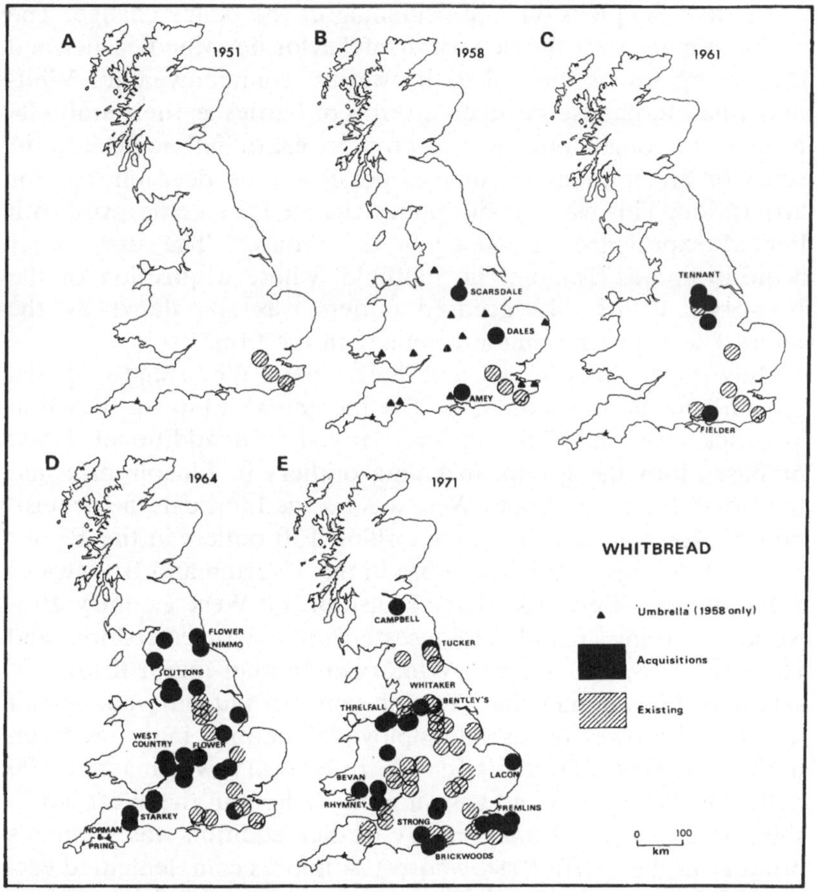

Source: Whitbread, *Brewery Manual, Brewers Almanack, Stock Exchange Year Book*.

added to Whitbread's market area in the 1950s, and its pattern of about 600 outlets in London and another 400 or so in Kent remained almost unchanged (Figure 8.7A). Two small firms in Hampshire (Amey) and Cambridgeshire (Dale's) had been acquired by 1956, and as late as 1960 the enterprise had further added only the very small firm of Scarsdale in Chesterfield. These acquisitions were primarily to enable the smaller entrepreneur to withdraw from the industry. In Cambridge the owner wished to retire and had no sons to inherit the business. The three additions represented no coherent growth policy, but simply reaction to a sudden crisis in the smaller firms.

Figure 8.7C picks out the beginning of the policy change. The major stimuli were the behaviour of Taylor described earlier and the setting up of the Allied Breweries 'commonwealth'. Whitbread had to choose between a series of battles as their umbrella firms were sought out by rival enterprises, or full acquisition of some or all of them as soon as possible. The decision was for acquisition. This was a major policy change for an enterprise with limited experience of managing tied houses. The first major acquisition was Tennant in Sheffield, where acquisition of the brewery and its 740 licensed outlets was stimulated by the interest of another London company in the firm.

Only in Figures 8.7D and 8.7E does Whitbread's spatial growth become more obvious. The merger with Flower, based in Warwickshire and Bedfordshire, brought an additional 1,500 premises into the group, including outliers in Lincolnshire and the North East. The South West was invaded through the acquisition of Norman and Pring, controlling 150 outlets in the Exeter area, and Starkey, Knight & Ford in the Tiverton and Bridgwater areas. In the West, too, the acquisition of West Country Breweries, serving mainly Gloucestershire, Worcestershire and Herefordshire, brought into Whitbread another major firm, considerably bigger than the Tiverton concern but only about half the size of Flower in capital employed. The final major addition in this period was Dutton's Blackburn Brewery, which added 800 outlets to Whitbread and gave it a major hold in the West Yorkshire and Lancashire markets. A further addition was Nimmo's brewery in the North East, whose 124 houses complemented earlier holdings acquired with Flower's brewery at Sunderland.

The final growth phase saw extension of the periphery, with additional outlets in Wales, the North and the South East. By 1967 about 50 per cent of Whitbread's sales were going to the tied trade[26] compared with 30 per cent in 1957.[27] The acquisition of Rhymney Breweries took Whitbread into Wales, and the initial interests were later extended by the acquisition of Bevan based in Neath (Figure 8.7E). To the north, Archibald Campbell, Hope & King in Edinburgh and Tucker in Gateshead were acquired. The north-western interests were considerably strengthened by the acquisition of Threlfall-Chester, with plants in Merseyside and Manchester-Salford, and Bentley's and Whitaker increased Whitbread's market share in Yorkshire.

The major changes were in the South East; the addition of over 750 outlets in Hampshire and Berkshire and Buckinghamshire through Strong and about the same number through Brickwood of Portsmouth gave new outlets in south-eastern England. In Kent, acquisition of outlets in Margate and Ramsgate was accompanied by the purchase of Fremlin's, based on Maidstone and Faversham, with about 400 to 500 properties. Finally, Lacon added 376 properties in the Yarmouth area.

The hectic pace of merger activity from 1962 through to 1971 has perhaps been emphasised by the complexity of this description, but it brought Whitbread to approximately the same size in 1971 (by tied outlets) as Watney and Allied. It is well represented by tied outlets and plants in most regions except the West Midlands.

The Interaction Process

These five cases of the spatial growth of an enterprise illustrate some interesting points about the interaction process discussed in Chapter 5, and the rest of the chapter, drawing on aggregate data for the enterprises and specific parts of the case studies, will illustrate inter-enterprise differences in the light of the interaction process.

Contrasts in spatial growth patterns are indicated by both the number and the timing of mergers. Such data tell nothing of the size of the different mergers, but they are the only data available for all firms. The most active acquirers were Bass-Charrington and Whitbread. Bass-Charrington acquired 27 firms and Whitbread 25. Measured another way Bass-Charrington by 1971 had absorbed 50 firms independent in 1951 and Whitbread 46. Thus these two enterprises together were in 1976 supplying outlets which twenty-five years earlier had been the province of almost 100 independent firms. Much less merger activity characterised the other three enterprises: Watney-Truman and Courage merged with 12 firms each and Allied with only 10. Watney-Truman supplied 27 formerly independent firms by 1976, Courage 21 and Allied a further 17. These figures suggest that there is a distinct difference between Bass-Charrington and Whitbread and the other three enterprises. This reflects the fact that Whitbread and the Charrington element of Bass-Charrington grew through the purchase of small breweries, whereas the other three enterprises purchased predominantly larger firms.

Satellite Role

The timing of mergers in the different enterprises can be related to the three phases of merger activity set out in Chapter 7. Watney-Truman, Courage, Allied and Bass-Charrington follow the overall pattern fairly closely: some activity in the early 1950s, a peak of activity around the turn of the decade and a decline thereafter. The one exception is Whitbread. It had acquired only 3 plants by 1958, only 7 in the peak period and 15 in the final phase. The timing, too, differed significantly ($p < 0.05$) from that of the other four, as Table 8.5 shows. This is clear evidence of its satellite role in spatial growth. The case study showed that this reflected undue confidence in the ability of its umbrella policy to secure its markets. Moreover, its initial acquisition of Tennant admittedly reflected sudden pressure from another firm, and the 'number one influence' on its overall change to an acquisition policy was the behaviour of Taylor and the Bass-Charrington enterprise. This late entrance too, probably explains its purchase of rather more and smaller plants than some of its rivals. Further, it operated its peak number of plants in 1967 and 1968 (22), much later than three of the others.

A satellite role, too, may be suggested for Courage. It still has a restricted area of tied outlets, it did not effectively break out of its primarily southern base until 1971, and even in the South some of its mergers were defensive rather than offensive: the Bristol firm is an example.

Leader Role

Identification of the leader role in spatial growth is more problematical, but it does not seem unreasonable to suggest that different enterprises occupied it at different times. Initially, in the 1950s, this was clearly occupied by Allied; as was shown, it was the largest and most widespread in its markets. Although left behind briefly in 1959 to 1961 by Watney, it quickly responded

Table 8.5: Inter-Enterprise Variations in Merger Activity, 1952–76

	1952–63	1964–76
Whitbread	10	15
Other four enterprises	41	20

$\chi^2 = 5.4*$ $n = 86$

with larger and more effective mergers, so that by 1962 it regarded its period of spatial growth as complete. It had achieved its objective of a comprehensive national market.

Watney's brief lead in 1959 to 1960 pre-dated the major merger boom, and gave the enterprise a temporary leading role. Like Allied it was able to buy relatively large firms, and quickly gained a sufficient base for a national market. It then, however, fell behind in developing its tied outlets, it was outbid for Truman and only in 1972 did it fully absorb its Yorkshire subsidiary.

There is little doubt that Bass-Charrington, too, occupied the leader role at some stages; indeed with the exception of Watney-Truman the other enterprises' initial merger activity was stimulated by Taylor. Its leader role, however, was played down by the fact, reported in the case study, that the traditional and larger firms were unwilling to co-operate with it. Nevertheless Taylor's aggressive growth strategy built up the largest UK brewing enterprise initially based on some small regional firms.

In sum, while two fairly clear cases of satellite roles can be identified, the leader role is less clearly cast. There seems, indeed, to have been some manoeuvring to maintain that role. Further, 'role' is assessed here in terms of spatial growth; other aspects of behaviour (e.g. pricing) might rank enterprises rather differently.

Competitive Behaviour

Within these roles some of the behaviour patterns suggested in Chapters 5 and 6 can also be explored. Evidence of collusion is almost impossible to obtain, particularly in an industry such as this characterised by very close formal and informal links between firms. Nevertheless, the predominant behaviour of the successful enterprises was competitive, while various smaller firms occupied passive positions. This competitive position is reflected partly in merger behaviour in response to merger behaviour in other firms, and more spectacularly in the battles between enterprises for specific smaller concerns.

The competitive response of the enterprises is reflected in the fact that some commentators believe firms were purchased for far more than they were worth. It was said of Whitbread's in 1970 that 'acquisitions have consistently been made on over-generous terms',[28] while Hawkins concluded that in Bass-Charrington's growth there is 'little doubt that some breweries were bought at prices which greatly exaggerated their real earning power'.[29]

The merger battles were more spectacular and only the feeling within the industry that 'gentlemen' did not outbid their rivals once an offer had been made kept the battles relatively few. Two were particularly fierce, those between United Breweries and Courage for Bristol Brewery Georges, and between Bass, Mitchells & Butlers and Watney for Bent's in Liverpool.

The Bristol Brewery Georges battle is described in detail by Hawkins.[30] Here Taylor, desperate to get some southern outlets, made an offer direct to the shareholders over the heads of the Directors of the Bristol firm, after they had turned down his informal approach. Almost immediately Courage made a counter-bid. United, trying to avoid a fight, suggested that they should split Bristol Brewery Georges assets with Courage, but this was turned down. Meanwhile Courage had gained sufficient acceptances of their offer to ensure their control, but a subsequent counter-bid by Taylor pushed the price up further. The market price of the shares prior to Taylor's initial bid was £5.75; Courage paid £9.25 – an expensive purchase, but indicative of the intense competition.

The Bent's battle was fiercer. Watney made an initial bid of £1.62½ per share in May 1967, but Bass made a surprise counter-bid of £1.81 and revealed they already had a shareholding in Bent's. Watney then met this offer and got the approval of the Bent's board but Bass were rapidly buying shares and had raised their stake from 5 per cent to 10 per cent. By the first week of June Bass raised the offer to £2.00, and both Watney's and Bass were buying Bent's shares. By mid-June, Watney's held 15 per cent, Bass 26 per cent. Bass won, but only with an offer of £2.45. Thus, the overall price of the offer had jumped from £17 million to £25 million.[31] This particular clash arose from Watney's desire to extend Wilson's activities into Merseyside, and Bass's recognition that Bent's provided them with possibly their last chance to get a small-to-medium-sized brewery in Merseyside.[32] These public fights are the surface signs of more intense competition at a private level, but they do indicate the competitive behaviour of the large enterprise.

Passive Behaviour

'Passive' behaviour was less common amongst the larger enterprises: Truman alone withdrew from its wider markets and concentrated mainly on one region. Truman, Hanbury & Buxton were predominantly regional brewers in south-east England: prior to contraction about 75 per cent of their tied outlets were in this area. At the turn of the century the company began to brew at Burton as well as London and purchased at least one small brewery outside the South East (Swansea) in 1926. Expansionist features were evident as late as 1965, when shares were acquired in a Sheffield company. In 1968 Truman's controlled about 3 per cent of the tied houses in south-east England, the market share rising to over 6 per cent in the London area. Elsewhere holdings were negligible except for South Wales, where the Swansea houses formed a compact block. Outlets were served from the 0.20 million barrel Burton brewery and the 0.60 million barrel Brick Lane brewery.

The company was then faced with the decision either to 'go national' or to intensify its market in the South East. It chose the latter. As a first step, in 1969, houses in the Newcastle and Sunderland area were exchanged for Whitbread houses in the Luton area 'as the cost of carriage from our Burton brewery did not allow us a proper return in the assets involved'.[33] Exchange rather than sale permits ready intensification and brewers (like Whitbread) are willing to exchange houses in areas where their holdings are strong.

The second stage was precipitated by the need to rebuild the London brewery at a cost of between £3 million and £6 million. To obtain maximum economies of production an output of approximately 1 million barrels per annum was desirable. This would increase the firm's overall capacity by about 50 per cent if the Burton brewery was retained – a market for this level of output did not exist.

A re-appraisal of the Burton brewery and Midlands and northern outlets of the company was undertaken. It was concluded, 'It has for some time been apparent that the production units and trading outlets of the company were dispersed over too wide an area of the UK which resulted in uneconomically high costs being incurred in the marketing and distribution of our products'.[34] All outlets in the Midlands and North (73 houses) were exchanged for 36 houses in the South East (from Courage) and £250,000. This, of course, rendered the position of the Burton brewery yet more anomalous and it was shut.

Thus, by the end of 1971, Truman's were essentially regional brewers based on a modernised London brewery and with holdings consolidated in the South East, apart from one major outlier in Swansea. This was retained because the close proximity of outlets in a small area made them relatively easy to supply. As was shown earlier, the result of this passive behaviour was acquisition by Grand Metropolitan Hotels, and subsequently integration with Watney's activities.

Conclusion

This chapter has considered the spatial growth of large industrial enterprises in the UK brewing industry. Enterprise behaviour was examined against the development sequence proposed in Chapter 6, and both aggregate and case-study data illustrate the increasing importance of the large enterprise, which is based in a major metropolitan area or a particularly favoured resource area, that merger partners are sought over an increasing distance, that multi-plant activities increase and that reorganisation of regional firms occurs. One of the five core enterprises did not fit this pattern.

Developing beyond the basic model, the evidence suggests that the leader role in the interaction process was occupied by different enterprises at different times. It was also possible to allocate some of the other enterprises to the satellite role. While evidence of collusive behaviour could not be provided, both competitive and passive behaviour appear to have had an important influence on the spatial growth of an enterprise.

One important caveat to these findings is that they are partly dependent on the methods used to trace the core enterprise back from the present enterprise. It was a mechanistic financial method, with little reference to the personnel involved, and other methods might well have produced a different pattern.

The process of market area change has reflected a steady increase in the areas in which an enterprise has its tied outlets. From the nature of the industry this extension of the market area produced also spatial growth of each enterprise's plant space. Not surprisingly, such growth was accompanied by adjustment of plants, a process examined in more detail in the next chapter.

Notes

1. J.E. Vaizey, *The Brewing Industry, 1886–1951*, 1960, London, p. 107.
2. M. Chisholm, 'Freight Transport Costs, Industrial Location and Regional Development', in M. Chisholm and G. Manners (eds.), *Spatial Policy Problems of the British Economy*, 1972, Cambridge, p. 231.
3. National Board for Prices and Incomes, *Costs, Prices and Profits in the Brewing Industry*, 1966, London, p. 5.
4. A. Weber, *Theory of the Location of Industries*, 1929, Chicago, pp. 62–3.
5. I have not been able to trace any quantitative evidence as to the 'life' of beer in the cask, or the extent of deterioration in cask beer quality as a result of long distance transport.
6. Based on industry output in 1951, and records of number of plants in operation in 1951.
7. R. Evely and I.M.D. Little, *Concentration in British Industry*, 1960, Cambridge, p. 308.
8. *Census of Production*, 1958 and 1963.
9. Allied Breweries, *Report and Accounts, 1963.*
10. Ibid.
11. Watney, Combe & Reid, *Report and Accounts, 1953.*
12. H. Janes, *The Red Barrel: a History of Watney-Mann*, 1963, London, p. 173.
13. Watney-Mann, *Report and Accounts, 1961.*
14. Courage and Barclay, *Report and Accounts, 1955.*
15. J. Pudney, *A Draught of Contentment: The Story of the Courage Group*, 1971, London, p. 97.
16. K. Hawkins, *The Brewers' Tale: A History of the Bass-Charrington Group* (privately published for limited circulation, 1978).
17. Hammonds United Breweries, *Report and Accounts, 1955.*
18. United Breweries, *Report and Accounts, 1961.*
19. Ibid.
20. *The Times*, 16 Jan. 1962.
21. Bass, Mitchells & Butlers, *Report and Accounts, 1967.*
22. *Brewers' Guardian*, August 1955, p. 10.
23. Whitbread, *Reports and Accounts, 1958.*
24. Ibid.
25. Anon, *The Story of Whitbreads,* 1964, London, p. 47.
26. Whitbread, *Report and Accounts, 1967.*
27. Whitbread, *Report and Accounts, 1962.*
28. *Investor's Chronicle*, Brewing Supplement, 13 November 1970, p. 3.
29. Hawkins, *The Brewers' Tale*, Chapter 5, p. 55.
30. Ibid., pp. 10–12.
31. *The Times*, June 1967.
32. Hawkins, *The Brewers' Tale*, Chapter 6, p. 33.
33. Truman, Hanbury & Buxton, *Report and Accounts, 1969.*
34. Truman, Hanbury & Buxton, *Report and Accounts, 1971.*

9 BREWING ENTERPRISES: LOCATIONAL ADJUSTMENT

The spatial growth of the plant space of the enterprises in the brewing industry was associated with major changes in the location, size and number of brewing plants. Greenall-Whitley, a market system firm, provides a simple example of the spatial evolution of a firm through the growth and adjustment process. By 1951 it had plants in Lancashire, Cheshire and Shropshire, with its main plant at Warrington. In 1959 it extended its plant space northwards by the acquisition of a Bolton plant, in 1961 eastwards to Salford and finally southwards to Wellington. From 1966 to 1969 it operated all seven plants, and then began a process of adjustment, closing the Chester and Wellington plants in 1969, Bolton in 1970, Salford in 1972 and St Helens in 1975. In the larger industrial system enterprises growth and adjustment were rarely as distinct as this, and generally new growth occurred before adjustments were complete.

Initial adjustments were rarely part of an overall production plan but resembled the adjustments undertaken by the beet-sugar enterprise described in Chapter 5. Towards the late 1960s three of the enterprises introduced major spatial rationalisation strategies, similar to that of the railway engineering enterprise described in the same chapter. This chapter focuses upon the spatial outcomes of the locational adjustment process, but begins with a synopsis of some technical changes which encouraged the expansion of some sites and the closure of others.

Technological Change

The changes took two forms: first, larger plants could be operated, and second, draught beer could be distributed over longer distances.

Plant Economies-of-Scale

Economies came principally from increasing the size of the individual units of a plant – mainly tanks and other containers. Evidence from Cockerill shows that such economies are more marked in the brewing industry than the usually accepted rules for other process industries would suggest.[1] The extent of these cost savings is indicated by the fact that the unit capital cost for a new plant of 0.1 million barrels would be five times that of a 1.0 million barrel plant. Increased size also reduces labour inputs, since increased size of capital equipment does not require a similar increase in the work-force. Over the same size-range described above labour costs would be three and a half times higher in the smaller unit.[2]

Evidence for changes in the minimum efficient scale of operations between 1951 and 1976 is difficult to obtain. Cockerill suggests that the chief development in brewing technology in the 1950s and 1960s was 'an improvement in the scheduling of production through the processing of smaller batches at a greater frequency than previously, and a consequent increase in the utilisation of large units of plants'.[3] This in itself would permit concentration of production in larger plants. At the lower end of the scale Vaizey argued that plants of less than 0.06 million barrels were uneconomical in the 1950s,[4] and this figure is probably much higher now. Estimates of the minimum efficient scale have risen; in the late 1960s it was seen as about 0.7 million barrels,[5] but Pratten, in 1971, put it at 1.0 million barrels, but thought that economies might not have been exhausted at that level.[6] Despite the limited evidence the conclusion that over the past twenty-five years there has been an economic justification for developing plants to give higher output seems reasonable. Capacity increase, however, in brewing is constrained by distribution costs, and labour disputes in very large plants have recently indicated an important disadvantage of concentrating production on a few sites.

Distribution Costs

Evidence of the potential for change in this area is more marked. Table 7.1 showed that in the 1960s keg beer increasingly replaced cask beer. The keg beers travel well, show little tendency to deteriorate and can be distributed more widely than the cask beers. As shown earlier, keg beers are also sold at a higher price. On the assumption that 10 per cent of the wholesale price goes to transport, the figures in Chapter 7 give £1.88 as available to distribute cask beer, but £2.56 to distribute keg. This may be partly offset by higher overheads (for example, advertising), but there is still room for spending more on transport of keg than of cask beers.

Increases in a plant's market area were aided also by the development of the motorway system and the adoption of more sophisticated distribution systems. A plant can attempt to reduce its distribution costs in several ways. First, deliveries can be focused on outlets with large sales; second, loads can be 'trunked' to depots and there split up into smaller vehicles for local delivery; third, tankers can replace trunk distribution in kegs; and fourth, the plant may use computer-based methods for vehicle scheduling and route planning.[7] Although these four possibilities are available, it is primarily the change from cask to keg beers and the development of better roads and motorways that have permitted the increase in the area served from a single plant.

If distribution costs are added to processing costs, the minimum efficient scale of plant today becomes around 1.0 million barrels. Because, however, spatial variations in demand for the output of a plant vary from one location to another, a unique scale of output at which the size of plant is at an optimum cannot be specified.[8] Further, plants of up to 2.5 million barrels are currently in operation in the United Kingdom, and of over 3 million barrels in the United States.

The marked scale economies in the industry encouraged large enterprises and small firms increasingly to concentrate their production capacity in fewer and larger plants, but distribution costs ensured that the larger multi-regional enterprises maintained plants in several regions, as Chapter 7 showed. A quantitative picture of the change is provided by the fact that, despite an increase in total output, the approximately 410 plants of 1951 had been reduced to about 140 by 1976, a decline of 66 per cent. One dramatic illustration of the scope for further change is the fact that all UK beer could be produced from fifteen 2.5 million barrel plants. This decline in plant numbers necessarily reflected a re-allocation of output among sites, and concentration of growth in particular parts of an enterprise's spatial structure.

The remainder of this chapter explores the aggregate patterns of locational adjustment and this, as in the last chapter, is followed by more detailed study of the five core enterprises. It concludes with a discussion of the contrasts among them in relation to the interaction process.

Aggregate Analysis

The development sequence in Chapter 6 envisaged a decline in plant numbers, which, as illustrated above, did take place. This decline was expected to be concentrated around the major metropolitan centre, and to affect primarily plants in smaller centres. In particular, it was predicted that a large enterprise would close a smaller proportion of plants acquired than the market system firms, that it would make a major contribution to the increase in mean plant size, and that it would focus its production in the very largest population centres. Each of these ideas can be explored with reference to the aggregate data. An earlier analysis of the data set has been reported elsewhere.[9] The discussion is restricted by the fact that it was impossible to build up a sufficiently accurate annual series of plant closure data.

Remoteness

For most of the development sequence more plants survived in the remoter part of the sector than in the area close to the metropolitan centre. Mark, also, has noted the effect of remoteness on survival,[10] and map evidence which shows that plants in West Wales, Cumberland and Cornwall have survived supports this idea. Further consideration of this point suggests that plants near a major centre could serve that centre and survive also. Middle-distance plants lacking a nearby market or the protection of remoteness should show a greater propensity to close.

Major market centres were defined as urban areas above the first clear break up the population size continuum of English cities with over 50,000 population in 1961. Scotland was excluded: it serves a distinct and separate market. Each plant's distance from its nearest major market centre was measured to the mid-point of Birmingham, Bristol, Leeds, Liverpool, London, Manchester or Sheffield. Identification of near, middle and remote distance groups was based on industry characteristics. 25 km (Figure 8.1) seemed to be about the limit beyond which a major market would be outside the range of a small town plant. The distance of 70 km is more arbitrary, but industry evidence suggests that this is about the distance over which major regional brewing plants were distributing most of their products in the 1960s. Road

Table 9.1: Distance from Metropolitan Area and Plant Survival, 1951–76

	km		
	0–25	26–69	>69
Survive	4	2	6
Not Survive	5	12	7

Source: *Stock Exchange Year Book*, *Brewery Manual*, *Brewers Almanack*.

transport data for 1962, which show that only 12 per cent (by weight) of beverages carried by road travelled over 80 km,[11] support it.

Table 9.1 illustrates the expected pattern, with survival rates of around 45 per cent in plants close to or distant from the major urban centres and of only 16 per cent in the middle-distance band. Inspection of the raw data revealed that all the survivors in the areas distant from the major metropolitan centres were market system plants. For technical reasons a test to identify significant differences is not possible, but an earlier analysis of the data set, involving closures only up to 1971, did identify a significant difference ($p < 0.05$).[12] This is not surprising as the effects of remoteness are more marked in the early stages of the sequence. The loss of plants in the middle distance category introduces an element which was not built into the development sequence.

Local Markets

Another aspect of the development sequence was that larger plants, located in the larger settlements, survived because the large surrounding markets enabled them to achieve economies-of-scale and extend their market areas. This point was developed by Riley.[13]

If this is so, plants located in very small centres should show a lower survival rate. Potential savings from any increased output would be offset by increased distribution charges attributable to an almost inevitable market area extension. A random sample from the 1951 list of plants was examined against the size of local market measured by a surrogate (the 1961 population). The Census of Population definition of a large centre (over 50,000

Table 9.2: Local Markets and Plant Survival, 1951–76

	Small Centres <50,000 Population	Large Centres ⩾50,000 Population
Survive	4	13
Not Survive	17	16

$\chi^2 = 3.6*$ One-tailed test n = 50

Source: *Stock Exchange Year Book*, *Brewery Manual*, *Brewers Almanack*, and *Census of Population, 1961*.

inhabitants) was used to distinguish two size groups (Table 9.2). The difference between large and small centres is significant ($p < 0.5$). Although location in a small centre decreased the chance of survival, however, a plant within a larger centre was almost as likely to shut as to remain open. This probably reflects the fact that larger centres had more than one plant, and these plants tended to merge with each other.

The decreased chance of survival in a small centre does not necessarily reflect the absence of a local market: it might, for example, be that the local labour market was insufficient to permit the plant to expand and thus survive. Given the increasing spatial extent of labour markets in small centres,[14] however, this seems unlikely. Table 9.2, then, may be interpreted in terms of the effect of small local markets on plant closure.

Site Value

The final variable to be considered in this first section is site value, which in Chapter 5 was thought to influence closure decisions. Closure rates for plants in the seven major urban centres in England, where competition for land should be most intense, were compared with closure rates in the remaining plants. There was not a significant difference; in fact the rates were virtually identical. The closure rate in London (73.7 per cent), however, was higher than in the other cities, and with a further closure imminent it will approach the level of the small population centres. Certainly, location in the major metropolitan centre does seem to encourage closure. This theme perhaps comes out more strongly in the case analyses later in the chapter.

Core Enterprises and Survival

So far, the plants have been treated independently of the enterprises operating them, yet it is the enterprises that have made the adjustments. For most of the period shown in the development sequence the retention of independence by regional firms meant that, as expected, regional plants showed a greater propensity to survive than plants absorbed into the major metropolitan enterprise. Table 9.3 compares the survival rate of absorbed plants with a random sample of twenty plants which were independent in 1951 and were not absorbed into the major enterprises. The survival rates differ significantly ($p < 0.01$). Plants remaining outside the orbit of the principal enterprises show a greater propensity to survive.

It was retention of independence that was all-important. Indeed, acquisitions by the market system firms were more likely to result in closure than those by core enterprises. This is seen in the last stage of the development sequence, where all acquired plants controlled by regional firms have been shut. This no doubt reflects the shorter merger distance of these market system firms (Chapter 8), whereas the core enterprise needs more plants to serve its wider markets. Empirical data confirm this general pattern. Of the 41 plants acquired by the market system firms operating in 1976 only 6 (15 per cent) were still brewing. This compares with a survival rate almost twice as great (28 per cent) for plants acquired by the core enterprises. Here distribution costs constrain the extent to which the spatial pattern can be moved towards one plant per enterprise.

Core Enterprises and Plant Size

One of the more obvious changes resulting from the growth of enterprises in the development sequence was the increase in plant size. Having no individual plant size data one cannot test for

Table 9.3: Acquisition and Plant Survival, 1951–76

	Acquired by Core Enterprises	Independent Firms 1951
Survive	39	13
Not Survive	82	7

$\chi^2 = 7.9^{**}$ n = 141

Source: *Stock Exchange Year Book*, *Brewery Manual* and *Brewers Almanack*.

significant differences in mean size. There was a 50 per cent increase in mean size during the first decade (from 0.06 to 0.09 million barrels) and over a 100 per cent increase in the second decade (0.09 to 0.20 million barrels), rising finally to 0.26 million barrels by 1976. Interpretation of the mean figures must be cautious because the plant size distribution is positively skewed at the beginning of the period and is probably bi-modal at the end. The significance of the large enterprises in the change is recognised by the fact that the mean plant size for the seven large enterprises was 0.57 million barrels in contrast to 0.06 for the remainder – which is just about the size which was termed the minimum viable capacity. Indeed, the general upward shift in plant sizes seems to be predominantly the work of the large industrial enterprise, especially since 0.06 was the mean size of all plants in 1951.

Core Enterprises and Local Markets

Surprisingly, the core enterprises showed no significant bias towards the closure of production sites in the smaller centres as defined previously; they closed about a third of their plants in both the larger and the smaller centres. There is, however, a bias towards the very largest towns within the over 50,000 category. This bias emerges whether the dichotomisation of the category is based on the discontinuity in urban size at about 400,000, or the median population size of 96,000. On the first, 70 per cent of the plants shut in the smaller towns compared with only 58 per cent in the larger; on the second, 66 per cent shut in the smaller towns and only 40 per cent in the larger.

This evidence suggests that the market system firms have played as important a role as the large enterprises in closing plant in the smaller centres. Where large enterprises did own such plants they were no more likely to be closed than the larger centre plants. The bias exerted by larger enterprises emerges more clearly *within* the larger centre category: the plants in the very largest towns show a greater propensity to survive.

These conclusions emphasise the important role of market system firms in the closure decision. Further, it is estimated that of all plant closures 39 per cent were closed by the five core enterprises, 31 per cent by small firms which they subsequently acquired, and 17 per cent by the present market system firms. (The remaining 13 per cent either ceased brewing without acquisition or were acquired by Scottish & Newcastle Breweries and by the Club breweries.) The core enterprises closed fewer than half the plants, but of course expanded considerably at sites they retained.

Core Enterprises and Locational Adjustment

The shift towards larger and fewer plants in the larger enterprises appears in the Census of Production evidence from 1963 to 1968. In the larger enterprise size groups the mean number of plants per enterprise fell markedly. In the 1,000–4,999 employees category the fall was from 12 to 5 plants per enterprise, in the over 5,000 employees category from 28 to 21. It should be remembered that the Census includes more than the brewing sites. Evidence from the enterprises for brewing sites alone, however, indicates a similar pattern. On average, the five enterprises reduced the maximum number of sites they operated by 38.6 per cent, a mean closure rate of 9 plants per enterprise after maximum plant numbers had been established.

New Entrants and New Plants

One element not included in the development sequence was the possibility of new entrants and new plants. Chapter 7 showed that there was only one new entrant to the industrial system enterprises from 1951 to 1976, but some seven new sites will be in operation by 1980. The most striking feature of all the new sites is their proximity to the motorway network, possibly reflecting the enterprises' general concern with distribution costs. These new sites are examined more closely in the case analyses, which also indicate some of the reasons for spacing the plants alongside the motorway network.

Summary

In the discussion of changes in plant locations the aggregate data show the expected tendencies for plant numbers to decline and for survival to be more likely in larger centres, except in the major metropolitan centre. More specifically, the areas in which core enterprises dominated saw more plant closures than areas where independent firms survived, but independent firms were more likely to close an acquired plant than the core enterprises. The core enterprises, while showing no bias in closure between large and small centres, did favour the very largest towns within the large centre category, and over the whole period considerably reduced the number of plants they were operating at any one time. In these ways the aggregate data fit the development sequence well.

It is not argued that these are the only regularities, but that they are the regularities that can be identified in the data available. Other constraints might well be more important than those discussed here; in particular an enterprise's organisational and spatial structures may influence adjustment behaviour, and only bivariate relationships have been examined. Some of the more complex inter-relationships emerge from the study of the adjustment process in the five core enterprises.

The Enterprises

In the small market system firms the post-merger adjustment problem was not particularly complex. The firm would face a retain/close decision rather than several plants from which to select an adjustment policy. Further, if only one or two firms were acquired over four or five years, they could be integrated slowly into the acquiring organisation. As shown earlier, these smaller firms were more likely to close plants than the core enterprises.

The problems the large industrial enterprise faced were more difficult. They often acquired many firms in quick succession, and time for reviewing and integrating operations was not always available; further, the enterprise frequently acquired several plants with one merger partner, and these plants of varying ages and locations needed careful assessment before any rationalisation strategy could be implemented.

All five large enterprises undertook adjustment of the distribution of their production capacity, and three introduced rationalisation policies in the last stages of the adjustment process. Since this account has focused on the location of brewing capacity rather than on ancillary features, such as malting, packaging, distribution or soft drinks activities, the policy of product specialisation is available only to a limited degree to the individual enterprise. Thus the basic problem is to identify the optimum number, size and location of plants.

The case studies show how the five enterprises adjusted these aspects of their activities. Some of the variations in their behaviour are brought out in the final section.

Allied Breweries

Adjustment within Allied Breweries presented few problems, as the very large regional concerns each provided a sufficient base for one or more major plants. Some early changes were undertaken by Ind Coope & Allsopp, who had by late 1958, reduced their 1951 total of seven plants to four (Figure 9.1), despite some acquisitions. The Plymouth and Burslem plants were early closures, as was the Liverpool plant closed in 1953. The reason for the latter closure was straightforward: it was to 'effect economies in production which would result from concentrating a larger proportion of group brewing at Burton'[15] and which would supply markets in Lancashire, Cheshire and North Staffordshire formerly served by Liverpool. Two plants acquired in the early 1950s (Shrewsbury and Watford) had contrasting fortunes. The Shrewsbury plant was closed before 1959, the Watford plant not until 1972.

The mergers between 1958 and 1963 added plants in Limehouse (London), Westerham, Brackley, Warrington, Leeds (2), Aston and Newport, increasing the number of production sites to a maximum of 12 in 1963. The plant numbers were reduced rapidly, only Warrington, Leeds and Aston still surviving in 1976. Adjustment not only closed the smaller plants, but expanded output in the four regional plants at Romford, Aston, Leeds and Warrington. At Romford a multi-purpose site was increasingly devoted to an enlarged brewing capacity, while in the mid-1960s new brew houses were built at Warrington and Leeds. In addition, at Burton-upon-Trent some £12 million was invested from 1968 to 1971, making it one of the largest UK plants in the industry – with a capacity of 2.5 million barrels, designed for increase to 4 million barrels for only another £5 million.[16] A £2.5 million Aston redevelopment project was announced in 1970.[17] Expansion in the plants was to meet increasing demand from 1961 onwards, and to take over production from closed plants. Watford's production, for example, was distributed between Burton and Romford.[18]

In these adjustments both land values and age of capital stock influenced the decision, but they were additional, though not crucial, factors. At Watford, for example, it was not 'economic to rebuild the 103-year-old brewery as it came to the end of its useful life',[19] but since Romford had already been selected as a major south-eastern production site the decision to close Watford

Figure 9.1: Locational Adjustment by Core Enterprises: Allied Breweries, 1951–76

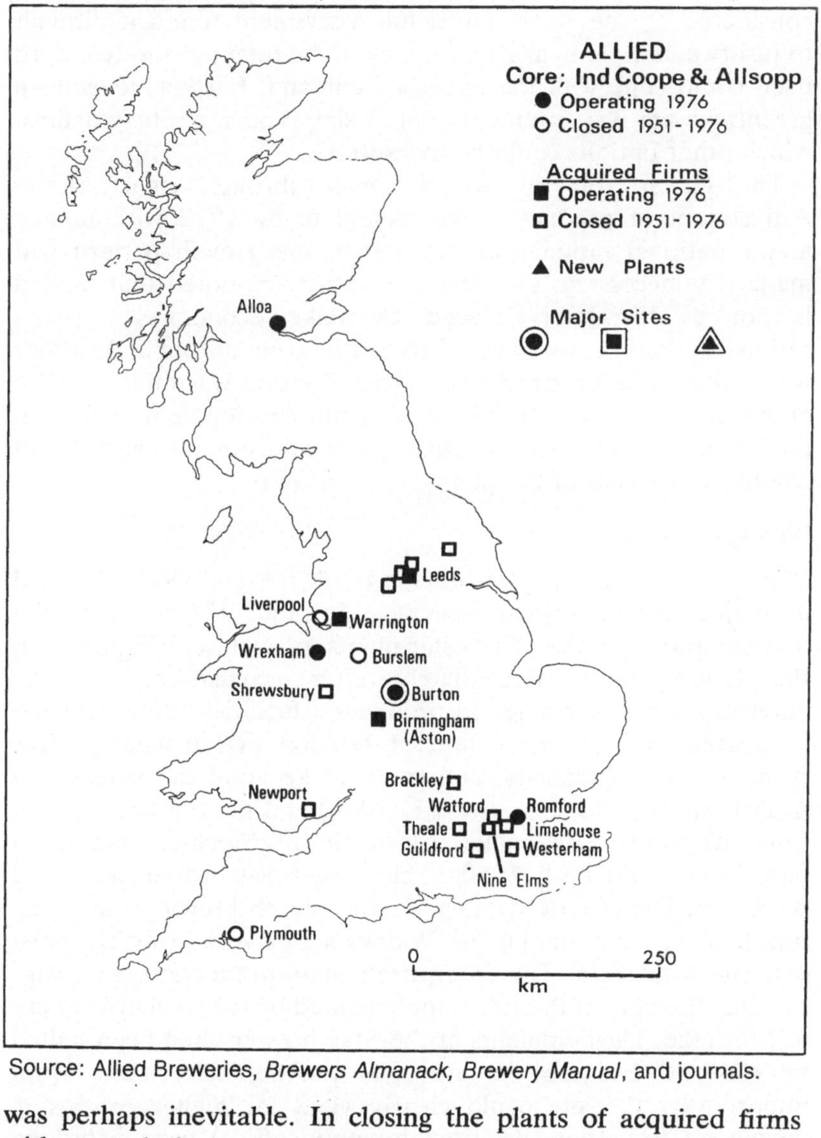

Source: Allied Breweries, *Brewers Almanack, Brewery Manual*, and journals.

was perhaps inevitable. In closing the plants of acquired firms with central city and peripheral sites, the city plant was closed first. The Nine Elms and Guildford plants (of Friary-Meux) were closed in 1964 and 1969 respectively, the Limehouse and Westerham plants (of Taylor-Walker) in 1960 and 1964, although a bad industrial relations record encouraged the Limehouse closure.

Plants acquired from major urban-based concerns, however, all permitted *in situ* expansion. A greenfield site west of London was considered at one stage, but a full assessment found it difficult to justify a new plant, as Romford was to be retained and Romford itself could cope with the increased demand. Further, it seems a greenfield site was often considered simply as a strategy against which other options could be measured.

The leader role of Allied comes through clearly here. Adjustment of production was complete by 1972 without any major national rationalisation scheme: the growth pattern had made it unnecessary. Financial commentators noted that 'Allied is not as favourably placed to make economies . . . [from rationalisation] . . . as some of its major competitors'.[20] In other words the scope for production rationalisation was minimal. The enterprise had gone the full cycle of the development sequence, market area extension and subsequent adjustments, and it had closed 80 per cent of the plants it had acquired.

Watney-Truman

Watney's piecemeal adjustments in the 1950s and 1960 preceded a major rationalisation scheme. In the 1950s both the Southampton and the Chichester plants were closed (Figure 9.2), the latter almost immediately after acquisition, but the enterprise's major change in production facilities came with the acquisition of a brewery in east London (Whitechapel). This plant had spare capacity, and could make good the inadequate facilities in the Mortlake (west London) and the Pimlico (central London) plants. The smaller Isleworth and Stockwell breweries had closed in the early 1950s. The merger was further motivated by the difficulties of owning a city centre brewing site. The problem was not unique to Watney's but was probably most extreme with them. The enterprise's main production sites were the Stag brewery in Pimlico, supplemented by the smaller brewery at Mortlake. Developments at the Stag brewery had been halted in 1949/50 because the site was proving too small. More importantly, the site could clearly yield far higher returns if developed for other (i.e. predominantly office) uses. Mortlake could provide some capacity increase, mainly by moving malting to East Anglia, but could not provide all the capacity lost when the Stag brewery closed. A greenfield plant was estimated to cost £4 million;[21] the only solution if the Stag site was to be sold was to merge with another firm, preferably one to the east to

Figure 9.2: Locational Adjustment by Core Enterprises: Watney-Truman, 1951–76

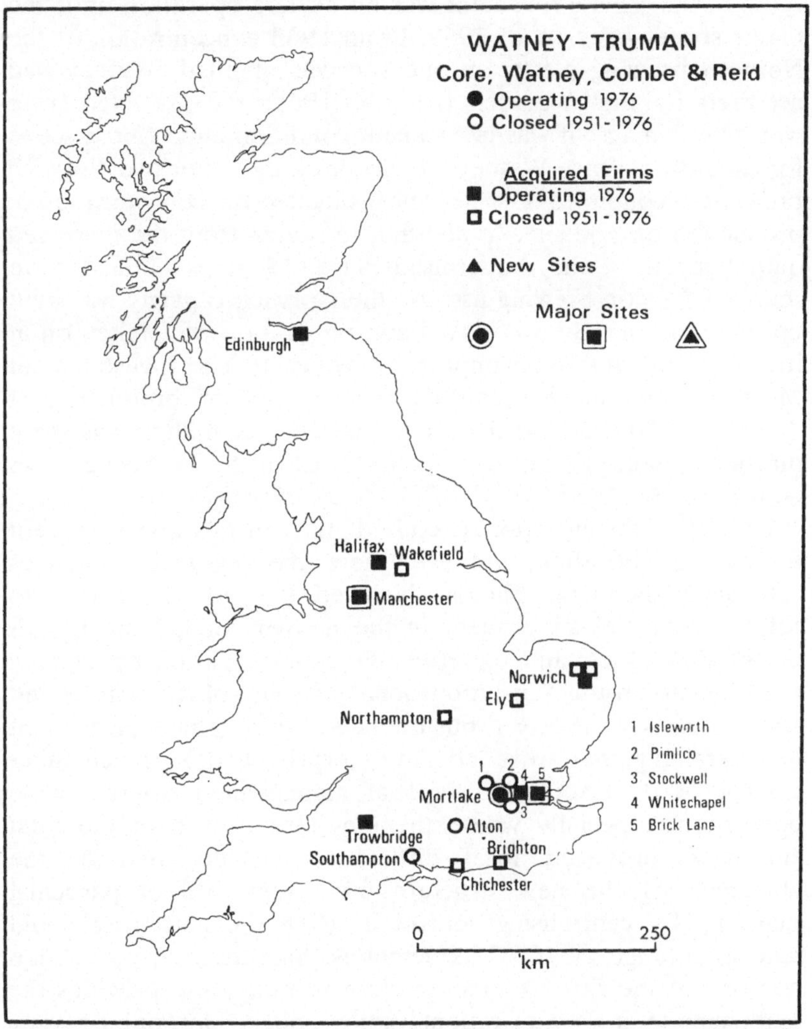

Source: Watney-Truman, *Brewers Almanack, Brewery Manual*, and journals.

complement Mortlake in the west. The merger with Mann in 1958 enabled brewing at Pimlico to cease, and the lease of the Stag site was sold for £2.75 million, most of this being put into capital investment at Mann's in Whitechapel and at Mortlake, the latter alone taking £1.5 million.

From 1959 to 1960, the city centre difficulties resolved, the Watney group turned to adjustment of their UK production facilities, which had been acquired through the spatial growth described earlier, the number of plants reaching a maximum of 12 in 1965. This adjustment was an ad hoc operation until the major strategy review of 1969. From 1963 concentration of the Norwich brewing plants on one site was planned. Watney had acquired its first Norwich plant in 1961; reconstructed after war-time damage, it was in excellent condition and offered scope for expansion. Once Watney had acquired the other two Norwich breweries economies-of-scale clearly dictated the concentration of production on one site. In addition to saving from the increased output levels of the modernised plant, 19 acres of land were released for non-brewing use. As the Norwich capacity was built up, the plant at Ely was closed and production was 'taken on at the Norwich and Northampton breweries'.[22] The investment at Mortlake eventually permitted phasing out of production at Alton in 1970,[23] and at the same time over £1 million was spent on the Edinburgh plant to cater for most of the Watney group's demand in Scotland.[24]

Until 1968 the enterprise exercised little central direction except for capital allocation, but even here the regional companies controlled spending. Thomas believed that the reluctance to rethink reflected an element in the mergers of helping friends out of difficulties, and therefore direct intervention by Watney was likely to arouse a disproportionate amount of resentment and resistance.[25] By the late 1960s the need for large new investment in several regional areas led the enterprise to take much fuller control of its resources. Regional management offered some opposition, especially where the long-term future of the total enterprise produced local difficulties; indeed, one of the objectives of the new structure was to get rid of parochial thinking. By centralising control in 1968 the enterprise could take long-range views of its activities. Significantly, production was one of the first to undergo close scrutiny, and provides the first example of a major rationalisation policy. This major review of production facilities was intended . . . 'to forecast demand ten years ahead and to give guidance as to the best size and location of our production and distribution facilities to meet this demand'.[26] The study, undertaken by the enterprise's Management Services section, examined production and distribution costs, minimising redundancies being an important constraint.

The review suggested that the 'least-cost solution would be the development over a period of years of major production centres at Mortlake . . . [and] Manchester'.[27] A future for Norwich and Edinburgh was, however, assured, although in part this was dictated by the earlier capital expenditure on those sites. The new Norwich plant began operation in 1971, and the other two Norwich plants were shut. Only one plant was recommended for immediate closure (Northampton); here economies-of-scale in production at Manchester, Mortlake and Norwich would offset increased distribution costs to the Midlands. The future of the other smaller plants was to be kept under review; and it was expected that when the £11 million Mortlake redevelopment was completed plants at Trowbridge, Brighton and Whitechapel would close. The expansion of Mortlake may seem strange considering the references to its 'limited capacity' in the 1950s. The changed evaluation of its potential reflected changed thinking in the industry as a whole. In the 1950s most plants had associated packaging facilities, in the 1960s major separate bottling and canning lines were well established, thus some functions could be removed from the Mortlake site to accommodate new brewing capacity. In addition to the Manchester and Mortlake plants, the enterprise has expanded the capacity of its Halifax site.

As Figure 9.2 shows, most of the plan has been implemented. The expanded Mortlake and Manchester plants were completed in the mid-1970s, and as new capacity came into use Northampton was shut in 1970, Brighton in 1973 and the Whitechapel plant was due for closure in 1977. The closure of Whitechapel was accelerated after the integration with Truman, as Truman had an under-utilised, but modern, 1 million barrel plant also in east London.[28] Only Trowbridge of the smaller plants still remains in operation, and the long-term objective is to operate only six plants.[29]

Courage

Courage by 1976 had acquired 19 plants to add to the two core units (Figure 9.3). In the mid-1950s five plants were operating, two in London, one in Alton, one in Maidstone and a smaller one at Kingston. Capacity acquired in Maidenhead and in Bexley was closed soon afterwards, while both the Kingston plant and one London plant were phased out, the latter in 1957. The 1960s

Figure 9.3: Locational Adjustment by Core Enterprises: Courage, 1951–76

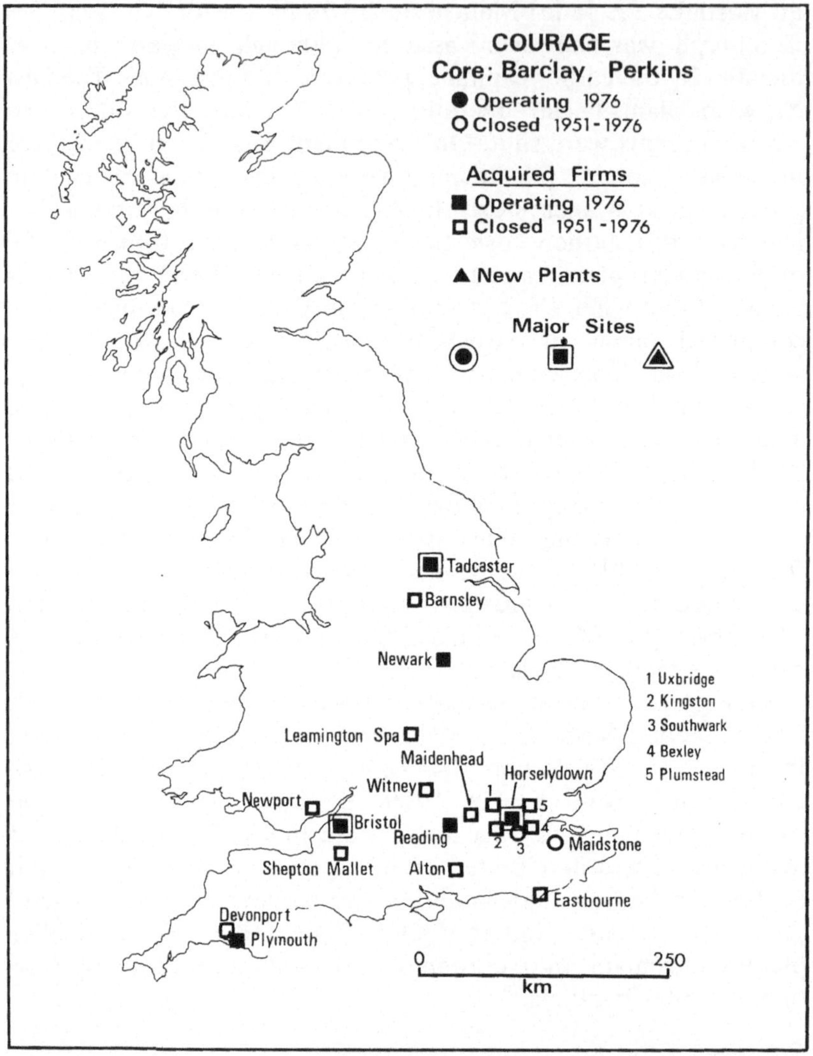

Source: Courage, *Brewers Almanack*, *Brewery Manual*, and journals.

expansion focused upon Horselydown and Bristol plants, with closures following the expansion of these two, the enterprise operating a maximum of 9 plants in 1963. In 1965 'the additional fermenting vessels in the Horselydown brewery . . . [were] . . . completed, which . . . enabled brewing at Maidstone to be discontinued and . . . [the] . . . brewery at Plumstead to be sold'.[30] Similarly in 1969, 'further fermenting capacity . . . was completed and Alton brewery . . . closed':[31] while, finally, the plant in Newport was closed as its capacity was replaced by Bristol.[32] Witney, Uxbridge and Eastbourne plants also closed in 1962, 1964 and 1967 respectively because of these investments in London and Bristol. So by early 1970 the enterprise had three major plants (two regional, one metropolitan) in Bristol, Reading and London, the latter having a capacity of over 1 million barrels. These plants were complemented by those in Newark and Devonport, the latter excellently illustrating the survival of a remote plant. Its value was recognised by the enterprise: 'Devonport is as far from Bristol as the latter is from London . . . yet it is still 80 miles [129 kms] from its farthest westerly delivery point at Penzance'.[33]

Up until 1969/70, although the group had planned and controlled production centrally, the general policy was for the regional subsidiaries to be self-sufficient in beer supplies, and the early adjustments were intra-regional. 1969, however, saw a 'thorough survey' of 'production plants . . . with special reference to the optimum means of providing future requirements'.[34] This scheme established the existing capacity of each brewery, and potential increases were worked out for London, Reading and Bristol, identifying possible stages in an expansion programme for each plant. These expansion stages were then related to sales forecasts and expansion plans drawn up for each of the three main plants. It was envisaged that the plants would be expanded in sequence, and consequently they would no longer be able to brew only for their local areas. For example, focusing expansion in period one on, say, Bristol might lead to a shortage in the London area; in a subsequent period priority for expansion in London might lead to shortages in the Bristol area. The chief change the report introduced was the introduction of group production planning (instead of plans for individual plants), and also, for the first time the group was able to quantify, on a comparable basis, the potential capacities of their different plants. This, of course, reflects a similar trend to centralisation as depicted in the Watney-Truman enterprise.

The report provided 'a firm foundation for future production planning'.[35] Yet over the next year or so the market area of the enterprise changed markedly, as was seen. Acquisition of another plant in the South West (Plymouth) permitted further rationalisation, and the Devonport plant was shut. Again age of capital stock was important. The newly acquired Regent Brewery had enjoyed capital expenditure shortly before acquisition, while the older Devonport plant needed more investment. Further, the site might have been vulnerable in the long term to the requirements of the nearby naval base. The plant was therefore closed in 1975. The merger with Smith's brought a two-plant firm, with sites in Tadcaster and Barnsley, into the enterprise. The inevitable phasing out of the smaller Barnsley plant took place in 1976. As the group Chairman noted, faced with major capital expenditure, the enterprise 'literally could not justify the expenditure of large amounts on two Yorkshire breweries so close to one another'.[36]

Rather like Allied and Watney, Courage were fortunate in being able to expand *in situ.* This was partly luck. For example, at Bristol they acquired 'a substantial site adjacent to the Bristol brewery which . . . [enabled] . . . modernisation and extension of existing production capacity to be carried out'.[37] Such expansion was not always straightforward. In London non-brewing activities were transferred from the Courage site to the Barclay Perkins site; some activities were transferred from Bristol to Avonmouth, and in the South East canning activities were undertaken at Alton.

Of all the sites Reading was the most restricted. In 1973 the enterprise announced a scheme to concentrate most of its production for the south of England in a greenfield complex somewhere between London and Reading. This appears to have originated in the 1969 rationalisation scheme, as sale of the Reading site was considered in the plan. The principal objective of a new site was to increase capacity as well as to achieve lower unit costs. It was envisaged the plant would come on-stream in the late 1970s.[38] In its final form this became a scheme to construct a new 1.5 million barrel complex on a site outside Reading. Although intended initially to give extra capacity and to replace the Reading plant, the site is big enough to take a much larger plant. A site further east might have provided for a more optimal distribution pattern, but increasingly there is competition for labour from London airport, and a Reading site can provide continuity of employment for employees, with little need for them to change place of residence or commuting patterns.

The Reading site is adjacent to an access point to the M4 motorway, and quite close to the existing Reading plant. Further north, the Tadcaster plant has considerable potential for expansion of brewing capacity. As indicated earlier, proximity to motorways appears also in the new complexes constructed by Bass-Charrington and Whitbread, and these enterprises are considered next.

Bass-Charrington

It was shown earlier how Bass-Charrington was built up from numerous firms, as a consequence acquiring 39 plants. The core firm, Hammonds, operated two main sites (Huddersfield and Tadcaster) and two smaller ones in 1951 (Figure 9.4). Of these smaller ones the Bradford plant was not closed till 1955, although closure had been planned since 1946 because of its congested central site.[39] Capacity was transferred to the two main plants. Southward expansion was followed quickly by closure of the Sheffield and Rotherham plants, as 'immediate steps were taken to absorb their production into the Tadcaster brewery';[40] but once major spatial growth was underway plant closures were infrequent. This reflected a conscious decision to go for spatial growth: as the Chairman explained at the end of 1961 'expansion must be the first aim in the conditions which surround our industry today; this means inevitably a period of organisational indigestion . . . the planning of long term benefits through expansion must, for a time, outstrip the benefits of rationalisation'.[41] Nevertheless some closures and expansions took place. In 1966, for example, 'the new brewhouse at Tadcaster was completed',[42] while in 1964 an enlarged Heriot Brewery had been opened in Edinburgh. As new capacity came on-stream so the improved facilities enabled the enterprise to 'shut down some of the older smaller breweries'.[43] Examples are Brighton, Hull, Yeovil and Derby, closed in 1963/4, the beers being produced 'from larger and more economical plants'.[44]

The merger with Bass, Mitchells & Butlers brought an already rationalised set of production sites into the enterprise. Indeed, Bass conducted the earliest major review of production patterns. In 1961/2 there had been 'a comprehensive survey by outside experts into the production methods, capacity, and efficiency ratings of all the breweries in the group . . . [focusing] . . . attention on possible operational economies'.[45] The chief result

Figure 9.4: Locational Adjustment by Core Enterprises: Bass-Charrington, 1951–76

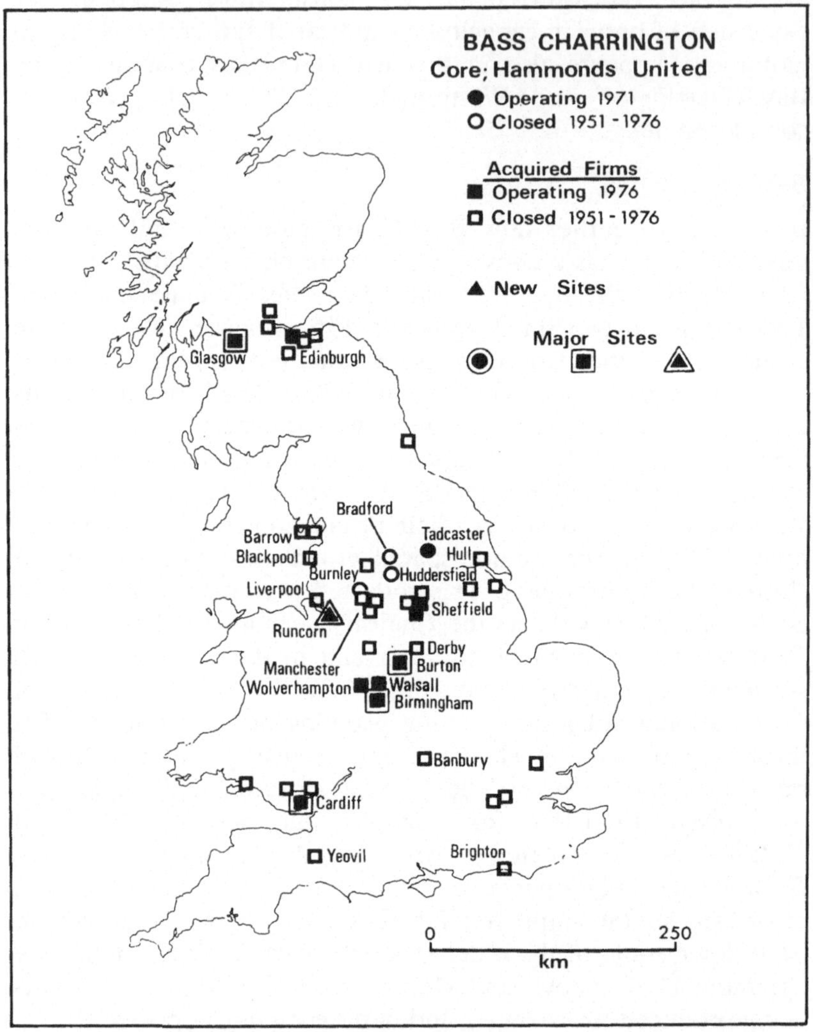

Source: Bass-Charrington, *Brewers Almanack, Brewery Manual* and journals.

was to concentrate the Burton-upon-Trent brewing plants on to one major site,[46] and in 1967/8 the rebuilt brewery was opened.

The merger of Charrington-United with Bass, Mitchells & Butlers brought valuable new expertise into the core enterprise. Taylor was an ideal generator of growth but not particularly interested in integrating the acquired plants into the enterprise's spatial structure, and it was left with a tremendous production rationalisation problem. The Bass, Mitchells & Butlers experience of rationalisation was utilised almost immediately with the setting up of the '1982 Committee' to prepare a production/distribution plan for 1982.

Before the plan was announced a change in the organisational structure concentrated production in a separate company, Bass-Charrington Production Ltd. This change, of course, parallels that made by Watney-Truman and by Courage. The rationalisation scheme emerged in 1970, when the number of the enterprise's plants was at its maximum, 20 (excluding Northern Ireland). It was the result of 'several years study of brewing techniques and changing patterns of the retail trade'.[47] A distinctive feature was the inclusion of a greenfield site. Four main sites were selected for expansion – Runcorn, Burton, Birmingham and Cardiff,[48] the last three being existing sites having room for expansion.

The purpose was to minimise production costs in the largest possible plant, subject to market constraint. Marketing considerations were expected to ensure the survival of at least one plant in Wales and in Scotland; in Scotland two plants were retained, as the smaller Heriot plant in Edinburgh had been recently modernised. In England it was decided to close all 'outdated' or 'poorly positioned' plants.[49] The most unusual aspect was to cease production in the South East. The London plant occupied a restricted site, but it had purchased, prior to acquisition, land at Silvertown (London) on which to build a new plant. Assessment of distribution costs from this relatively central site suggested it would be cheaper to supply the South East from a West Midlands plant, and possibly from the new Runcorn site.

Choice of a Runcorn location for the new plant emerged from the existing situation. A major new brewing complex was clearly necessary, partly because the enterprise's acquisitions had brought small plants with limited potential for expansion. A northern location was expected to give water and effluent costs significantly less than in the South. It then became a question of finding an available 100-acre site in proximity to a motorway. This was found at Runcorn, which had the additional advantage that the enterprise's existing plants in the region occupied particularly difficult sites. The new Runcorn plant has a capacity of 2.5 million barrels, but is designed for expansion up to 3.6

million.[50]

Since 1970 five plants in the North West (Barrow, Liverpool, Manchester, Burnley and Blackpool) have been closed, while the Birmingham plant has taken on most of the production for the South East. Not all small plants have closed. The Edinburgh plant has been cited; another example is the Hope & Anchor plant in Sheffield, which had been built on an entirely new site just before the outbreak of World War II. Possibly its relatively new construction encouraged survival; in the survival of these two plants age of capital stock again appears important. The group has also retained three small plants, at Wolverhampton, Walsall and Sheffield.

The scale of the rationalisation changes is reflected in a doubling of the enterprise's mean plant size and the reduction of plants from 20 to 11 between 1970 and 1976.

The enterprises discussed so far all experienced spatial growth at an early stage, but with Whitbread the spatial outcomes of locational adjustment had, by 1976, been less well marked.

Whitbread

Not surprisingly, Whitbread, occupying a satellite role in spatial growth, has a similar position in locational adjustment which, indeed, partly explains why it operates so many more plants than the other enterprises. There seems also, however, still to be a feeling that some advantages lie with the smaller plants. Col. Whitbread in fact admitted he was reluctant to close plants, as it was 'most important to retain the prestige, tradition, and goodwill of the merged firms'.[51]

Overall, in the early 1960s adjustment of production patterns was not a Whitbread goal. Perhaps growth seemed vital, and any available capital went into acquisition rather than rationalisation. In 1964 the enterprise admitted that it had been its policy not to concentrate 'their production in one large brewery but to dispose it into efficient reasonably sized units throughout the country. The result of this has been that in the event of a merger we have seldom closed a brewery'.[52] It did not reach its peak plant number (22) until 1967/8. Nevertheless, as Figure 9.5 shows, numerous plants have been closed. In the later period, plants acquired were placed in one of two categories, immediate closure or retention for at least five years. Yet, as with Bass-Charrington in the early 1960s, Whitbread felt in 1969 that 'with so many

Figure 9.5: Locational Adjustment by Core Enterprises: Whitbread, 1951–76

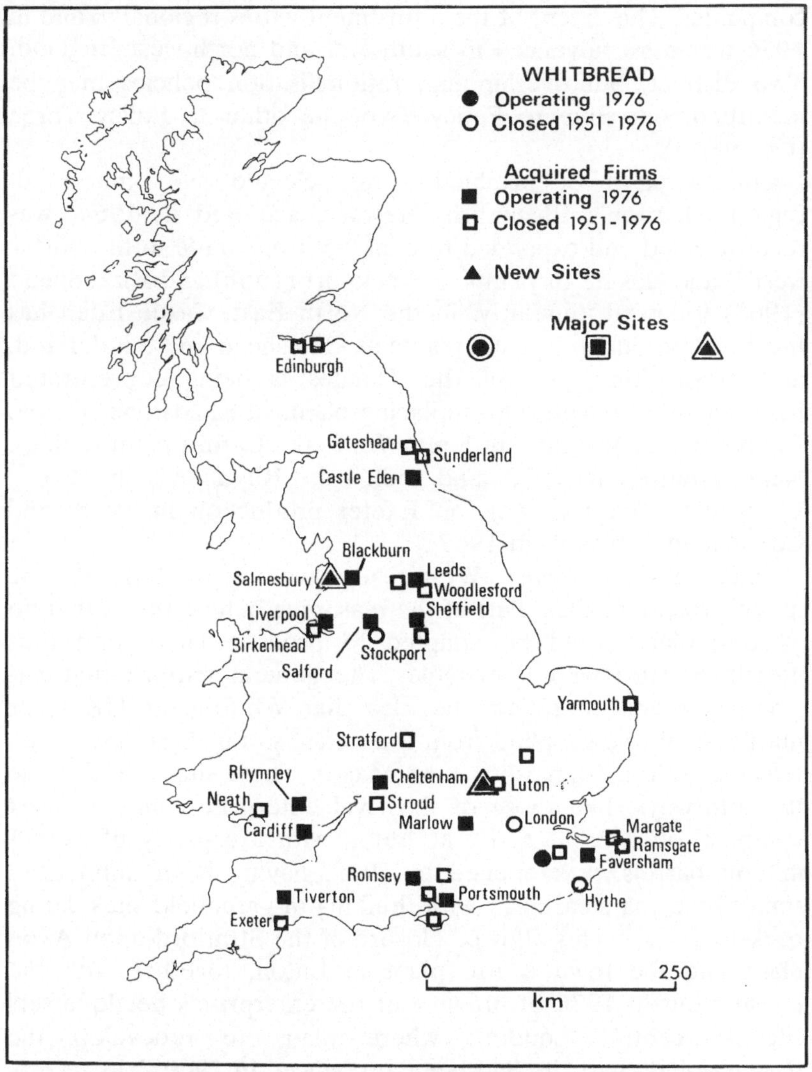

Source: Whitbread, *Brewers Almanack, Brewery Manual*, and journals.

companies coming into [the enterprise], it . . . needs continual reorganisation, especially in production, distribution and management'.[53]

After the mid-1960s, adjustment began within a regional framework, probably reflecting the fact that Whitbread is probably the least centralised of the five enterprises, with production and distribution closely integrated within regional companies. The extent of the adjustment varies regionally, and in 1976 was most advanced in south-east and north-west England. Two distinct, but overlapping, rationalisation policies may be identified, one akin to Policy Two, the other to Policy Three (Chapter 5).

Concentration of production on selected sites marks all regions. Dutton's Blackburn Brewery, acquired in 1964, was reconstructed and expanded to deal 'with our trade in the north-west'[54] and closure of plants at Stockport (1965) and Birkenhead (1968) followed. Similarly, in the North East, Castle Eden has taken on production of the plants at Gateshead and Sunderland, and production south of the Thames is being concentrated increasingly at Faversham, replacing plants at Maidstone, Hythe, Ramsgate and Margate. In South Wales the Cardiff plant took on Neath's output in 1972, and took over Rhymney's in 1978.[55] Elsewhere, Tiverton took on Exeter production in 1968, and Cheltenham, Stroud's in 1967.

Since 1969, however, Whitbread have favoured developing major greenfield sites. Part of the reasoning behind this is that no existing plant could be adapted to produce lager, and thus greenfield sites were inevitable. The general pattern that has emerged seems to reflect the idea that Whitbread's UK lager market could be supplied from four sites; so far three have been selected, Luton, Salmesbury and Magor. These sites are all close to motorways, like those of the rival enterprises, and the first complex, on a 25-acre site at Luton with a capacity of over 1 million barrels, was opened in 1969, having been announced some three years earlier,[56] with thinking of greenfield sites dating back to 1963.[57] This allowed closure of the Stratford-upon-Avon plant and the town centre plant at Luton, together with the phasing out in 1976 of brewing at the enterprise's headquarters site in central London, where plans to redevelop the six-and-a-half-acre site had been announced in 1969.[58]

In 1972 the Salmesbury plant on a 55-acre site in the North West was opened. This was intended to replace three older plants in the area,[59] but with rapidly growing demand for lager Salmesbury was devoted to lager production and the older plants retained. The third plant, at Magor in South Wales, is expected to begin production in the late 1970s. Although this has been announced as a lager plant, it offers scope for concentrating production in the South West and Wales on a single site.

Despite its greenfield sites Whitbread still does not have a fully rationalised pattern of plants, and has not at any stage announced a formal rationalisation strategy. Adjustments appear to take place within a regional framework. Plant closures accelerated in the late 1960s, one in 1967, but four in 1968 and seven in 1969. Indeed, the number of closures in 1969 led to a questioning within the enterprise as to 'whether we are not going too fast with the closure of breweries and depots'.[60]

Inter-Enterprise Contrasts

An overview of the activities described in the five cases brings out some interesting contrasts in the number of plants acquired, the number still operating and their mean size. Table 9.4 summarises these first two contrasts.

The striking difference in the number of plants acquired can be explained by their roles and behaviour in the interaction process during spatial growth. Allied, Watney-Truman and Courage acquired between 14 and 19 plants; Whitbread and Bass-Charrington 35 to 39 plants. This difference reflects the satellite role of Whitbread and the competitive behaviour of Bass-Charrington, discussed in the last chapter.

A rather different grouping of enterprises appears if one considers the current number of plants operated. Table 7.3 showed that, except for Whitbread, all the enterprises operate between 6 and 11 plants, Whitbread operating significantly more at 17. Whitbread clearly has room for further adjustment of its production units, again partly reflecting its later entry into the spatial growth process.

The most marked changes have been implemented by the

Table 9.4: Enterprises and Plant Closures, 1952–76

	Core Plants	Closures		Acquired Plants	Closures	
		Number	Per Cent		Number	Per Cent
Allied	7	3	42.8	16	13	81.3
Watney-Truman	6	5	83.3	14	7	50.0
Courage	2	2	100.0	19	13	68.4
Whitbread	4	3	75.0	35	21	60.0
Bass-Charrington	4	3	75.0	39	28	71.8

leaders in the spatial growth process: Allied has closed the highest proportion of acquired sites, and Bass-Charrington almost three-quarters. Allied's position is perhaps not surprising, since its spatial expansion was essentially complete by the mid-1960s, but the Bass-Charrington achievement is more spectacular, as it has had to deal with many more plants, and indicates the efficiency of its rationalisation strategy.

Perhaps the most striking differences are those in plant sizes of the groups, given that a plant of minimum efficient scale should now probably produce over 1 million barrels. Table 9.5 shows estimates of plant capacity and mean plant size. The figures are estimates only but, while the absolute figures are liable to error, the relative size of the plants and output appears to be reasonably accurate. Just as Allied took the leader role in spatial growth, these plant size figures suggest that with a mean size of plant 50 per cent larger than that of the others it has succeeded best in concentrating production in a few large plants. Bass-Charrington, Courage and Watney-Truman have similar-sized plants, but Whitbread's satellite role is reflected here too. On average its plant size is half that of three of the enterprises, and only one-third the size of Allied plants. The mean figures, of course, tend to hide the fact that Whitbread operates two plants with over a million barrels capacity at Luton and Salmesbury and that Bass-Charrington's figures are inflated by the two very large plants at Warrington and Burton-upon-Trent.

The mean size may seem small when set against the very largest 2.5-million-barrel plant, but they are large when compared with the mean size, only 0.06 million barrels, for market system firms.

Table 9.5: Enterprise Output and Mean Plant Size, 1976

Enterprise	Output (millions of barrels)	Mean Output per Plant, 1976
Allied Breweries	6.19	0.88
Bass-Charrington	7.17	0.60
Watney-Truman	4.89	0.61
Courage	3.59	0.59
Whitbread	4.89	0.28

Sources: Outpu⁺ estimated for 1976 from A.J. Cockerill, 'The Merger Movement in the Brewing Industry', *Journal of Industrial Affairs*, 4, 1976, p. 14; and Anon, Brewing and the UK Beer Market, Part I', *Retail Business*, 174, p. 21.

These comparative data on differences in plant numbers and plant size of enterprises indicate that one possible spatial outcome of the interaction process is major contrasts in plant size and number between leader and satellite enterprises, and different plant numbers have produced different overall patterns (summarised in Figure 7.2). In the long run, as all enterprises move towards an optimum production strategy, these differences may disappear, but since the long run may reach thirty years the interaction process is helpful in explaining such contrasts as do exist at any particular time.

Chapter 5 argued that the detailed form of locational adjustment patterns reflected the potential of existing sites, an enterprise's spatial structure and its organisational structure. These elements have been illustrated clearly in the preceding cases. Wherever possible the enterprises have expanded *in situ*, and if necessary non-brewing operations were removed to other sites. This was so for Allied, Watney-Truman and Courage. The effects of alternative uses for brewing sites emerge most clearly in Watney-Truman and Whitbread, though hints of their influence appear also in the other three. The strength with which enterprises are tied to existing sites is seen most clearly in the very small number of greenfield developments.

Part of the reason for this behaviour is the character of the physical plant and equipment occupying the site. The influence of the age of capital stock is seen both in closure and in retention decisions. As has been shown, the older run-down plants become sites for closure, whereas quite small plants with modern equipment are retained, and may even receive further modernisation. Although it has been possible to examine only this one characteristic of an enterprise's spatial structure, its importance in influencing the pattern of spatial change is clear.

In the final stages of the adjustment process rationalisation of plants required the necessary organisational structure to permit recognition of needs and implementation of non-programmed decisions. The general tendency in the 1950s and early 1960s was to control acquired firms through holding companies (cf. Figure 2.5). This was followed by geographical divisions, and then in the late 1960s by increased emphasis on centralisation. Allied and Watney's were the leaders. In 1968 'all production was concentrated under one company'.[61] Allied Breweries (Production) Ltd was established, but regional names, such as

Tetley and Ansell, for example, were retained for marketing purposes. In Watney-Mann, after the centralisation of control functions the group, as was shown, achieved an overview of its production activities. The change in Bass-Charrington came slightly later, when an 'organisation with direct responsibility for brewing, processing and packaging' was set up.[62] Courage began centralised production planning in 1969/70, but Whitbread's still has a strong regional emphasis, with each regional company seen as a separate profit centre.

An important consequence of the relatively late change in the organisational structures is that rationalisation policies, which replaced piecemeal adjustments, began to appear only in the late 1960s and the major changes came after 1970. Probably recognition of the need to co-ordinate and integrate production facilities nationally was a prime factor encouraging the structural reorganisation, the new flow of information within the enterprise permitting the development of corporate rationalisation policies. To Allied this was of little importance: Allied had adjusted its production patterns adequately within a decentralised framework. Nevertheless, it perhaps indicated to the other enterprises the direction in which a move was desirable.

Most of the adjustments, and the sub-set of activities called rationalisation, concentrated upon the selective expansion of existing sites, Policy Two of the rationalisation policies discussed in Chapter 5. Whitbread, however, which in growth and adjustment occupied a satellite role, took a leader role in developing greenfield complexes. As shown in the case study, it first began to think of these in 1963 and will shortly have three in action. This may give it greater adaptability to cope with future change, and thus justify its decision to build 'the first [large] brewery . . .[to be] . . . built on a completely new site in the British Isles for many years'.[63]

Conclusion

In these three chapters the spatial outcomes of the evolution of large industrial brewing enterprises in the United Kingdom have been explored against concepts discussed in earlier chapters. Of course it has not been possible to examine all aspects of the spatial behaviour of large industrial enterprises in this limited context. These limitations flow partly from data problems which excluded study of linkages, and partly from the nature of the industry, which consisted of enterprises that had grown primarily through external methods.

Nevertheless the spatial behaviour of these large enterprises is responsible for many changes in the location of the industry's plant. Change has not resulted from the behaviour of myriads of independent actors, as is characteristic of the market system, but from the growth of large enterprises seeking merger partners over increasing distances, acquiring plants over greater distances than market system firms and also extending their plant space by larger steps to build up multi-regional, multi-plant concerns. They then proceeded to adjust their production patterns, at first *ad hoc* and then as part of structured rationalisation policies. The net result was the survival and expansion of selected plants in larger towns with a concomitant closure of plants in medium-size towns; surprisingly, plants in small centres were not more likely to close than those in medium and large towns taken together. The large enterprises were more likely to retain a plant after acquisition than the market system firms, and consequently they contributed less to closures than their market system partners. Nevertheless they were a major force in the upward shift in mean plant size. Underlying the whole of this process of change was the interaction process characteristic of many large industrial enterprises which operate in oligopolistic environments. Here the roles and behaviour patterns, over the past twenty-five years, appear to have influenced the present contrasts in the enterprises, which express themselves in plants of varying size and varying numbers. This interaction process was seen in both spatial growth and locational adjustment by the enterprises.

Notes

1. A. Cockerill, 'The Merger Movement in the Brewing Industry', *Journal of Industrial Affairs*, 4, 1976, pp. 12–13.
2. A. Cockerill and G. Rainnie, *Economies of Scale in the Brewing Industry: A Comparative Study*. Unpublished manuscript, c. 1968.
3. A. Cockerill, 'The Merger Movement', p. 12.
4. J. Vaizey, *The Brewing Industry, 1886–1951*, 1960, London, pp. 94–5.
5. A. Cockerill and G. Rainnie, *Economies of Scale*.
6. C.F. Pratten, *Economies of Scale in Manufacturing Industry*, 1971, Cambridge, pp. 72-6.
7. Cockerill and Rainnie, *Economies of Scale.*
8. Cockerill, 'The Merger Movement', p. 16, fn 14.
9. H.D. Watts, 'Market Areas and Spatial Rationalisation: the British Brewing

Industry After 1945', *Tijdschrift voor Economische en Sociale Geografie*, 68, 1977, pp. 224–40.

10. J. Mark, 'The British Brewing Industry', *Lloyds Bank Review*, 112, 1974, p. 36.
11. Ministry of Transport, *Survey of Road Goods Transport, 1962. Final Results: Geographical Analysis*, 1966, London, p. 98.
12. Watts, 'Market Areas and Spatial Rationalisation', p. 236.
13. R.C. Riley, 'The Brewing Industry', in R.C. Riley, *Industrial Geography*, 1973, London, pp. 149–67.
14. H.D. Watts, 'The Character and Origin of Industry in a Rural Area', *Yorkshire Bulletin of Economic and Social Research*, 18, 1968, pp. 120-31; H.D. Watts, 'The Industrial Journey to Work in a Rural Area', *Journal of the Town Planning Institute*, 54, 1968, pp. 79–80.
15. *Brewers Guardian*, Feb. 1953, p. 48.
16. *Financial Times*, 16 June 1971.
17. *Financial Times*, 2 Feb. 1970.
18. *The Times*, 18 Sept. 1970.
19. Ibid.
20. *Guardian*, 6 Jan. 1971.
21. *The Economist*, 190, 1959, p. 539.
22. Watney-Mann, *Report and Accounts, 1967.*
23. Watney-Mann, *Report and Accounts, 1968.*
24. Watney-Mann, *Report and Accounts, 1969.*
25. D. Thomas, 'What Watney's Wants', *Management Today*, May 1971, pp. 58–69.
26. Watney-Mann, *Report and Accounts, 1969.*
27. Watney-Mann, *Report and Accounts, 1970.*
28. *Investor's Chronicle*, 17 Mar. 1972, p. 856.
29. *Guardian*, 17 Oct. 1973.
30. Courage, Barclay & Simonds, *Report and Accounts, 1965.*
31. Courage, Barclay & Simonds, *Report and Accounts, 1969.*
32. Ibid.
33. *Brewers Guardian*, Feb. 1962, p. 61.
34. Courage, Barclay & Simonds, *Report and Accounts, 1970.*
35. Ibid.
36. *Guardian*, 19 May 1973.
37. Courage, Barclay & Simonds, *Report and Accounts, 1964.*
38. *Financial Times*, 25 Aug. 1973.
39. *Brewers Guardian*, Feb. 1955, p. 4.
40. Hammonds United Breweries, *Report and Accounts, 1956.*
41. Charrington-United, *Report and Accounts, 1961.*
42. Charrington-United, *Report and Accounts, 1966.*
43. Charrington-United, *Report and Accounts, 1963.*
44. Charrington-United, *Report and Accounts, 1964.*
45. Bass, Mitchells & Butlers, *Report and Accounts, 1962.*
46. Bass, Mitchells & Butlers, *Report and Accounts, 1963.*
47. Bass-Charrington, *Report and Accounts, 1970.*
48. *The Times*, 9 Apr. 1970.
49. Bass-Charrington, *Report and Accounts, 1970.*
50. *North West and North Wales Industrial Review*, 2, Mar./Apr. 1972, p. 48.
51. Whitbread, *Report and Accounts, 1962.*
52. Whitbread, *Report and Accounts, 1963.*
53. Whitbread, *Report and Accounts, 1969.*
54. Whitbread, *Report and Accounts, 1966.*

55. *Guardian*, 22 Oct. 1977.
56. Whitbread, *Report and Accounts, 1965.*
57. Whitbread, *Report and Accounts, 1963.*
58. *The Times*, 9 Dec. 1969.
59. *Guardian*, 24 Jan. 1973.
60. Whitbread, *Report and Accounts, 1968.*
61. Allied Breweries, *Report and Accounts, 1969.*
62. Bass-Charrington, *Report and Accounts, 1970.*
63. Whitbread, *Report and Accounts, 1968.*

Part Four

SPATIAL POLICY IMPLICATIONS

10 ENTERPRISES, CITY–SYSTEMS AND REGIONS

Large industrial enterprises, or large organisations in general are thought to have a major influence on the differential growth of regions and of cities, and on the mix of economic and social activities within them. Attention to the non-industrial context in which an enterprise is working considerably widens the scope of the study. It particularly overlaps with the analysis of city-systems, recently summarised by Pred,[1] and with the closely related study of communications and office location typified by the work of Goddard[2] and Daniels.[3] Clearly, this extensive literature cannot be summarised here; instead, some of the more important relationships between large enterprises and city-systems and regions are described.

The widespread linkages of large industrial enterprises make it difficult to view large industrial enterprises solely in an intra-regional context, as 'the regional framework does not correspond to [a] firm's action space'.[4] Two examples illustrate this point. In the case of Boeing only 10 per cent of its processing sector inputs come from the immediate vicinity of the plant (the Puget Sound area) and developments at Boeing contributed importantly to expansion at Hartford, over 3000 km from Washington State.[5] The Chrysler plant in Linwood, Scotland, is similar. True this is a branch plant established in an area with no tradition of motor vehicle manufacture, but only 4.5 per cent of purchases of vendor supplied parts come from within the region and only 14 per cent from within 322 km.[6]

Warneryd argued that the growth of enterprises of this kind was part of the 'organisational changes in society [which] lead to increases in the mutual dependence between separate regions'.[7] This chapter recognises the importance of this mutual dependence and begins by examining the nature of city-systems, the present distribution of control functions within them and the recent trends in the location of such functions within the system. The second part examines the evidence for and against spatial bias in the behaviour of large enterprises, and considers its implications for the central and peripheral parts of the city-system. Finally, some of the social implications of the spatial behaviour of large industrial enterprises are examined.

Centralisation of Control

A concise definition of a city-system is

> a set of cities which are interdependent in such a way that any significant change in the economic activities, employment structure, total income and/or population in one member city will directly or indirectly bring about some alteration in the economic activities, occupational structure, total income, and/or population of one or more other set members.[8]

The spatial structures of city-systems and those of large industrial enterprises are not dissimilar. In both, a hierarchy of units exists. This was seen in the spatial structure of an enterprise (Chapter 2), and it is widely accepted as a characteristic of the urban system. Further, it is usually assumed that in both systems information flows down the hierarchy from larger to smaller units, although a counter-flow allows higher levels of the hierarchy to supervise or monitor the performance at the lower levels. It is the spatial coincidence of these two hierarchies, or the lack of it, that affects the way in which large industrial enterprises impinge on city-system development. The possible inter-relationships between city-systems and enterprises were explored initially by Warneryd, whose ideas have been developed extensively by Pred.[9] Their basic argument is that where there is a one-to-one correspondence, or something approaching it, between the hierarchical structures of enterprise and city-systems cumulative advantages accrue to the first ranking city centre because it receives an increasing share of the control functions of large industrial enterprises.

The links between an enterprise's sites and the links between the different parts of a city-system are made up partly of the physical flow of products and materials, and partly of flows of information. The latter are thought to have most influence on city-system development. This influence comes not from the day-to-day routine items transmitted by letter, telephone or telex associated usually with programmed decisions, but from the flows resulting in face-to-face contact external to an individual's place of work and concerned with non-programmed decisions. Tornqvist argues rightly that the routine contacts 'are probably scarcely capable of affecting the location of ... activities' and that 'it is only the direct personal contacts which have a perceptible influence on the location of activities and therefore also on the regional development of employment'.[10] As was shown earlier it is these face-to-face contacts associated with non-programmed decisions that are found primarily in an enterprise's control units.

The extent of the centralisation of the control functions of large industrial enterprises can be assessed at the simplest level by either examining the inter-regional distribution of head-offices or, rather less satisfactorily, by examining the degree to which manufacturing employment in a region is in plants owned by firms based outside that region. In this context emphasis is placed on the former, partly because the evidence relates directly to large industrial enterprises rather than to all firms and partly because the evidence relating to external ownership is available only for a few regions.[11] Whatever form of evidence is used it must be paralleled by an assessment of the extent to which the concentration of head-offices is a reasonable indicator of the degree of centralisation of control functions.

The evidence in Chapter 2 showed that because of their contact-intensive functions the control units (in this case head-offices) have special locational requirements. As has been shown earlier although operating functions are spread widely through the city-system, control units are not — they are located primarily in the highest ranking centres in the city-system. In the United Kingdom of the 100 largest industrial enterprises 80 have their head-offices in the South East; in France just over 90 of the 100 largest manufacturing organisations had their head-offices in Paris. These are the two extreme cases. The dominance is less marked elsewhere, and indeed in the larger space economy of the United States the headquarters of the top 500 manufacturing organisations are spread over 29 metropolitan complexes, but the manufacturing belt had over 60 per cent of the headquarters.[12] The reasons for these concentrations have already been discussed.

Even among firms with control units outside the highest ranking centre, non-routine business activities are focused upon that part of the urban system. Tornqvist found that in Sweden about half the head-office contacts of three non-Stockholm firms were with the town in which they were located, but the remaining contacts were not principally with the nearest large towns but with the centre with the highest contact potential (Stockholm). The data disaggregated by job level showed the contacts of the higher-status jobs were characterised by more links with Stockholm or overseas than lower-status jobs.[13] Should this be a general feature of contact patterns, flows of information and the information fields of the decision makers in high-status positions can be influenced by the location of the dominant parts of the urban system.

Cumulative advantages of the contact-intensive parts of the urban system result in an increasing concentration of control units in them. This can be traced in the United Kingdom in the data for the 100 largest industrial enterprises between 1969/70 and 1976/7. Over this period (Table 10.1) the expected fall in the number of control units in the periphery paralleled a rise in the number of units in the principal metropolitan region (South East).

The concentration of control functions in selected parts of the city-system is emphasised further by the rate of change in the numbers employed in contact-intensive functions. In many industrial enterprises the manpower engaged in production is falling, reflecting increased automation and increased productivity, but the contact-intensive functions, such as information and public relations, planning and administration of group training programmes, are growing. This growth rate varies between enterprises, being partly dependent upon the technology the enterprise employs. Since many of these contact-intensive functions are head-office located, growth in their numbers is indicative of growth in head-office employment.

Table 10.1: Head-Offices of the 100 Largest UK Industrial Enterprises by Turnover, 1969/70 and 1976/7

	South East	Rest of Centre	Periphery
1969/70	72	10	18
1976/77	80	9	11

Note: The areas are defined in Table 2.4.
Source: *The Times 500, 1969–70*, *The Times 1000*, *1976–7*.

This growth is influenced further by increases in related personnel for monitoring (market research) and processing (computer specialists) information.[14] The change in emphasis within an enterprise need not promote changes in the number of its sites but may well encourage a decline in the work-force at some sites and a parallel increase elsewhere.

The constituents of this kind of pattern can be seen in numerous enterprises. It was illustrated in the brewing enterprises discussed in Chapter 8, and some further examples are now presented. Unilever, with 60 per cent of its manual jobs located in Assisted (i.e. peripheral) Areas of the United Kingdom in 1972, had only 40 per cent of its other jobs in these areas. As the enterprise reports, 'head-offices and the newer research establishments are heavily concentrated in the South. Many Unilever companies, including nearly all the largest, even those with a high proportion of plant capacity located in the assisted areas, have their head-offices in London and the Home Counties.'[15] Similarly, data for the Swedish firm of Pripp-Bryggerierna (Table 10.2) indicate this trend: management, office and technical workers are over-represented in either Goteborg or Stockholm. In North America, Pred shows that jobs in plants owned by the 100 largest manufacturing enterprises in several metropolitan centres were (with the exception of New York) in plants owned by enterprises based outside the city in which the plants were located. In Buffalo, the most extreme case examined, 95 per cent of such jobs were owned by enterprises based elsewhere in the United States.[16]

Table 10.2: Regional Distribution of the Employees of Pripp-Bryggerierna AB., 1965

Region	Labourers	Management	Office	Technical
	Percentage of each group			
Malmo	19	14	14	9
Goteborg	21	26	22	*49*
Norrkopping	8	6	8	4
Eskilot	15	11	12	4
Stockholm	33	*39*	*42*	30
Falun	4	4	2	4

Source: S. Follin and I. Uvebrant, *Fran ab Pripp and Lyckholm till Pripp-Bryggerierna AB.*, 1967, p. 58.

That these patterns are characteristic of large industrial enterprises emerged from Figure 2.6 which showed the over-concentration of white-collar (control) jobs in south-east England for the 13 largest industrial enterprises in the United Kingdom.

All the evidence clearly demonstrates that large enterprises do concentrate many of their higher-level activities in the central parts of the city-system, and that many production sites are located some way from the head-office of the enterprise which owns them. What the evidence does not do is to indicate the extent to which the head-offices constrain plant behaviour. As Tomkins and Lovering point out, the location of 'real control . . . does not ultimately depend upon the location of the head-office'[17] but on the extent to which head-offices in centres outside the region regard their regional establishments as near autonomous profit or investment centres. The extent to which a head-office location reflects the location of control may vary from one economy to another. In North America highly centralised control appears to be common but Granick provides evidence of an independent role for lower-level managers in the UK system. He concluded from a study of an admittedly small number of large industrial enterprises in the United Kingdom that 'managerial weakness in decision making seems to be displayed primarily at the central level of the companies . . . top company managements were characterised by the avoidance of decisions in general, and particularly by the avoidance of such decisions as would have required major alteration in the way that their companies' affairs were conducted'.[18]

Some authorities have explored the overall degree of plant autonomy, most of the evidence being drawn from regions where the plants were owned by firms based outside the region. It shows that the degree of autonomy accorded to branch or subsidiary plants varies considerably. In a study in Wales most plants could appoint their own staff, almost half could vary their product mix or make their own capital expenditure; and for well over half the plants a separate profit figure was established. There is no evidence of their degree of autonomy on supply decisions, but a fifth of the plants carried out their own marketing.[19] These data and Granick's work suggest that plants owned by large industrial enterprises perhaps have more autonomy than is usually implied in the literature. This has been confirmed elsewhere, and both Townroe[20] and the Northern Region Strategy Team[21] find this autonomy is higher where a subsidiary firm operates the plant.

While these findings must cast doubt over the extent of the centralisation of control, the subjective views of the Welsh investigators tend to support it. In visiting the plants Tomkins and Lovering 'gained the impression that there were not so many autonomous . . . [plants] . . . among those establishments visited as one might suppose from the examination of the data'.[22] Further, Townroe, in a study of branch plants only, found their freedom to invest very limited, though it increased with distance from the parent plant. Out of 60 plants moving over 40.2 km, 41 could not spend over £1,000 without reference to the parent plant, but despite this 'no link could be found between the degree of delegation of authority, and the level of investment undertaken in the new establishment after the initial financial commitment'.[23]

Clearly, the location of head-offices provides only a very crude indication of the degree of centralisation of control within the city-system. Similarly, assessments of the consequences of the increasing spatial concentration of control and the associated loss of control from the peripheral parts of the city-system are still, to some considerable extent, based on speculation rather than on hard fact. In essence, the argument has been put that large industrial enterprises show a bias in favour of the centre of the system, and that this bias works mainly, but not exclusively, against the peripheral part of the system.

Spatial Bias in Enterprise Behaviour

Spatial bias in the behaviour of large industrial enterprises within a city-system expresses itself partly in the linkages of its plants and partly in the employment patterns it creates. Behind this concept of spatial bias lies the view that decision makers in the control units, being more familiar with their immediate spatial environment than with areas further away will feel that risk and uncertainty will be reduced by developments close at hand. Since the control units are in the central part of the system, the bias will favour that part. Risk and uncertainty reduction may also play a part in ensuring a plant favours other plants in the enterprise in its supply and purchasing arrangements and this restricts a plant's ability to develop links with the local economy in which it is set.

The evidence relating to the extent of spatial bias in large enterprise behaviour is examined in two parts. First, and briefly, linkage patterns are considered and second a detailed examination of employment characteristics is undertaken.

Linkages

It was shown in Chapter 2 that a high proportion of the material linkages of a large enterprise's plants may be with other plants of the enterprise. Since most large enterprises are multi-regional in their operations a bias against linkages with the local region might be expected in plants owned by enterprises based outside the region in which the plant is located.

Evidence for bias in linkage behaviour comes from the study of branch plants. It was noted earlier that the establishment of branch plants produced few linkage adjustments by the enterprise except perhaps where long-distance moves were involved. This is reflected in the degree of local linkage recorded for branch plants by Lever in his study of some Scottish plants. The percentage of Scottish purchases varied from 23.7 in indigenous plants to 18.5 in branch plants. Similarly, 88 per cent of the branch-plant sales were to non-Scottish destinations, as against 65 per cent for indigenous plants.[24] These differences, while small, are in the expected direction, and Chapter 3, which showed that foreign-owned plants had fewer links with the local economy than their indigenous counterparts, gives further support.

Data collected by McDermott from part of the Scottish electronics industry present a similar picture. Indigenous plants had 36 per cent Scottish inputs compared with 23 per cent of plants owned by firms based outside Scotland, while Scottish-owned plants sent 49 per cent of their output to Scottish markets compared to only 37 per cent for the remaining firms.[25] Gilmour, too, took a single industry (paints and varnish) and explored the linkage pattern of four plants in Montreal. One was owned by a single-plant firm, one by a Canadian enterprise based elsewhere, and two by non-Canadian enterprises. In all four the main inputs showed similar linkage patterns, but the less important input linkages were drawn from non-local sources except for the plant owned by the single-plant firm. The other plants used intra-enterprise sources rather than local suppliers.[26]

Much of this evidence is drawn from the peripheral parts of the city-system and different linkage patterns may well exist in the centre. Nevertheless within these peripheral areas plants owned by firms based elsewhere were less well integrated into the local economy than their indigenous counterparts. This has the important implication that any growth-inducing effects that might be transmitted to a region by the plant's material linkage system will be damped down.

Only the evidence collected by Leigh & North presents an opposing view. They found that most acquiring firms 'regarded material purchase as a middle-to-low management function that is best left at the level of the acquired firm or factory, and so established patterns tend to be retained'.[27] Thus acquisition may well have advantages for supply firms in a region when the acquired plants are expanded. In marketing, also, little post-acquisition change was identified, except to extend the acquired firm's market area and thus probably diversifying its markets so contributing to a stabilisation of a region's prospects.

In turning to information linkages it has already been seen (Chapter 5) that acquisition of a firm in a region leads to the replacement of its links to local business services by services provided by an enterprise's head-office, and branch plants may rely on head-office links for similar types of service. In a study of non-Toronto branches in Ontario, Britton identified a pronounced metropolitan effect in legal, auditing and broker's facilities and in loan finance. More than half the branches in the sample obtained 'some of their high-order service linkages in such a manner that the location of other company offices is reflected directly'.[28] Evidently, ownership of plants by firms based outside a region reduces the demand for local services, and this is especially marked in the peripheral parts of the city-system.

Thus there is a gradual removal from the periphery of the system of back-up services, for example specialised financial, legal and banking operations, as well as the more specifically industrial services, such as industrial consultants and computer bureaux. These functions, as was shown, are provided by, or sought through, a plant's head-office. Those which do survive have less expertise and fewer contacts than their counterparts near the centre and may therefore meet their clients' needs less adequately. Agreed, all these disadvantages can be overcome, but only at a cost. It is likely that in this information deficient environment, the probability of a small firm's survival is reduced, and the region's potential for attracting future growth of high-level functions shrinks. The general exception to this line of argument is the small firm or large industrial enterprise headquartered in a specialised industrial complex where it is itself a member of the dominant industrial sector. Here specialist information gains outweigh more general information losses resulting from peripherality of location.

Despite the limited evidence it is possible to conclude tentatively that where a plant on the periphery of a city-system is owned by a large industrial enterprise it will have less links with the local economy than a similar locally owned enterprise. This will be most marked in its pattern of service linkages. The likely extent of the difference remains to be established by examining a wider range of places and enterprises.

Employment

It does not seem unreasonable to argue that the employment characteristics of the plants of a large industrial enterprise will be influenced strongly by the characteristics of the enterprise itself and its role in the national economy. Many of these enterprises take on the features of a lead enterprise (or 'lead firm' as it is called in the literature). These features are an increasing output, an increasing market share, productivity increases above the national average and marked innovative behaviour. The concept of the 'lead firm' develops from the work of Perroux[29] and Rosenfeld[30]. In the national (aspatial) economy lead firms make up the growth sectors (poles) around which the economy can develop and Erickson, argues these lead firms 'direct the nature and processes of regional economic growth'.[31]

The innovative behaviour characteristic of lead firms is a striking feature of many large industrial enterprises. There are a number of difficulties in interpreting data on innovations, but the evidence suggests that large enterprises are more innovative and adopt innovations earlier than small firms. Two examples of the relationship between size and innovation illustrate this point. Between 1945 and 1970, 1,102 innovations were made in UK industries examined by Freeman and 80 per cent were introduced in enterprises with over 1,000 employees. Small firms with less than 200 employees were responsible for only 10 per cent of the innovations despite providing one-fifth of the net output and one-quarter of the employment.[32] Similarly, Mansfield showed that the hypothesis that 'large firms are quicker on the average, than small ones to begin using new techniques' was acceptable.[33]

While innovation is important in the lead firm idea, size is its 'cornerstone'.[34] Some small firms may have many of the described lead firm characteristics, but because of their size they can have little effect on the economy and thus lack a 'lead' effect. The sheer size of the lead firm is emphasised throughout the literature, and Erickson stresses, 'lead firms are generally considered to be large-scale . . . production units'.[35]

Yet what is important from the viewpoint of a city-system is the extent to which a lead firm's national characteristics are replicated in its plants in the different parts of the system. Quite conceivably a lead firm's performance in a specific region might not mirror its national performance. A lead firm, for example, might be highly innovative but not all regions will gain equally from that innovative behaviour. Pred, for example, assumes that innovations must flow out from a head-office site[36], but there are few data to support the idea.

The only aggregate data that have been traced are in Luttrell's study, which suggests that head-office plants are more likely than branches to be selected to take a new product beyond the prototype stage.[37] A similar trend has been noticed in large enterprises such as Boeing[38], and Chapter 4 also showed that Watties tended to introduce new crops for their processing plants in their core region. Nevertheless, new products may be developed in a core region and then put into full production in other regions. Between 1900 and 1959 Westinghouse Electric developed ten new product groups at their East Pittsburgh Works, which were subsequently relocated elsewhere.[39] It seems reasonable to conclude that initially products new to an enterprise may be concentrated, if not at the headquarters site, at least in the core region. This, in turn, may provide greater employment stability in that part of the city-system.

Before a consideration of employment stability it is useful to begin with an examination of the overall employment patterns and employment mix controlled by large industrial enterprises within a city-system. These patterns have raised considerable interest and Holland has argued that large industrial enterprises favour the more developed part of a city-system. He claims that 'the leading firms in the economy tend to be located in its leading regions'[40] and that they and 'their subsidiary plant are located in, and *continue to locate in* [present author's italics] more developed regions'.[41] He also extends his argument to state that 'analysis dramatically shows the extent to which [foreign] multi-nationals concentrate their activities in more developed regions'.[42]

Chapter 2 showed that at the present time in the United Kingdom leading enterprises are no more likely to be located in leading regions than are other firms. Similarly, Chapter 3 showed foreign firms have a propensity to locate outside the central parts of the system. Indeed, foreign firms (in total) favoured the periphery in the late 1960s. These chapters gave a further discussion of the evidence on which these conclusions are based but it seems that in the allocation of their *total* employment large industrial enterprises in the United Kingdom at the present time are no more likely than small firms to favour some parts of the city-system at the expense of other parts, or, if they do, they favour its periphery rather than the centre. This general pattern agrees with Keeble's argument that manufacturing in the United Kingdom as a whole favoured peripheral areas from 1966 to 1971.[43]

Nevertheless, the concentration of control functions in some parts of the city-system has contributed to a change in the employment mix in various parts of the system. The periphery has seen an increase in the proportion of manual jobs, and it is sometimes suggested that the branch plants in these areas employ semi-skilled labour, often female, on products subject to wide fluctuation in demand, rather than skilled, more highly paid male jobs which last.[44] This is a reflection of an assumed tendency for the mature and later stages of the product-cycle to be located in peripheral areas (Chapter 2). Massey notices a de-skilling effect in the re-structuring process[45] and Townroe shows that peripheral areas fared rather badly by attracting a high proportion of female jobs, but also that labour reserves were essentially female until male unemployment began to rise in the 1970s, so this was perhaps not surprising.[46]

Paralleling the rise in the proportion of manual jobs in the periphery has been the increase in the relative importance of administrative and professional jobs in the centre. Westaway has traced this shift within the United Kingdom. He identified three groups of male occupations from UK Census data (Professional, Administrative and Manual) and examined their changing distribution over 112 Metropolitan Economic Labour Areas (MELAs) between 1961 and 1966. At one end of the scale the South East stands out as an area with marked increases in professional jobs. The special nature of the South East was also seen in its important concentration of MELAs with a higher-than-average share of managerial and administrative jobs. These results, albeit over a decade ago, suggest that even in the early 1960s the job-mix in the South East was changing towards an emphasis on white collar jobs.[47]

The ideas relating to the overall distribution of employment and its occupational mix are relatively new. A more established view is that branch plants and recently acquired plants, often set up or acquired by large industrial enterprises are more susceptible to fluctuations in employment and closure than locally controlled firms. This view tends to be emphasised by press announcements of major closures, but analysis of aggregate change suggests the view may be inappropriate, at least for those areas for which data are available. Most studies have focused on closures but a more general investigation of this problem by Clark shows that in the County of Skaraborg in Sweden plants owned by firms based outside the county were less sensitive to employment fluctuations than indigenous firms, and this was particularly true of the larger plants.[48]

The closure data present a similar picture. In the Northern Region of the United Kingdom the expected difference between branches and indigenous firms emerged but it was small; 18 per cent of the indigenous plants in 1962 had closed by 1973, compared with 22 per cent of the externally controlled plants.[49] In a more interesting study Atkins compared the performance of some UK branches with their parent plants.[50]

Only branches over five years old were examined, to remove the effects of growth in the early stages of a plant's life. Atkins's figures show two important elements:

(1) approximately the same proportion of branch plants as of parent plants closed in the period 1966–71;

(2) employment declined more severely in parents (17.2 per cent) than in branch units (6.1 per cent).

These branch plants may not be typical of those of large industrial enterprises as Atkins had to exclude 23 branches of large nationals because of the difficulty of identifying the parent enterprise, but if this exclusion has not biased the results then branch plants of large industrial enterprises are not as unstable as was once thought. Perhaps the undue emphasis on presence/absence data, with its lack of concern for plant size, together with the failure of short-lived branches, accounts for the established picture of instability in branch employment. As Townroe observes, 'fears of the propensity-to-close of branch plants seem to have little justification'.[51]

One further aspect of this problem, however, needs investigation. Branches or subsidiaries in some parts of the city-system are possibly more likely to close than those in other parts. Here, the evidence suggests a bias in favour of the peripheràl parts of the city-system. Sant shows that from 1966 to 1971 branch plants in peripheral areas were less likely to close than all movers, and much less likely to close than branch plants in other areas.[52] Atkins's more carefully controlled investigation is less favourable, but at least she establishes that closure rates for peripheral and non-peripheral branches were identical.[53] The unfavourable image is partly explained by the fact that in the 1950s, as Sant and Keeble indicate branch plants in peripheral areas were more likely to close than those elsewhere.[54]

Data on the performance of plants acquired by large industrial enterprises is still fragmentary, although Leigh & North's view of the immediate post-acquisition period hints that a long-term view of subsidiaries may not indicate instability. Chapter 5 showed expansion to be as common as closure, and further evidence shows that where closure did occur in three-quarters of the instances the resources were transferred to plants elsewhere in the region. The same study shows little evidence of spatial bias in post-acquisition closure and concludes 'there is certainly nothing to suggest that manufacturing output in the peripheral regions of the UK suffered at the expense of that of the central regions'.[55] Similarly, data taken from Massey's study of the reorganisation of production activities by enterprises in the electrical engineering industry indicated that the greatest losses occurred not in the periphery, but in the other parts of the city-system as is described later (Table 11.1).

It appears that the principal economic implications of the growth of large industrial enterprises on the city-system are the reduced demand for industrial services and a decline in the relative importance of white-collar jobs in the peripheral parts of the system.

Lever tried to examine the aggregate effect of linkage and employment when he calculated an income multiplier for branch and indigenous plants in Scotland. He selected 24 plants in six different industries and within each industry he controlled for plant size and divided plants by organisational status (indigenous to region or branch) and found that 'whilst there are significant differences between industries these are outweighed in importance by differences between plants'. If the not unreasonable assumption is made that the branch plants belong to large industrial enterprises, the multiplier effects of the plants of large industrial enterprises and of other plants can be compared. Lever's findings suggest that the presence of large industrial enterprises' plants enhance a regional economy, as the branch plant income multiplier (1.22) not only surpassed that for indigenous plants (1.09) but was also significantly different at the 1 per cent level.[56]

This discussion has emphasised several important implications of spatial bias in large enterprise behaviour; there may well be others which deserve further attention but for which few data are available. Two obvious ones are the flows of non-wage income arising from the activities of the large industrial enterprises, and the extent to which the financial resources and innovative capacity of the large industrial enterprise are able to stimulate a regional economy through its branch plants. In this respect an exciting new area being developed is the examination of the role of the large industrial enterprise in transmitting technological innovations between regions.[57] The ideas in this field are still highly speculative, but over the next five years it is likely that the results of empirical research will begin to appear.

Social Implications

The social implications of large enterprise behaviour flow directly from its effect on the economic system. For the periphery of the system and, indeed, for some cities in the centre the most obvious social repercussion is that once control is removed from a particular city or community that city or community loses some of its ability to influence an enterprise's behaviour. The managers can no longer react to the informal pressures of the communities in which they live, and even given a managerial desire to meet local needs a policy geared to such needs can be changed by head-office. More subtly, because of potential contacts between workers and local managers in a community, a greater sense of common interests may emerge than when managers are constrained by 'them' located elsewhere. The problems of distant control affect both local managers and the work-force.

The brewing industry in north-east England provides an example. A large Newcastle plant, now controlled from an Edinburgh headquarters, was acquired in 1960 and like other brewing enterprises, Scottish & Newcastle has undertaken an integration and rationalisation of its activities. The Tyneside (North East) managers said that 'industrial relations decisions taken in Newcastle were too frequently over-ruled by Edinburgh . . . and that in some respects the North East . . . was expected to comply more closely with company policy than other regions'.[58] The workers' representatives expressed similar views. This illustrates a conflict between local and distant control, and long distance relationships being forced to follow formal rules (company policy) rather than more flexible informal systems. This is only one example, but supports the expected trend. Of course, such distant control is not confined to the large industrial enterprise; the labour-force may be constrained by nationally negotiated agreements which over-ride plant bargaining structures.

It is difficult to test the consequences of this loss of control, but intuitively one might expect that informal solutions to problems in a locally based firm might be replaced by more open conflicts and disputes in the plants of a large enterprise controlled from outside. Steuer and Gennard, who compared the labour disputes in foreign firms with those in domestic enterprises, provide some evidence of this. In 1963 foreign firms provided just over 10 per cent of UK employment, and after adjustment for different industrial structures foreign firms suffered 3.6 per cent of stoppages, involving 1.9 per cent of the workers and 1.8 per cent of the total working days lost. Similar data for 1968 indicate that foreign firms were still experiencing less than their 'share' of disputes.[59] If one accepts that increased disputes illustrate some of the social effects of loss of local control, then certainly this does not seem to be supported by this evidence on foreign firms, although no adjustment was made for variation in size between foreign and domestic firms.

These findings have not gone unchallenged, and in Forsyth's study of US firms in Scotland their strike performance was 'markedly worse both in general and in the majority of the industries' groups in which they operated than that of indigenous firms'.[60] While this might reflect the possibility of regional variations in the strike record of foreign-owned firms, it does provide some evidence at least that plants owned by firms based elsewhere experience worse labour relations than locally based firms.

The loss of the higher-level jobs also reduces the middle-class component in regional social structures. Barlow argues that this is not necessarily a disadvantage.[61] Reduction in the middle-class group can reduce imports into a region, and free other goods from consumption within the region, thus improving the region's trade balance. However valid this argument may be, there seems a general consensus that the loss is important for several reasons.

The loss of managerial and professional jobs from some regions and their concentration in others affects the degree of opportunity in different places. Where 'top' jobs are removed the occupational ladder is stunted. Incentives to advance are lost as better jobs are not available locally for those moving up the ladder, while those educated to a high level may be forced outside their city to seek a job appropriate to their ability. In sum, lack of incentives means wasted ability within the peripheral parts of the city-system, or the selective migration of the better qualified away from them. A further direct effect on industrial growth is that loss of the better qualified removes entrepreneurs who might have created the growth of new small firms. Yet the loss of high-level jobs to the centre of the system does not necessarily bring only advantages to those central cities for, in the long run, it may produce a marked over-representation of high-level jobs and low-level service jobs in the central regions. In turn, those in the lower-level jobs find difficulty in obtaining accommodation in the high-price congested central areas, this congestion reflecting the space and transport demands of the high-level functions.[62]

A strong middle-class group has further advantages to the periphery of the system which may be lost if it is under-represented. As Hannah and Kay observe, 'for the provincial world . . . the preservation of independent centres of initiative which are not dominated by a metropolitan elite . . . is an important objective'.[63] The strong middle-class group can provide the information and expertise for community groups; they can establish pressure groups aimed at influencing the development of social structures. An informed element can attempt to manipulate the bureaucracies that dominate health, education and local government. The manipulation may or may not be in the best interests of a community as a whole, but at least some criticism of city-system bureaucracies should emerge.

To see these trends solely as the result of the growth of large industrial enterprises is, of course, an exaggeration. They are but one of a group of large organisations, such as the civil service, trade unions, building societies and banks. To blame the large industrial enterprise alone for disparities between the central and peripheral parts of the city-system is unreasonable, but it has some responsibility.

Conclusion

This chapter has illustrated the relationship between the spatial structures of large industrial enterprises and city-systems. There is clear evidence of an increasing concentration of control units in the higher-ranking centres of the system. It has been paralleled by a loss of control from the peripheral part of the system. Closer systematic investigation of the degree of autonomy enjoyed by branch plants suggests that the removal of local control from the periphery is perhaps less marked than the loss of control units would suggest.

Overall, the removal of control appears to have had little effect on the distribution of production, but white-collar jobs have tended to become more centralised. The production units might tend to purchase from and supply less to their immediate vicinity than their independent counterparts; they certainly make less use of local services. The social implications of the growth of large enterprises seem, subjectively, more significant, even if difficult to measure.

Although it is of interest to study inter-regional relationships within a city-system framework, and despite the increasing interest in the loss of control from the peripheral parts of the city-system, substantive evidence that the growth of large enterprises has militated against the periphery of a space economy is found only in the bias in information and material links and the loss of white-collar jobs. The absence of many of the expected relationships may in part reflect the small spatial extent of the United Kingdom, from which most of the evidence is drawn but, intuitively, it seems more likely to result from the close relationship between large industrial enterprises and the state since World War II and this is examined in the final chapter.

Notes

1. A. Pred, *City-Systems in Advanced Economies*, 1977, London.
2. J.B. Goddard, 'Organisational Information Flows and the Urban System', *Economie Appliqué*, 128, 1975, pp. 125-64. J.B. Goddard, *Office Location in Urban and Regional Development*, 1975, London.
3. P.W. Daniels, *Office Location: An Urban and Regional Study*, 1975, London.
4. R.A. Erickson, 'The Lead Firm Concept: an Analysis of Theoretical Elements', *Tijdschrift voor Economische en Sociale Geographie*, 63, 1972, p. 434.
5. R.A. Erickson, 'The Spatial Pattern of Income Generation in Lead Firm, Growth Area Linkage Systems', *Economic Geography*, 51, 1975, pp. 17-26.
6. Expenditure Committee, *Regional Development Incentives*, HC327, 1973, London, p. 45.
7. O. Warneryd, *Interdependence in Urban Systems*, 1968, Goteborg, p. 112.
8. A. Pred, 'The Growth and Development of Systems of Cities in Advanced Economies', in Pred and Tornqvist, *Systems of Cities and Information Flows*, 1973, London, p. 11.
9. Warneryd, *Urban Systems*, Pred, *City-Systems*.
10. G. Tornqvist, 'Flows of Information and the Location of Economic Activities', *Geografiska Annaler*, 50B, 1968, pp. 99–107; developed more fully in G. Tornqvist, *Contact Systems and Regional Development*, 1970, Lund.
11. C. Tomkins and J. Lovering, *Location, Size, Ownership and Control Tables for Welsh Industry*, 1973, Cardiff; J. Firn, 'External Control and Regional Development: the Case of Scotland', *Environment and Planning A*, 7, 1975; Northern Region Strategy Team, *Changes in the Corporate Structure of Manufacturing Industry in the Northern Region*, Working Paper, Project A9, 1976, Newcastle.
12. A. Pred, *Major Job-Providing Organisations and Systems of Cities*. Commission on College Geography, Association of American Geographers, Resource Paper No. 27, 1974, Washington, p. 19.
13. Tornqvist, 'Flows of Information', p. 100.

14. R. Crum and G. Gudgin, *Non-manufacturing Activities in U.K. Manufacturing Industry*, 1976, Norwich, especially pp. 1-92.

15. Expenditure Committee, *Regional Development Incentives*, p. 227.

16. Pred, 1974, *Major Job-Providing Organisations*, pp. 47 and 52.

17. Tomkins and Lovering, *Location, Size, Ownership*, p. 10.

18. D. Granick, 'Use of Corporate Divisional Headquarters: a Peculiar American Innovation', *Business Topics*, 22, 1974, p. 15.

19. Tomkins and Lovering, *Location, Size, Ownership*, p. 14.

20. P.M. Townroe, 'Branch Plants and Regional Development', *Town Planning Review*, 46, 1975, p. 51.

21. Northern Region Strategy Team, *Changes in the Corporate Structure*, p. 31.

22. Tomkins and Lovering, *Location, Size, Ownership*, p. 13.

23. Townroe, 'Branch Plants'.

24. W.F. Lever, 'Regional Multipliers and Demand Leakages at Establishment Level', *Scottish Journal of Political Economy*, 21, 1974, p. 120.

25. P.J. McDermott, 'Ownership, Organisation and Regional Dependence in the Scottish Electronics Industry', *Regional Studies*, 10, 1976, p. 326.

26. J.M. Gilmour, 'External Economies of Scale, Inter-Industrial Linkages, and Decision-Making in Manufacturing', in F.E.I. Hamilton (ed.) *Spatial Perspectives on Industrial Organisation and Decision-making*, 1974, London, pp. 354-6.

27. R. Leigh and D. North, 'Regional Aspects of Acquisition Activity in British Manufacturing Industry', *Regional Studies*, 12, 1978.

28. J.N.H. Britton, 'Environmental Adaptation of Industrial Plants: Service Linkages, Locational Environment and Organisation' in Hamilton (ed.), *Spatial Perspectives*, p. 386.

29. F. Perroux, 'Note on the Concept of Growth Poles', in D.L. McKee *et al.* (eds.), *Regional Economics: Theory and Practice*, 1970, New York, pp. 93-103.

30. F. Rosenfeld, 'L'industrie motrice dans la région et dans l'espace économique intégré', *Economie Appliquée*, 19, 1966, pp. 511-30.

31. R.A. Erickson, 'The Regional Economic Impact of Growth Firms: the Case of Boeing, 1963-68', *Land Economics*, 50, 1974, p. 127.

32. C. Freeman, *The Role of Small Firms in Innovation in the United Kingdom since 1945*, Committee of Enquiry on Small Firms, Research Report No. 6, 1971, London.

33. E. Mansfield, *The Economics of Technical Change*, 1969, New York, pp. 123-4.

34. Erickson, 'The Lead Firm Concept', p. 429.

35. Erickson, 'The Case of Boeing', p. 127.

36. A. Pred, 'The Inter-Urban Transmission of Growth in Advanced Economies: Empirical Findings Versus Regional Planning Assumptions', *Regional Studies*, 10, 1976, pp. 151-72.

37. W.F. Luttrell, *Factory Location and Industrial Movement, Volume 1*, 1962, London, p. 128.

38. G. Krumme and R. Hayter, 'Implications of Corporate Strategies and Product Cycle Adjustments for Regional Employment Changes', in L. Collins and D.F. Walker, *Locational Dynamics of Manufacturing Activity*, 1975, London, p. 349.

39. G.P.F. Steed, 'Forms of Corporate-Environmental Adaptation', *Tijdschrift voor Economische en Sociale Geografie*, 62, 1971, p. 92.

40. S. Holland, *The Socialist Challenge*, 1975, London, p. 95.

41. S. Holland, *Capital versus the Regions*, 1976, London, p. 140.

42. S. Holland, *The Regional Problem*, 1976, London, p. 33.

43. D. Keeble, *Industrial Location and Planning in the United Kingdom*, 1976, London, p. 18.
44. Firn, 'External Control and Regional Development', p. 411.
45. D. Massey, 'A Structural Approach to Industrial Location', *Centre for Environmental Studies, WN454*, 1977, p. 5.
46. Townroe, 'Branch Plants', pp. 52-4.
47. J. Westaway, 'Contact Potential and the Occupation Structure of the British Urban System', *Regional Studies*, 8, 1974, pp. 57-73.
48. U.E.G. Clark, 'The Cyclical Sensitivity of Employment in Branch and Parent Plants', *Regional Studies*, 10, 1976, p. 297.
49. Northern Region Strategy Team, *Changes in the Corporate Structure*, p. 14.
50. D.H.W. Atkins, 'Employment Change in Branch and Parent Manufacturing Plants in the United Kingdom, 1966-71', *Trade and Industry*, 30 August 1973, pp. 437-9.
51. Townroe, 'Branch Plants', p. 57.
52. M. Sant, 'Inter-Regional Industrial Movement: the Case of the Non-Survivors' in B.J. Turton and A.D.M. Phillips (eds.), *Essays in Honour of S.H. Beaver*, 1975, London, p. 365.
53. Atkins, 'Employment Change'.
54. M. Sant, 'The Case of the Non-Survivors'; D. Keeble, 'Industrial Decentralisation and the Metropolis: the North-West London Case', *Transactions of the Institute of British Geographers*, 44, 1968, p. 48.
55. Leigh and North, 'Regional Aspects of Acquisition Activity', pp. 227-45.
56. Lever, 'Regional Multipliers', p. 120.
57. M.D. Thomas, 'Growth Pole Theory, Technological Change and Regional Economic Growth', *Papers and Proceedings of the Regional Science Association*, 34, 1975, 3-25.
58. Advisory Conciliation and Arbitration Service, *Scottish & Newcastle Breweries Ltd.*, 1977, London, pp. 16-17. I am indebted to Suzanne Richbell for drawing my attention to this reference.
59. M. Steuer and J. Gennard, 'Industrial Relations in Foreign Owned Firms', in J.H. Dunning (ed.), *The Multi-national Enterprise*, 1971, London.
60. D.J. Forsyth, *U.S. Investment in Scotland*, 1972, London, p. 205.
61. A. Barlow, 'A Comment on the Concentration of Manufacturing Corporations and Regional Growth', *Area*, 4, 1972, pp. 274-5.
62. J. Westaway, 'The Spatial Hierarchy of Business Organisations and its Implications for the British Urban System', *Regional Studies*, 8, 1974, pp. 148-52.
63. L. Hannah and J.A. Kay, *Concentration in Modern Industry*, 1977, London, p. 40.

11 LARGE INDUSTRIAL ENTERPRISES AND THE STATE

A nation's concern with large industrial enterprises arises, primarily, because the power and influence of the enterprises challenges the power and influence of the democratically elected governments. What is good for a large enterprise is not necessarily good for the state. Most advanced Western-type economies are concerned with the role of these large enterprises, as Vernon's review *Big Business and the State* demonstrates,[1] and there have been fears that the enterprises' spatial policies may not fit with the state's. Since policies vary markedly among states, this chapter focuses solely upon the United Kingdom.

The relationship between large enterprises and the state is complex, and only the elements which seem to be of particular relevance in this context can be picked out. Three basic questions arise. The first is whether large enterprises as a group have been more (or less) responsive to regional policy measures than their smaller counterparts; the second is whether aspatial policy measures aimed at the large enterprise have had any marked spatial repercussions, and the third is what are the spatial responsibilities of large enterprises?

Regional Policy

Some speculative ideas and the occasional spectacular example suggest that large enterprises are less responsive than their smaller counterparts to regional policy measures. One popular view is that an enterprise, rather than the government, has the final say, partly because of a large enterprise's bargaining strength derived from its multi-national operations (Chapter 3). It is frequently illustrated by the IBM production facilities at Havant. Their establishment apparently reflects this implicit bargaining: if the British government said 'I am sorry, but you cannot go to Havant', the Chairman of IBM in New York would have replied 'All right. We will not go to the United Kingdom'.[2]

A less extreme reaction by an enterprise to government

control is to attempt to negotiate a 'package' deal, with some of the expansion on a preferred site and the remainder in an area less attractive to the enterprise in order to meet the government's requirements. Examples are recorded by both Ford and Courtaulds. Ford 'was granted an Industrial Development Certificate to expand at Basildon . . . on condition that further expansion would be located in Development Areas'.[3] Courtaulds' agreement with the government was less of a deal and more a running 'dialogue' so that 'a certain bunch of IDCs would receive approval side by side with an expansion going ahead, say at Spennymoor'.[4]

The implication of this evidence, despite its anecdotal nature, is that large industrial enterprises are able to wring concessions from powerless governments. Yet some small firms were also able to escape the government's influence. Reliant, for example, refused a location in the North West and after a seven-year delay obtained an IDC for their preferred site.[5] Similarly, some large concerns were directed to peripheral areas with little public hint of a package deal, Rootes' (now Chrysler's) dismissal to central Scotland being one example.

The aggregate data, discussed in Chapters 2, 3 and 10, indicate that in overall job provision these enterprises have patterns which do not differ from those of smaller firms or that they show a bias towards the periphery of the system, where regional policy incentives have been highest. Keeble summarises these incentives (and associated controls).[6] Admittedly a bias towards the peripheral areas does not necessarily reflect the effectiveness of controls and incentives but it does indicate that in the recent past large enterprises (particularly those under foreign control) have been showing the kind of pattern that regional development policies deem desirable. They are neither exerting their power to maintain the status quo nor working in the opposite direction.

The evidence presented here and in earlier chapters suggests that there is no strong case for a regional policy aimed specifically at the large industrial enterprise on the grounds that it is concentrating its employment in the centre of the city-system. Other features, however, indicate such a policy might be necessary. These are the concentration of their white-collar jobs in the centre of the system and the limited dependence on local inputs and markets, which may create difficulties for the peripheral parts of the system. Further, the enterprises with their multi-locational, multi-regional activities may have greater flexibility than their smaller counterparts to discriminate between different parts of the system. Finally, and perhaps more attractively to government, focusing regional assistance on selected large enterprises might be cheaper than the present generous granting of aid to all comers.

A move towards a policy focused upon large enterprises began tentatively in 1974 with schemes to introduce Planning Agreements between the government and large public and private-sector enterprises. The agreement becomes a realistic way of managing the economy only when economic power is concentrated in a few large enterprises. Such agreements are expected to cover a wide range of enterprise activities, including the proportion of an enterprise's investment that is to go to Assisted Areas, analysis of the scope for increasing employment in Assisted Areas, and changes in the level of employment in those areas.[7] It is too early to assess the likely effects of this policy, but by April 1976 Agreements were being discussed with certain industries (process plant and turbo-generators) rather than enterprises.[8] By 1977 only Chrysler was prepared to sign a Planning Agreement in return for major government financial assistance.[9] Except where the government can offer large enterprises a financial incentive to sign such an agreement little progress, apparently, will be made.

Regional policy has a particular side effect which was not foreseen. Large enterprises can exploit peripheral areas to gain either grants from the state (indigenous enterprises) or access to the UK market (foreign enterprises). Chapter 5 illustrated the latter in the UK aluminium-smelting industry. As Krumme and Hayter observed 'the corporate planner . . . tends to exploit the . . . regional authorities utilising his . . . inter-regional mobility of capital . . . and economic power derived from the size, diversity, and status of his . . . national activities'.[10] Clearly a threat to close a plant in a peripheral area is more likely to secure government help to avert the closure than is a plant closure in a prosperous centre. Similarly, it is difficult to refuse entry to the United Kingdom of foreign firms which have already promised employment provision to a specific peripheral area, even if the long-run effect will be to reduce employment in existing firms. Even if it is refused, production elsewhere in the EEC might ultimately have the same effect without any compensating provision of employment.

Aspatial Policies

The large industrial enterprise's role in the development of city and regional systems is but one of its roles in national affairs. Indeed, its national significance may well have tended to hide its regional influence. Special non-spatial policies were well established by the mid-1960s, and these are discussed under four heads: the Monopolies Commission, industrial strategy, the Industrial Reorganisation Corporation (IRC) and public ownership. The role of the Restrictive Practices Act of 1956 is not explored, but it may well have rendered illegal many forms of collusive behaviour.[11]

The aims of these different policies may sometimes conflict. For example, the Monopolies Commission could and does investigate and discourage the growth of enterprises which wish to increase their market shares in particular industries. In contrast, the IRC sought to encourage industrial concentration to increase the international competitiveness of British industry. Thus the various aspatial policies may have worked in different directions, but did they influence the spatial behaviour of large industrial enterprises?

Monopolies Commission

Although the Monopolies Commission dates from 1948, its powers were strengthened considerably by the Monopolies and Mergers Act of 1965.[12] Until 1965, companies which produced one-third (reduced to one-quarter in 1974) of the goods of a particular industry could be investigated but from 1965 it was empowered to investigate prospective or actual mergers if the combined assets involved reached £5 million. Further the appropriate government body could delay, forbid or unscramble a merger. Britain was late in introducing this type of legislation, which dates in the United States from 1890.

Gribbin shows that 576 mergers in the manufacturing sector were referred to the Takeover Panel of the Department of Industry from 1965 until the end of June 1973.[13] Of these only 13 were referred to the Monopolies Commission for investigation. The principal interest lies probably in those which the Commission found were against the public interest, and those which were abandoned during the Commission's investigation. Two major proposals in the first category were those between the pulp and paper interests of Reed and Bowater (1971), and between Beecham and Glaxo (1972). Second-category examples are those of Marley and Redland Tiles (1969) and of Glynwed and Armitage Shanks (1973). In these cases, without the Monopolies Commission, the mergers might well have taken place, with consequential adjustments in both plants and linkage patterns. While it is not possible to decide whether the pattern existing now differs from what would have occurred, the evidence suggests that the Commission may well influence the spatial patterns of large industrial enterprises.

These data could underestimate the role of the Commission, since its very existence may deter merger proposals. For example, plans to merge the interests of any two of the brewing enterprises discussed earlier would certainly stimulate a Commission enquiry.

Industrial Strategy

The government has frequently attempted to assist established industries facing contraction or to promote new industries to strengthen the economy. The Cotton Industry Act of 1959[14] was intended to ease the decline of that industry and the Shipbuilding Industry Board to create more viable firms in the industry.[15] The Industrial Expansion Act of 1968 aimed at establishing new science-based industries and assisted the UK computer industry to survive as International Computers.[16] Another product of the Act was a considerable expansion of the aluminium-smelting industry (Chapter 5).

In the 1970s strategy has become more comprehensive, focusing upon setting up 37 sector working parties to identify means of fostering increased output and exports.[17] Government-financed schemes have been developed to stimulate product development and the modernisation and rationalisation of facilities. It is recognised that the 300 leading enterprises in the strategy sectors must play a vital role in stimulating change. These changes may clash with the demands of regional policies, but such conflicts have not, as yet, emerged publicly. The work of the earlier Industrial Reorganisation Corporation throws light on some problems which the strategy may create.

Industrial Reorganisation Corporation

The Industrial Reorganisation Corporation (IRC) operated from 1966 to 1971 and was intended primarily as an agency for drawing firms' attention to merger possibilities.[18] It could, if necessary, provide loans to assist the merger activities. There seems to be no evidence that it was conscious of the spatial outcomes of its policies, but its task of promoting the 'concentration and rationalisation' of British industry ensured selective expansion or contraction of plants. The most prominent effects of the IRC were the creation of British Leyland, and the emergence of an enlarged GEC (including Associated Electrical Industries and English Electric). It also influenced some smaller firms, such as the creation of RHP discussed in Chapter 5.

The most extensive criticism of the IRC's work arose from redundancies it appeared to create. Young and Lowe observe that 'detailed post-merger plant closures and rationalisation schemes do not seem to have been worked out in detail before a merger was supported'.[19] IRC certainly claimed that regional factors were taken into account, but 'the claim seems dubious . . . with a few exceptions the decision to close factories was made on commercial grounds without social considerations being taken into account'.[20] Nevertheless, more recent work indicates that, while these factors may not have been considered, there was a spatial bias against the central parts of the city-system in the employment changes resulting from rationalisation.

Massey studied some 25 cases of restructuring under IRC auspices, focusing upon the electrical engineering, electronic and aerospace industries. She identified three different types of problem: Group 1, firms in sectors facing a marked fall in demand (power engineering, supertension cables and aerospace); Group 2, firms in industries seen as crucial to productivity in other sectors (for example, computers); and Group 3, firms in industries where sheer size would improve their international competitiveness (scientific instruments). In each there is a bias in favour of the Assisted Areas (Table 11.1), where they were either declining less or growing more. As far as is known this did not reflect conscious policy by the IRC, nor of course can all the changes be attributed solely to IRC intervention.[21] Nevertheless, this illustrates very clearly the

Table 11.1: Employment Change from Industrial Restructuring After 1966

	Group 1	Group 2	Group 3	Total
Development Areas	−6,610	+1,650	−880	−5,840
Rest of UK	−17,503	+100	−4,406	−21,809

Source: D. Massey, 'A Structuralist Approach to Industrial Location', Centre for Environmental Studies, Working Note 454, 1977.

spatial impact of an essentially aspatial policy.

Policies implemented through regional incentives, the Monopolies Commission, industrial strategies and the IRC involved only a tinkering with the private-enterprise system. Yet, the enterprises concerned are so large and so crucial to the economy as well as to particular regions that a complete collapse or major contraction of such enterprises is politically unacceptable. In a crisis, the taking into state ownership of these concerns is perhaps inevitable. A logical extension to this argument for some is that state ownership might be more valuable if it took over before, rather than after, a crisis.

Public Ownership

The special problems of public-sector enterprises have not been explored in any detail in the earlier chapters; public-sector enterprises probably deserve a book to themselves. Nevertheless UK experience does bear out the view that, once an enterprise reaches a specific size, it will not be allowed to shut down its operations completely. Examples are the nationalisation of Rolls-Royce and British Leyland and the input of large sums into the UK operations of Chrysler. The government observed of British Leyland that they were 'in no doubt that there was no practical alternative to large-scale finance from public sources if British Leyland was to continue to operate on a scale which would meet the requirements of the national interest'.[22] More carefully structured schemes created the British Steel Corporation,[23] British Shipbuilders and British Aerospace.

The National Enterprise Board, established in 1974/5 to extend public ownership, is intended, in part, to stimulate the restructuring of private industry.[24] It is perhaps a logical extension of the work of the Industrial Reorganisation

Corporation. Extension of public ownership, however, does not necessarily result in immediate spatial changes, as the brief discussion of the steel and railway engineering enterprises in Chapter 5 makes clear. Nor does the sad post-nationalisation history of British Leyland suggest that nationalisation will bring rapid solutions to an enterprise's problems. Virtually all the nationalised concerns have faced major problems of spatial rationalisation in the past or will do so in the immediate future. In British Leyland, the government hopes to assist 'where necessary in the rationalisation of plants and reduction of assembly capacity, recognising the needs to minimise the effects on employment'.[25] Yet once such problems are faced disinvestment decisions become more emotionally charged: some feel that public-sector enterprises should be more responsive than private-sector concerns to the social and economic requirements of the areas in which they are set. The history of British Steel's endeavours to rationalise its production facilities is perhaps indicative of the difficulties a nationalised concern faces.[26] The attempts by nationalised concerns to adjust their spatial structures draws attention to the spatial responsibilities of a large industrial enterprise, yet these responsibilities should perhaps differ little between those enterprises in the public sector and those in the private sector.

Spatial Responsibilities of an Enterprise

The spatial responsibilities of large industrial enterprises place their leaders in a dilemma very similar to that experienced by the UK government from 1966 to 1970, when, as was seen, the IRC was promoting growth of large enterprises and the Monopolies Commission sometimes working against it. In the long run increased size or rationalised production facilities probably means lower costs and stronger international competitiveness, thus improving the economy as a whole and strengthening the enterprise. It is, however, difficult for the redundant executive or shop-floor worker to appreciate his or her small contribution to the national good. In the short run, the relevant period for most politicians, investment by an enterprise may mean fewer jobs, and as in the brewing industry, fewer plants. The number of workers in manufacturing is now steadily declining, and many adjustments by an enterprise result in an output increase but in job loss. Here it is suggested that large industrial enterprises have certain social responsibilities of a spatial nature, which possibly exceed those which they are bound to follow by law.

While a major expansion project requires warning to permit development of appropriate public investment, if needed, the planning period of this type of investment decision plus the construction period give adequate warnings of proposed changes. This is not so with plant closure decisions, although public-sector concerns are less guilty here. While the occasional panic measure may be justified, plant closures are often announced with little warning, leaving little time for re-adjustment by individual or local economies. Plessey and Courtaulds provide two examples.

In March 1977 Plessey gave the minimum 90 days' notice required by the Employment Protection Act that it was to create 4,000 redundancies in north-west and north-east England. It was claimed that although the possibility of closures was known three months earlier the Manpower Services Commission had been unable to take any jobs initiative as it could not find out the enterprise's intentions about redundancy.[27] Similarly, some six months earlier Courtaulds announced 3,000 redundancies one day in October 1976, followed by the announcement of a further 1,300 redundancies less than a week later. Again, these closures gave only slightly over the minimum notice period, and the announcement in two stages gave scope for further misunderstandings. The impact of these closures was heightened by the fact that most were in two centres—Flint and Skelmersdale.[28]

The social responsibilities this kind of closure creates are two. The spatial context of the proposed plant must be considered in detail. There are cases where product line or the need for re-equipment make a particular plant the only candidate for closure, but where the differences between plants are relatively small, the environmental setting of the various plants that are potential closure candidates needs careful examination. The plant in a small town, or the major employer in a new town, should, other things being equal, have more in its favour than a plant in a diversified centre. Even where cost differences between plants are large, these differences need to be set out for both government and employees to show why plant A was selected instead of plant B, or indeed why both plants could not be contracted by a similar amount.

Secondly, adequate warning should be given of closure, although what is adequate will vary from case to case. A long warning presents problems in that the best members of the work-force may be lost. Further, costs rise if enterprises phase redundancies over a period instead of a complete shut down at one time, but gradual reduction of staff is particularly important if the number of redundancies in one place is large. From an enterprise viewpoint, long warning and phased run-down are likely to present a prolonged period of move and counter-move by government, unions and the enterprise, and a carefully scheduled scheme makes it more difficult for the enterprise to compromise. With minimum notice and complete shut down promised, an enterprise has ample negotiating moves to utilise.

While some socially and politically difficult decisions will have to be made, a closer awareness of the enterprise's spatial structure and its relationship to the city and regional system may help to avoid some problems. Long-term plans might attempt to ensure that plants dominating an urban area maintain high work-loads, or that new plants are introduced into centres where the abandonment of an existing production unit is a possibility. Indeed, an enterprise will find it politically easier to close a plant in a prosperous region than in an Assisted Area. Similarly, positive action might be taken to counteract the trend to concentrate control functions of the enterprise in the more developed part of the city-system. Above all, an enterprise should be seen to be assisting in the development of the peripheral parts of the city-system. Certainly, no examples have been discovered of an enterprise emphasising this in its nationwide publicity material or in Annual Reports.

Conclusion

Large enterprises may well behave in a spatially responsible manner even if they are not singled out for special treatment. Certainly, as shown earlier, they appear to have responded at least as well as smaller firms to regional incentives. There remain, however, important areas which need to be monitored, if not controlled, by government. Since governments are now expected to rescue the failed or failing enterprise, they must be able to monitor change with accurate information provided by the enterprises. The system of Planning Agreements described earlier is a move in this direction.

Yet, one area of enterprise behaviour, interaction between enterprises, the Planning Agreement system may not tackle effectively. Chapter 5 discussed the general nature of this interaction and it was examined in the case analyses from the brewing industry. It is difficult to see how organisational gamesmanship can be controlled without very close state intervention, which could be unacceptable, but certainly it is an area where governments might attempt to intervene.

Notes

1. R. Vernon, *Big Business and the State: Changing Relations in Western Europe*, 1974, London.
2. Expenditure Committee, *Regional Development Incentives*, HC 327, 1973, London, p.16.
3. Ibid., p.78.
4. Ibid., p.311.
5. Ibid., pp.60-9.
6. D. Keeble, *Industrial Location and Planning in the United Kingdom*, 1976, pp.220-33.
7. Department of Industry, *The Regeneration of British Industry*, Cmnd 5710, 1974, London, p.4; Anon, 'The Subject Matter of a Planning Agreement', *Trade and Industry*, 8 Aug. 1975, pp.340-2.
8. *Trade and Industry*, 23 Apr. 1976, p.194.
9. Department of Industry, *Public Expenditure on Chrysler U.K. Ltd*, Cmnd 6745, 1977, London, pp.13-14.
10. G. Krumme and R. Hayter, 'Implications of Corporate Strategies and Product Cycle Adjustments for Regional Employment Changes', in L. Collins and D.F. Walker (eds.), *Locational Dynamics of Manufacturing Activity*, 1975, London, p.329.
11. D. Swann et al., *Competition in British Industry: Restrictive Practices Legislation in Theory and Practice*, 1974, London.
12. A. Sutherland, *The Monopolies Commission in Action*, 1970, Cambridge.
13. J.D. Gribbin, 'The Operation of the Mergers Panel Since 1965', *Trade and Industry*, 17 Jan. 1974, pp.70-3.
14. C. Miles, *Lancashire Textiles: a Case Study of Industrial Change*, 1968, Cambridge.
15. This board followed the Board of Trade, *Shipbuilding Industry Enquiry Committee*, Cmnd 2937, 1966, London.
16. Ministry of Technology, *Industrial Expansion*, Cmnd 3509, 1968, London; ibid., *The Computers Merger Project, 1968*, Cmnd 3660, 1968, London; Board of Trade, *The Production of Primary Aluminium*, Cmnd 3819. 1968, London.
17. Department of Industry, *An Approach to Industrial Strategy*, Cmnd 6315, 1975, London; Anon, 'An Approach to Industrial Strategy', *Trade and Industry*, 7 Nov. 1975, pp.322-6; 'Industrial Strategy – a Progress Report'. *Trade and Industry*, 12 Nov. 1976, pp.410-12.
18. S. Young and A.V. Lowe, *Intervention in the Mixed Economy*, 1974, London.

19. Ibid., p.117.
20. Ibid.
21. D. Massey, 'A Structuralist Approach to Industrial Location', Centre for Environmental Studies, Working Note 454, 1977, London.
22. Department of Industry, *The British Motor Vehicle Industry*, Cmnd 6377, 1976, London, p.8.
23. D.W. Heal, *The Steel Industry in Post-War Britain*, 1974, Newton Abbott, pp.145 et. seq.
24. Department of Industry, *The Regeneration of British Industry*, Cmnd 5710, 1974, London, pp.6-11.
25. Department of Industry, *The British Motor Vehicle Industry*, Cmnd 6377, 1976, London, p.4.
26. Heal, *The Steel Industry*; K. Warren, 'British Steel: the Problems of Rebuilding an Old Structure', *Geography*, 61, 1976, pp.1-7.
27. *Guardian*, 8 Mar. 1977.
28. *Guardian*, 23 Oct. 1976 and 28 Oct. 1976.

POSTSCRIPT

The preceding chapters have illustrated that increasingly research workers are examining the spatial behaviour of large industrial enterprises. Some important parameters for measuring this behaviour seem to have been isolated, and the book has tried to take stock of what has, and what has not, been achieved. Such a stock-taking seemed to be essential before further case studies or analyses of aggregate behaviour are begun. There were, and are, data problems, which will be reduced if the required data are specified carefully. Such careful specification could prevent lack of data from restricting the kind of investigation undertaken and could lead, in turn, to deeper and more penetrating enquiries into the spatial behaviour of large enterprises.

Some vital limitations stand out in the material summarised earlier. There is a focus on case analyses rather than on aggregate data, and the case analyses of spatial *behaviour* have concentrated on enterprises in a narrow range of industries processing farm or forest products or the closely related food and drink industries. There is still scope for case studies of the behaviour of enterprises in industries where space plays a less obvious role, but such studies are not of prime importance. Urgently needed is the study of one particular group of phenomena, or even one phenomenon, over a large group of enterprises, perhaps the largest hundred employers or the top five enterprises in each of the most highly concentrated industrial sectors. Studies of the spatial behaviour of large industrial enterprises must move away from the case study to the analysis of aggregate data. Analysis of this type will not only make it much easier to generalise from the results but will also extend the industrial coverage from the restricted range of industries so far explored.

Clearly, too, very little is known about the making of spatial *decisions* in large enterprises. Such a study would involve a detailed examination of all the individuals and groups providing, monitoring and transmitting data to the control unit, together with an awareness of any bias introduced at each level of decision making. Interviewing one or two individuals tells little of the real decision process: it gives simply two individual views of decision making in an organisation. Here the case study will still be invaluable; it may even need a full-time research team within the organisation to monitor and investigate the process.

In the future greater emphasis on the diversity of products within large enterprises might be expected. Most of the studies reported here have examined either single-product enterprises, or only one product group of an enterprise. Yet the basic decision to allocate resources to one product division rather than another will eventually trickle down through an enterprise's structure to express itself in space. A decision to expand product A at the expense of product B may eventually see the closure of a plant in town Y and major expansion in town Z.

This leads to another important theme missing from most of the discussion. Although city-systems were defined, their relationships with enterprise systems were discussed in only the crudest spatial terms of centre and periphery. The next stage is to examine large enterprises at a much finer spatial scale than has been possible here. Two such clearly important scales are the urban and intra-urban. Some research on this theme is already in progress and in the near future more will be known about the behaviour of large enterprises in the inner city and in towns of different sizes.

Moreover it is probably important to widen the study beyond the large industrial enterprise to all large organisations, particularly the multi-regional organisations which own retail outlets, entertainment, banking and insurance. Through their distant head-offices they control the fortunes of many other essential economic activities in cities and urban areas. Here again perhaps case studies are still required. High priority should be given to examining the spatial structure and evolution of enterprises in the primary, tertiary and quaternary sectors to parallel the studies of industrial activity summarised in the earlier chapters.

Despite the obvious gaps in our knowledge of large industrial enterprise behaviour, which in themselves suggest avenues for future research, some positive statements about the spatial behaviour of large industrial enterprises are possible. These assertions might provide useful stepping stones towards the kind of aggregate analysis recommended above. The assertions made in this postscript must not be read in isolation but in the light of the caveats, limitations and evidence presented earlier. Nor should they be treated as the only conclusions to emerge from this work; more detailed findings were summarised at the end of each chapter.

Large industrial enterprises distribute their employment in the same manner as smaller firms, with the exception of their control unit jobs, which tend to be spatially concentrated. The sites that contribute to the spatial structures of the enterprises can be classified by product cycle, best-practice or function, and in each category plants have different locational characteristics and different employment records. There are marked variations in intra-enterprise material links between the plants of an enterprise, and enterprises, too, structure the flows of information within their organisations in various ways, and these different organisational structures appear to influence an enterprise's spatial behaviour. The foreign-controlled sub-set of large industrial enterprises depicts a greater propensity to create spatial concentrations of white-collar jobs, and their plants have fewer links with regional economies than their indigenous counterparts. Nevertheless in overall employment provision they pay greater regard to peripheral areas than do indigenous firms.

An enterprise's spatial evolution reflects both the spatial growth of its plant space and locational adjustment within it. Spatial growth results both from the establishment of branch plants and from acquisition of other firms, and such outward growth may be stimulated by disadvantages in an enterprise's core region or by positive advantages of new materials, new markets or labour resources. Space appears to be an important constraint in spatial growth by branch plants, but it influences only certain types of merger behaviour. Different growth methods appear to produce different spatial patterns. Adjustments after growth are less likely to affect the material links of an enterprise's plants, but marked changes in information links are usual. Post-merger rationalisation is as likely to produce expansion as closure, while more general adjustments are made first within existing sites. Once the potentialities of existing sites have been exhausted more major changes occur, and characteristic types of rationalisation behaviour can be identified, but this behaviour is still constrained by the existing spatial structure (particularly age of capital stock) and an enterprise's organisational structure. Further, a large enterprise's spatial behaviour may be strongly influenced by its rivals' behaviour.

General ideas about the evolution of large industrial enterprises have been put together in model form, and three models are now available. They clearly represent only the beginning of efforts to conceptualise the spatial evolution of large industrial enterprises. Certainly the case analyses present strong support for the new hypothetical development sequence proposed here, at least within the limited range of industries to which it was expected to apply.

The case analyses, too, demonstrate the dichotomy between industrial system and market system firms, a distinction central to the isolation of large industrial enterprises as an important sub-group of firms. The five multi-regional, multi-plant enterprises described adopted primarily a single- or related-product growth strategy, and selected an external growth path. Compared with their market system rivals large industrial enterprises acquire more firms, extend their plant space over longer distances and grow in larger steps. These characteristics influence industrial location patterns, since large firms are more likely to retain acquired plants than small firms, but an area dominated by large firms is likely to have fewer production sites than one of similar size dominated by small firms. The description of inter-enterprise interaction illustrated clearly the importance of this formerly neglected aspect of the spatial behaviour of large industrial enterprises.

The social and regional consequences of the growth of large industrial enterprises, or at least the most obvious manifestations, are now clear. There has been a centralisation of control functions in the economy and a consequential removal of control from the periphery. The implications for job provision, however, appear confined to the lack of white-collar jobs on the periphery and of material and information links between a large enterprise's plants and their local economy. Production jobs in large enterprises are no more concentrated in the centre than those of smaller firms, externally controlled plants seem no more susceptible to employment fluctuations than those of indigenous firms, and despite their lack of independence they have access to the finance and expertise of large industrial enterprises. Nevertheless the lack of white-collar jobs does reduce the choice of jobs for residents in peripheral areas. Other possible effects of large enterprises have been hypothesised, such as the de-skilling of jobs in the periphery and the concentration of innovative behaviour in the centre, but there is as yet no strong empirical evidence of this tendency.

The evidence presented also suggests that in aggregate, large enterprises, in the spatial allocation of their employment, do not misuse their bargaining strength with governments and do not select sites wherever they wish. In the United Kingdom they have consistently either worked in the direction that regional policy desired or, sometimes, created more than their share of employment in areas receiving regional aid. Studies of the spatial effects of aspatial policies by government are few, but where they are available they confirm that the policies have not worked against the less-favoured parts of a city-system. Nevertheless it might be argued that because of their size, expertise and flexibility large industrial enterprises should attempt to take a long-term spatial view of their operations to attempt to mitigate the effects of any plant closure decisions.

While the large industrial enterprise, with its multi-regional system of plants, has grown in importance over the past decades, so it has been monitored by individuals, research teams and governments. The work on the spatial patterns of plants, employment provision and linkages of large industrial enterprises has been discussed in the preceding chapters, but this synthesis is not a final report but a dispatch from the middle of an exciting, and rapidly expanding, research area.

SELECT BIBLIOGRAPHY

The bibliography brings together the geographical literature on the spatial behaviour of large industrial enterprises. It excludes many of the papers discussed in the text, including those from other disciplines and those which touch on the theme of the book only in passing. Also excluded are mimeographed materials. The papers listed were all published before the end of 1976, with the exception of one or two items I was privileged to see before publication.

Atkins, D.H.W., 'Employment Change in Branch and Parent Manufacturing Plants in the United Kingdom, 1966 to 1971', *Trade and Industry*, 30 August 1973, pp.437-9

Barlow, A., 'A Comment on the Concentration of Manufacturing Corporations and Regional Growth', *Area*, 4, 1972, pp.273-5

Bater, J.H., and Walker, D.F., 'Aspects of Industrial Linkage: the Example of the Hamilton Metal Working Complex, Ontario', *Revue de Géographie de Montréal*, 28, 1974, pp.233-43

—, 'Foreign Ownership and Industrial Linkage', in D.F. Walker and J.H. Bater (eds.), *Industrial Development in Southern Ontario*, 1974, Waterloo, pp.101-25.

Beyers, W.B., 'On Geographical Properties of Growth Centre Linkage Systems', *Economic Geography*, 50, 1974, pp.203-18

Blackbourn, A., 'The Location of Foreign-Owned Manufacturing Plants in the Republic of Ireland', *Tijdschrift voor Economische en Sociale Geografie*, 63, 1972, pp.438-43

—, 'The Spatial Behaviour of American Firms in Western Europe', in F.E.I. Hamilton (ed.), *Spatial Perspectives*, pp.245-64

Britton, J.N.H., 'Environmental Adaptation of Industrial Plants: Service Linkages, Locational Environment and Organisation', in F.E.I. Hamilton (ed.), *Spatial Perspectives*, pp.363-92

—, 'The Influence of Corporate Organisation and Ownership on the Linkages of Industrial Plants: a Canadian Enquiry', *Economic Geography*, 52, 1976, pp.311-24

Buswell, R.J., and Lewis, E.W., 'The Geographical Distribution of Industrial Research Activity in the United Kingdom', *Regional Studies*, 4, 1970, pp.297-306

Cadden, P.G., 'Multi-Plant Firms and Commodity Flows: the Case of the Western Canadian Flour Milling Industry', in B.M. Barr (ed.), *Western Canadian Research in Geography: the Lethbridge Papers*, 1975, Vancouver, pp.11-20

Chapman, K. 'Oil Based Industrial Complexes in the United Kingdom', *Tijdschrift voor Economische en Sociale Geografie*, 61, 1970, pp.157-72

—, 'Agglomeration and Linkage in the UK Petrochemical Industry', *Transactions of the Institute of British Geographers*, 60, 1973, pp.33-68

—, 'Corporate Systems in the United Kingdom Petrochemical Industry', *Annals of the Association of American Geographers*, 64, 1974, pp.126-37

Clark, U.E.G., 'The Cyclical Sensitivity of Employment in Branch Plants', *Regional Studies*, 10, 1976, pp.293–8

Collins, L., and Walker, D.F. (eds.), *Locational Dynamics of Manufacturing Activity*, 1975, London

de Smidt, M., 'Foreign Industrial Establishments Located in the Netherlands', *Tidjschrift voor Economische en Sociale Geographie*, 57, 1966, pp.1-19

Derrieux-Cecconi, F., 'Les espaces de la firme: le cas de Creusot Loire', *L'Espace Géographique*, 2, 1973, pp.21-36.

Dicken, P., 'Some Aspects of Decision-making Behaviour in Business Organisations', *Economic Geography*, 47, 1971, pp.426-37

—, 'The Multi-Plant Business Enterprise and Geographical Space: Some Issues in the Study of External Control and Regional Development', *Regional Studies*, 10, 1976, pp.401-12

—, and Lloyd, P.E., 'Geographical Perspectives on United States Investment in the United Kingdom', *Environment and Planning A*, 8, 1976, pp. 685-706

Erickson, R.A., The 'Lead-Firm' Concept: an Analysis of Theoretical Elements, *Tijdschrift voor Economische en Sociale Geografie*, 63, 1972, pp.426-37

—, 'The Regional Impact of Growth Firms: the Case of Boeing, 1963-8', *Land Economics*, 50, 1974, pp.127-36

—, 'The Spatial Pattern of Income Generation in Lead-Firm,

Growth Area Linkage Systems', *Economic Geography*, 51, 1975, pp.17-26

Evans, A.W., 'The Location of the Headquarters of Industrial Companies', *Urban Studies*, 10, 1973, pp.387-95

Expenditure Committee, *Regional Development Incentives*, HC 327, 1973, London

Firn, J., 'External Control and Regional Development: the Case of Scotland', *Environment and Planning A*, 7, 1975, pp.393-414

Fleming, D., and Krumme, G., 'The Royal Hoesch Union: Case Analysis of Adjustment Patterns in the European Steel Industry', *Tijdschrift voor Economische en Sociale Geografie*, 59, 1968, pp.177-99

Goddard, J.B., *Office Location in Urban and Regional Development*, 1975, London

—, 'Organisational Information Flows and the Urban System', *Economie Appliquée*, 128, 1975, pp.125-64

Goodwin, W., 'The Structure and Position of the British Motor Vehicle Industry', *Tijdschrift voor Economische en Sociale Geografie*, 56, 1965, pp.145-56

Hamilton, F.E.I. (ed.), *Spatial Perspectives on Industrial Organisation and Decision-Making*, 1974, London

—, 'A view of Spatial Behaviour, Industrial Organisations and Decision Making', in F.E.I. Hamilton (ed.), *Spatial Perspectives*, pp.3-43

—, 'Multi-National Enterprise and the EEC', *Tijdschrift voor Economische en Sociale Geografie*, 67, 1976, pp.258-78

Hayter, R., 'Corporate Strategies and Industrial Change in the Canadian Forest Products Industries', *Geographical Review*, 66, 1976, pp.209-28

Heal, D.W., *The Steel Industry in Post-War Britain*, 1974, Newton Abbott

—, 'Ownership, Control and Location Decisions: the Case of the British Steel Industry Since 1945', in F.E.I. Hamilton (ed.), *Spatial Perspectives*, pp.265-86

Hoare, A.G., 'Foreign Firms and Air Transport: the Geographical Effect of Heathrow Airport', *Regional Studies*, 9, 1975, pp.349-68

Jansen, A.C.M., 'Enkele aspekten van het ruimtelijk gedrag van grote industriële concerns in Nederland, 1950-71', *Tijdschrift voor Economische en Sociale Geografie*, 63, 1972, pp.411-25

Keeble, D., *Industrial Location and Planning in the United*

Kingdom, 1976, London, especially pp. 162-72 and 181-91
Krumme, G., 'Notes on Locational Adjustment Patterns in Industrial Geography', *Geografiska Annaler*, 51B, 1969, pp.15-19
—, 'Toward a Geography of Enterprise', *Economic Geography*, 45, 1969, pp.30-40
—, 'Comments on Inter-Regional Sub-Contracting Patterns and Bi-Lateral Feedbacks', *Journal of Regional Science*, 13, 1970, pp.237-42
—, 'The Inter-Regional Corporation and the Region', *Tijdschrift voor Economische en Sociale Geografie*, 61,1970, pp.318-33
—, 'Corporate Growth Through Spatial Decentralization: Triumph's Expansion Path', *International Geography*, vol. 1, 1972, Montreal, pp.554-6
—, and Hayter, R., 'Implications of Corporate Strategies and Product Cycle Adjustments for Regional Employment Changes', in L. Collins and D.F. Walker (eds.), *Locational Dynamics*, pp.325-6
Labasse, J., 'The Geographical Space of Big Companies', *Geoforum*, 6, 1975, pp.113-24
Le Heron, R.B., 'Best-Practice Technology, Technical Leadership and Regional Economic Development', *Environment and Planning A*, 1973, 5, pp.735-49
—, 'Best-Practice Firms and Productivity Changes in the Pacific North-West Plywood and Veneer Industry, 1960-72: Some Regional Growth Implications', *Environment and Planning A*, 8, 1976, pp.163-72
—, and Schmidt, C.G., 'An Exploratory Analysis of Linkage Change Within Two Regional Industries', *Regional Studies*, 10, 1976, pp.465-78
—, and Warr, E.C.R., 'Corporate Organisation, Corporate Strategy and Agribusiness Development in New Zealand', *New Zealand Geographer*, 32, 1976, pp.1-16
Leigh, R., and North, D.J., 'Acquisition in British Industries: Implications for Regional Development', in F.E.I. Hamilton (ed.), *Contemporary Industrialisation. Spatial Analysis and Regional Development*, 1978, London, pp.158-81
—, 'Regional Aspects of Acquisition Activity in British Manufacturing Industry', *Regional Studies*, 12, 1978, pp.227-45
McDermott, P.J., 'Ownership, Organisation and Regional Dependence in the Scottish Electronics Industry', *Regional*

Studies, 10, 1976, pp.319-35

McNee, R.B., 'Towards a More Humanistic Economic Geography: the Geography of Enterprise', *Tijdschrift voor Economische en Sociale Geografie*, 51, 1960, pp.201-5

—, 'Regional Planning, Bureaucracy and Geography', *Economic Geography*, 46, 1970, pp.190–8

—, 'A Systems Approach to Understanding the Geographic Behaviour of Organisations, Especially Large Corporations', in F.E.I. Hamilton (ed.), *Spatial Perspectives*, pp.47-76

Moore, C.W., 'Industrial Linkage Development Paths in Growth Poles: a Research Methodology', *Environment and Planning A*, 4, 1972, pp.253-71

—, 'Industrial Development Linkage Paths', *Tijdschrift voor Economische en Sociale Geografie*, 64, 1973, pp.93-107

North, D.J., 'The Process of Locational Change in Different Manufacturing Organisations', in F.E.I. Hamilton (ed.), *Spatial Perspectives*, pp.213-44

Parsons, G., 'The Giant Manufacturing Corporation and Balanced Regional Growth in Britain', *Area*, 4, 1972, pp.99-103

Pred, A., 'Major Job-Providing Organisations and Systems of Cities', *Commission on College Geography*, Resource Paper No. 27, 1974, Washington

—, 'Diffusion, Organisational Spatial Structures and City System Development', *Economic Geography*, 51, 1975, pp.252-68

—, 'On the Spatial Structure of Organisations and the Complexity of Metropolitan Interdependence', *Papers of the Regional Science Association*, 33, 1975, pp.115-42

—, 'The Inter-Urban Transmission of Growth in Advanced Economies: Empirical Findings Versus Regional Planning Assumptions', *Regional Studies*, 10, 1976, pp.151-72

—, and Tornqvist, G., *Systems of Cities and Information Flows*, 1973, Lund

Ray, D.M., 'The Location of United States Manufacturing Industries in Canada', *Economic Geography*, 47, 1971, pp.389-400

Rees, J., 'The Industrial Corporation and Location Decision Analysis', *Area*, 4, 1972, pp.199-205

—, 'Decision-Making, the Growth of the Firm and the Business Environment', in F.E.I. Hamilton (ed.), *Spatial Perspectives*, pp.189-211

—, 'Oligopoly, Investment and Spatial Growth of Multi-National Enterprise', in F.E.I. Hamilton (ed.), *The Organisation of Spatial Industrial Systems*, IGU Working Group on Industrial Geography, 1976, London, pp.189-91

Schmidt, C.G., 'Firm Linkage Structure and Structural Change: a Graph Theoretical Analysis', *Economic Geography*, 51, 1975, pp.27-36

Steed, G.P.F., 'The Changing Milieu of a Firm', *Annals of the Association of American Geographers*, 58, 1968, pp.506-25

—, 'Forms of Corporate-Environmental Adaptation', *Tijdschrift voor Economische en Sociale Geografie*, 62, 1971, pp.90-4

—, 'Internal Organisation, Firm Integration and Locational Change: the Northern Ireland Linen Complex, 1954-64', *Economic Geography*, 47, 1971, pp.371-83

—, 'Locational Implications of Corporate Organisation of Industry', *Canadian Geographer*, 15, 1971, pp.54-7

—, 'Plant Adaptation, Firm Environment, and Location Analysis', *Professional Geographer*, 23, 1971, pp. 324-8

Stewart, J.C., 'Linkages and Foreign Direct Investment', *Regional Studies*, 10, 1976, pp.245-58

Taylor, M.J., 'Organisational Growth, Spatial Interaction and Locational Decision Making', *Regional Studies*, 9, 1975, pp.313-23

Thomas, M.D., 'Growth Pole Theory, Technological Change, and Regional Economic Growth', *Papers of the Regional Science Association*, 34, 1975, pp.3-25

—, and Le Heron, R.B., 'Perspectives on Technological Change and the Process of Diffusion in the Manufacturing Sector', *Economic Geography*, 50, 1974, pp.231-51

Thorngren, B., 'How Do Contact Systems Affect Regional Development?', *Environment and Planning A*, 2, 1970, pp.409-27

Tornqvist, G., 'Flows of Information and the Location of Economic Activities', *Geografiska Annaler*, 50B, 1968, pp.99-107

—, *Flows of Information and the Location of Economic Activities*, 1968, Lund

—, *Contact Systems and Regional Development*, 1970, Lund

Townroe, P.M., 'Branch Plants and Regional Development', *Town Planning Review*, 46, 1975, pp.47-62

Wärneryd, O., *Interdependence in Urban Systems*, Göteborg, 1968

Warren, K., 'Recent Changes in the Geographical Location of the British Steel Industry', *Geographical Journal* , 135, 1969, pp.343-64

—, 'Heavy Industry With Special Reference to the Chemical Industry', in M. Chisholm and G. Manners, *Spatial Policy Problems of the British Economy*, 1971, Cambridge, especially pp.194-211

—, 'British Steel: the Problems of Rebuilding an Old Industrial Structure', *Geography*, 61, 1976, pp.1-7

Watts, H.D., 'The Location of Aluminium Plant in the United Kingdom', *Tijdschrift voor Economische en Sociale Geografie*, 61, 1970, pp.148-56

—, 'The Location of the Beet-Sugar Industry in England and Wales, 1912-36', *Transactions of Institute of British Geographers*, 53, 1971, pp.95-116

—, 'Further Observations on Regional Growth and Large Corporations', *Area*, 4, 1972, pp.269-73

—, 'Locational Adjustment in the British Beet-Sugar Industry', *Geography*, 59, 1974, pp.10-23

—, 'Spatial Rationalisation in Multi-Plant Enterprises', *Geoforum*, no. 17, 1974, pp.69-76

—, 'The Market Area of a Firm', in L. Collins and D.F. Walker (eds.), *Locational Dynamics*, pp.357-83

—, 'Market Areas and Spatial Rationalisation: the British Brewing Industry After 1945', *Tijdschrift voor Economische en Sociale Geografie*, 68, 1977, pp.224-40

—, 'Inter-Organisational Relations and the Location of Industry', *Regional Studies*, 12, 1978, forthcoming

Westaway, J., 'Contact Potential and the Occupation Structure of the British Urban System', *Regional Studies*, 8, 1974, pp.57-73

—, 'The Spatial Hierarchy of Business Organisations and its Implications for the British Urban System', *Regional Studies*, 8, 1974, pp.145-55

Yannopoulos, G.N., and Dunning, J.H., 'Multinational Enterprise and Regional Development: an Exploratory Paper', *Regional Studies*, 10, 1976, pp.389-400

AUTHOR INDEX

SUBJECT INDEX